Mohammad Hashim Kamali

FREEDOM, EQUALITY AND JUSTICE IN ISLAM

ISLAMIC TEXTS SOCIETY

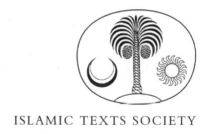

This edition published 2002 by The Islamic Texts Society
22a Brooklands Avenue, Cambridge CB2 2DQ, U.K.

ISBN 1 903682 0 10 paper
ISBN 1 903682 0 29 cloth

First published 1999 by Ilmiah Publishers, Kuala Lumpur, Malaysia

British Library Cataloguing in Publication Data
A catalogue record for this book is available from the British Library

ABOUT THE AUTHOR

Mohammad Hashim Kamali, born in Afghanistan in 1944, is currently Professor of Law at the International Islamic University, Malaysia, where he has taught Islamic law and jurisprudence since 1985. He studied law at Kabul University, where he was later appointed Assistant Professor, and completed his LL.M. and doctoral studies at London University, specializing in Islamic Law and Middle Eastern Studies. He has also held a faculty position at the Institute of Islamic Studies, McGill University, a Research Associateship with the Social Sciences and Humanities Research Council of Canada, and was a Visiting Professor at the Law School, Capital University, Ohio. He has authored *Law in Afghanistan: A Study of the Constitutions, Matrimonial Law and the Judiciary* (Leiden: E.J. Brill, 1985); *Principles of Islamic Jurisprudence* (Cambridge: The Islamic Texts Society, 1991, and Kuala Lumpur: Ilmiah Publishers, 1998); *Freedom of Expression in Islam* (Cambridge: The Islamic Texts Society, 1997 and Kuala Lumpur: Ilmiah Publishers, 1998); *Punishment in Islamic Law: An Enquiry into the Hudud Bill of Kelantan* (Kuala Lumpur: Institute for Policy Research, 1995); *Islamic Commercial Law: An Analysis of Futures and Options* (forthcoming), and numerous articles in reputable international journals. He has twice received the Ismāʿīl al-Fārūqī Award for Academic Excellence, first in 1995, when the award was initiated jointly by the International Institute of Islamic Thought and the International Islamic University, Malaysia, and second, in May 1997 for his work entitled *Istiḥsan (Juristic Preference) and Its Application to Contemporary Issues* (Jeddah: Islamic Research and Training Institute, 1997). Dr. Kamali wishes to acknowledge that he prepared the present edition of this book during his stay at the Institute for Advanced Study, Berlin, where he was fellow for the academic year 2000-2001.

بسم الله الرحمن الرحيم

Contents

Introduction

The subjects that are addressed in this volume are the concern of every legal system, and are not, therefore, peculiar to the *Sharīʿah*. Their relationship to one another and to the general theme of human rights hardly needs elucidation. Justice and equality are closely interrelated insofar as the one cannot be meaningfully implemented without the other. For justice often means equal treatment and the equal distribution of advantages and burdens, or a commensurate correction of an imbalance that is caused by deviant behaviour. Similarly, neither equality nor justice can be a meaningful reality without freedom. For justice presumes the moral autonomy of individuals and their liberty to act as they will. Justice can, therefore, have little meaning if it is applied to a person or a group of persons who are deprived of their freedom, or compelled to a course of action that is beyond their control. Equality also acquires much of its substance only in an environment where freedom is a reality. To treat two prisoners equally does make some sense but equality before the law in different situations and among people of different calibre and status is where equality becomes more meaningful.

A perusal of the Universal Declaration of Human Rights, or of any chapter on the basic rights and liberties enshrined in a contemporary constitution will show that numerous and varied as they are, almost the entire range of these rights and liberties are predicated on freedom, equality and justice, the most fundamental, so to speak, of all the recognised rights and liberties.

The first chapter on freedom in this volume is mostly concerned with a conceptual analysis of freedom, its manifestations in theological, social and political contexts, and the various shades of meaning it has been given by commentators from different disciplines. Freedom has a basic meaning, and this is why any serious distortion or deviation from its core concept has not commanded general acceptance. Yet beyond this basic clarity, the meanings and implications of freedom vary considerably and tend to become increasingly complex. This is borne out by the fact that a comprehensive and all-embracing definition of freedom eludes us. The conceptual analysis of freedom has not received as much attention from Muslim jurists as it has in the writings of Western scholars on the subject. Part of the reason for this might be that the basic parameters of freedom in Islam are determined by reference to the normative evidences of the Qur'ān and *Sunnah*, but there is considerable variation in the understanding of these evidences and the manner in which commentators have related them to theological, legal and political subjects. This presentation provides a review of the basic evidence on freedom and the contributions of Muslim scholars to the development of ideas on the subject.

The chapter on equality that is presented here is also concerned mainly with an analysis of the normative evidence of the Qur'ān and *Sunnah*, which Muslim jurists have elaborated in reference to particular themes. Equality, like freedom, is an integrated concept, which is indivisible and averse to compromise. Yet neither freedom nor equality are absolute in the sense that both are amenable to the influences of context and circumstance. In addition to a general characterisation of equality and its evidential basis in the *Sharīʿah*, this presentation also looks into the application of equality to two other subjects, namely women and non-Muslims, and examines the way in which they are treated in Islamic legal literature. It is of interest to note a certain contrast, highlighted in this presentation, between earlier juristic writings on these themes, and the works of contemporary *ʿulamā'* and scholars. Muslim jurists of the twentieth century have made a significant contribution to the understanding of the source evidence of the *Sharīʿah* on equality in conjunction, particularly, with the changing realities of contemporary Muslim societies. They have not hesitated, for instance, in taking a totally different stand on women's issues from many classical scholars, and advancing a different perspective on equality in the *Sharīʿah* for all citizens, regardless of their race, language or religion. It is clearly in these areas that the substance of the modern reformist thought in the *Sharīʿah* makes its presence unmistakably visible.

Justice is the sum-total, in a sense, of all recognised rights and duties, as it often consists of nothing more than a balanced implementation of rights and duties, and of due regard for equality and freedom. The Qur'ān is emphatic on the objectivity of justice, so much so that it defies any level of relativity and compromise in its basic conception. A perusal of the Qur'ānic evidence on justice leaves one in no doubt that justice is integral to the basic outlook and philosophy of Islam, within or beyond the *Sharīᶜah* itself. It is therefore not incorrect to say that the *Sharīᶜah* is committed to justice as one of its cardinal goals and objectives, to the extent that the veracity of the *Sharīᶜah* itself can be measured by its effectiveness in administering justice. This is the understanding, in fact, that the renowned Ḥanbalī jurist, Ibn Qayyim al-Jawziyyah (d. 1350), has conveyed in his widely-quoted statement that 'Islam will always stand for justice and any path that is taken towards justice is bound to be in harmony with the *Sharīᶜah* and can never be against it'.

The *Sharīᶜah* shows the way to justice and this way must be followed as far as possible. In the event, however, that the established rules of the *Sharīᶜah* do not offer sufficient guidelines by which to administer justice, one may take any route, including for example, those of natural rights and natural justice, or the general rules of equity and fairness, or that of a judicious policy (*siyāsah sharᶜiyyah*), in order to secure justice, and the result that is arrived at is *a fortiori* in accordance with the *Sharīᶜah* and cannot be held to be contrary to it.

The chapter that is presented here on justice consists essentially of a review and analysis of the basic evidence of the Qur'ān and *Sunnah* on the subject. It seeks to depict, in particular, the Qur'ānic outlook or universal justice which reaches beyond the particularities of any rigid framework that might restrain the humanitarian call and substance of justice in Islam.

CHAPTER ONE

Freedom (*al-Ḥurriyyah*)

I. Introductory Remarks

Despite the obvious significance of, and the sustained preoccupation of all legal and philosophical traditions with freedom, there is little agreement on its precise meaning. To a reader of constitutional law, freedom means something different from what it might mean to a philosopher or a mystic. Whereas the philosophically-oriented Muᶜtazilah and the Ashᶜariyyah were preoccupied with the freedom of the human will versus predestination and determinism (*al-jabr wa'l-ikhtiyār*), to the Sufi and mystic, freedom primarily means freedom from the desires of the self, which releases one from dependence on the material world, and is freedom from everything except God and devotion to Him.[1] More than any other factor, it is the animal desires of the animal nature in man that render him unfree. The struggle with those desires, and this final victory over them, makes man free. Ultimately, freedom from desires is a facet of human perfection, something that raises man to the level of the angels and outlasts his physical life.[2]

The jurist and the reader of political science are mainly concerned with the struggle between authority and freedom. Freedom in this context has primarily meant the ability of the individual to lead a life of security, free from the tyranny of oppressive governments and rulers. To the reader of fundamental rights and liberties, it is the struggle between authority and freedom that gives freedom much of its meaning. This is a focal theme of many a modern Constitution, and the emphasis that is given to it is typical of the era of constitutionalism and government under the rule of law. But even here, there has, over time, been a considerable adjustment of the notion of the relationship of individual liberty to the authority of the state. Individual freedom was initially conceived as a limiting factor on government power, and was seen necessary for limiting the power of various organs of government in order to protect individual liberties. But that perception of bipolarity seems to have given way to a vision which sees it as the duty of the state to be an active participant in the protection of liberties. The initial view of conflicting interests is thus changing to one of the essential unity of interests.[3] The Declaration of the Rights of Man issued by the leaders of the French Revolution of 1789, which was later attached to the French Constitution of 1791, declared freedom to be the right of the individual to do what he wishes, provided that this does not cause harm to others, and that any limits imposed on freedom are not valid unless validated by the law. It was similarly declared that freedom and equality were the natural rights of all human beings.[4]

We are also concerned here with the close relationship between equality and freedom. To achieve objectivity and balance in understanding the basic notions of equality and freedom is often a question of accommodation and compromise between them. The compromise here is essentially between individual and communal interests. The individual is naturally inclined towards freedom, but his untrammeled desire for freedom is prone to lead to inequality, and the concern here how to limit the individual freedom in order to secure some of the valid objectives of equality. In this sense, the history of human rights has been one of 'continuous struggle for compromise between freedom and equality, between individual rights and considerations of social justice'.[5] It need not be overemphasised that a hungry man can make little use of his freedom. Considerations of social justice thus affect the substance of freedom in individual cases. Whereas liberalism puts freedom before equality, socialism and its allied doctrines have emphasised equality to a greater extent than freedom. Freedom has undoubtedly been and will remain the most important of all the rights of man. Yet without equality, freedom is likely to become a privilege of the few, and can easily be turned into an instrument of abuse.[6]

II. Definition and Scope

Historically, Muslim jurists have not addressed the subject of freedom in a comprehensive manner. Instead of advancing a theoretical understanding of the general concept of freedom, they often spoke about some of its manifestations, such as the freedom of opinion, belief and ownership. Muslim philosophers such as Farabī (d. 339/950) and Ibn Rushd (d. 595/1198) took limited notice of freedom as a political term, whereas it has received much attention in Sufi thought and literature. But Sufi thought is mainly preoccupied with the question of spiritual refinement and the extent to which a person can be free from dependence on the material world. The *ᶜulamā'* of theology and *kalām* have on the other hand debated issues such as how much freedom can be attributed to human beings in view of the omnipotence of God.[7]

The word '*ḥurr*' in classical Arabic implies 'free' as opposed to *ᶜabd* (slave), but is also used as a qualitative term denoting nobility of origin and character. The phrase '*rajulun ḥurrun*' did not only mean a free man as opposed to a slave, but also a man of noble character and descent, in the same way as *farasun ḥurrun* means a pedigree horse. Similarly, the phrase '*huwa min ḥurriyāt qawmihi*', means 'he is among the most noble of his people'; and '*ḥurr al-kalām*' means speech of high literary quality. In order to stress the moral meaning of *ḥurr*, it is frequently paired with *karīm* (noble, generous); *al-ḥurr al-karīm* thus means a true gentleman, a person who is pure in his human dignity, a person of integrity possessing a free conscience unrestrained by material considerations. It seems that the word '*ḥurriyyah*' was not as commonly used by the classical jurists as it is now being used by modern writers in Arabic. Thus the current usage of *ḥurriyyah*, which conveys the full force of the concept of 'freedom', is of relatively recent origin.[8] The word '*ikhtiyār*' (choice, free will) is more commonly used in the writings of Muslim mystics and philosophers than '*ḥurriyyah*', and one occasionally finds derivatives of *khalaṣa* (to release, to free) and *ᶜataqa* (to free, as of a slave) used as synonyms of *ḥurriyyah* in the various contexts and discourses of freedom. Muslim jurists have, in turn, used a variety of other terms, such as *ibāḥah* (permissibility), *al-barā'ah al-aṣliyyah* (original non-liability) and *ᶜafwah* (exemption, pardoning), which convey equivalent meanings to that of *ḥurriyyah*. There will be occasion to elaborate on these terms in the following pages.

The word '*ḥurriyyah*' does not occur in the Qur'ān itself but other derivatives of the same root, such as '*al-ḥurr*', 'a free man' (cf. al-Baqarah, 2:178), and '*taḥrīr*', 'releasing' (in the context mainly of manumitting a slave by way of atonement—*kaffārah*), occur frequently in it (cf. al-Mā'idah, 5:89, and al-Mujādilah, 68:3).

In its English usage, 'freedom' is distinct from 'independence': whereas freedom refers to the position of the individual within a group, independence is used in reference to the group itself. Freedom thus means the immunity of the individual from arbitrary and illegal action by the government, and his right to participate in the formation and conduct of government. Independence, on the other hand, refers to the position of a group in relation to other groups.[9]

Ibn ʿĀshūr has defined *ḥurriyyah* as 'the opposite of slavery and the independent disposition of a prudent man to manage his own affairs by his own free will; his ability, in other words, to manage his personal affairs as he wishes free from the opposition and hostility of others'.[10] This definition of *ḥurriyyah* is clearly focused on the freedom for the individual to manage his personal affairs free of the interference of others.

ʿAbd al-Wahhāb Khallāf has defined personal freedom (*al-ḥurriyyah al-shakhṣiyyah*) as 'the ability of a person to manage his own affairs free from oppression and the interference of others, while enjoying the safety of his person, honour, property, home and all the rights that belong to him, provided that the manner of his management does not amount to hostility or prejudice against others.'[11] Commenting on this, Mutawallī noted that the three component elements of personal freedom in the terms of this definition are freedom of movement, the right to personal safety, and the right to privacy.[12] Khallāf himself is not so specific and subsumes these and the freedom of religion, freedom of expression, freedom to own property, and the right to education, under personal freedom. Personal freedom is thus assured for the individual who enjoys all of these liberties.[13] Maḥmaṣṣānī has defined freedom as 'a person's ability to act in a certain way or avoid acting without violating the rights of others or the limits laid down by the law'.[14] For ʿAbd al-Karīm Zaydān, 'personal freedom means the individual's freedom of movement and the freedom to protect himself against aggression on his personal security including unlawful arrest, persecution and imprisonment. It also means his freedom to move into, leave, or return to, the country of his origin'.[15] This definition of personal freedom is obviously focused on freedom of movement and personal safety against aggression. Kāmil Laylah has taken a similar view when he states that: 'Personal freedom means that a person enjoys the right of movement within the state in which he resides and is also able to leave it or to return to it when he wishes; it also means immunity from arrest, detention and punishment unless it be in accordance with the provisions of the law.'[16] In my opinion, Khallāf's more comprehensive approach to personal freedom is preferable, as the different aspects of liberty are interrelated, and compromise on one is likely to have a bearing on the integrity of the others.

Abū Zahrah has considered personal freedom to be the first and most important manifestation of freedom, but adds that 'the liberty of the individual to believe in, and to express what seems right to him pertaining to the affairs of the society in which he lives, as well as his ability to act in pursuit of his welfare without interference or compulsion from others, is the essence of his personal freedom'.[17] Abū Zahrah's definition of personal freedom is similar to the ones noted earlier, although Abū Zahrah tends to give a higher profile to the freedom of expression and belief over the other manifestations of personal freedom, such as personal safety and freedom of movement, which were accentuated by Khallāf. Attainment of personal freedom in both these definitions subsumes the entire range of basic rights and liberties including the freedom to work, political freedom and the right to vote as well as participation in government and so forth.

ᶜAbd al-Munᶜim Aḥmad speaks of a three-fold division of basic rights and liberties into (a) personal rights and liberties (*al-ḥuqūq wa'l-ḥurriyyāt al-shakhṣiyyah*); (b) intellectual rights and liberties (*al-ḥuqūq wa'l-ḥurriyyāt al-maᶜnawiyyah*); and (c) socio-economic rights and liberties (*al-ḥuqūq wa'l-ḥurriyyāt al-iqtiṣādiyyah wa'l-ijtimāᶜiyyah*). Of these three types, the first is considered to be the most important and constitutes the bedrock of all other rights and liberties. The most important of all personal rights and liberties, in turn, are the ones that relate to personal safety, and the rights to privacy and movement. 'For what good it will do to an individual to enjoy the freedom of ownership and work if he is in the meantime denied his freedom and right of movement!'[18] Intellectual rights and liberties include the freedom of religion (*ḥurriyyat al-ᶜaqīdah*), freedom of education and dissemination of knowledge (*ḥurriyyat al-taᶜallum wa'l-taᶜlīm*), and freedom of speech (*ḥurriyyāt al-ra'y wa'l-bayān*). And lastly, the most important areas of socio-economic liberties are freedom of ownership (*ḥurriyyat al-tamalluk*) and freedom of work (*ḥurriyyat al-ᶜamal*).[19] Wāfi and Sibāᶜī have both employed an alternative phrase, namely *al-ḥurriyyah al-madaniyyah*, or civic liberty, as an equivalent to 'socio-economic liberty'. Civic liberty as a category thus includes the liberty of the individual to choose the work he wishes to do for a living, the liberty to pursue knowledge and specialise in a field of learning or profession, the individual's capacity and freedom to take part in contracts and transactions, including the choice of spouse, and the freedom to choose the place where one wishes to live, free of fear and interference from ruling authorities. The term *al-ḥurriyyah al-madaniyyah*, being the equivalent of *droit civil*, is often used in contradistinction to *droit naturelle*, or natural rights and liberties, which unlike civic liberties, are acknowledged to belong to every human being at all times and circumstances. Civic liberty for Sibāʿī includes a person's liberty to choose the work or the profession he or she wishes to pursue; the freedom of an adult man or woman to choose his or her partner in marriage; freedom in regard to the choice of locality and residence, and freedom of education. These are the classes of liberties in which the state must not interfere except where it is deemed necessary in order to ensure their integrity.[20] Sanhūrī has mentioned a broad classification of freedom into two general categories, one of which is personal liberty (*al-ḥurriyyah al-shakhṣiyyah*), which signifies the liberty of the individual vis-à-vis other individuals, and the other is his liberty in regard to the use of objects, and this is known as the freedom to own property (*al-ḥurriyyah al-milkiyyah*).[21]

The different classification, terminology and contents of personal liberties are partly a function of their susceptibility to change over time and circumstance, as well as the type of political philosophy and system of government under which they operate. Some of the liberties that are now commonly known to both Western and other legal systems, such as freedom of association and the freedom of the press, were added to the list only after the inception of democracy and its political doctrines following the French Revolution of 1789. These differences of perception and approach are also seen in the applied constitutions of various countries which are not entirely consistent in the terminology and contents of the different classes of rights and liberties.[22]

Political systems and philosophies have also differed in the relative weight they have attached to equality and freedom. The fine balance that is sought between individual interests and those of the community as a whole has often been influenced by the different perceptions of equality and freedom. The individual is naturally inclined towards freedom, whereas the community's interest requires a certain degree of restraint on individual freedom. This struggle between diverging interests is also felt today between the concerns of free economic enterprise and those of equality and social justice.[23]

According to a more simplified definition, '*ḥurriyyah* means that the individual is free to act in whatever way he wishes provided that others are not harmed by his action'.[24] Al-ᶜĪlī tends to concur with this characterisation of *ḥurriyyah* when he writes that Islam's view of *ḥurriyyah* is rooted in the postulate that the individual enjoys liberty in all things provided that this does not violate the rights of others and the collective interest (*maṣlaḥah*) of the community. When liberty exceeds these limits, it turns into transgression and becomes liable to restriction or even a total ban. Based on the *ḥadīth-cum-legal maxim* that 'harm may neither be inflicted nor reciprocated', the law should not interfere with individual liberty, and should confine its intervention to regulating instances of conflict with other rights and interests.[25] When the exercise of freedom by one person harms another, it becomes an instrument of *ḍarar*, in which case it must be eliminated or curtailed.

Islam's affirmative stance on freedom has been vividly expressed in the writings of many commentators on the subject. ᶜAbd al-Qādir ᶜAwdah has thus noted that '*ḥurriyyah* is one of the foundational principles of Islam, and it finds one of its most fascinating and comprehensive manifestations in the *Sharīᶜah*.'[26] Fatḥī ᶜUthmān has similarly observed that 'Islam sanctifies the liberty of the individual and makes it an integral part of the dignity of the believer. Fear is due only to God Most High and to no one else [...] Islam rejects compulsion even if it be the only way to Islam itself'.[27] In ᶜAbd al-Wāḥid Wāfi's assessment, 'Islam takes *ḥurriyyah* as one of its basic norms that affects almost every part of its legislation [...] It is deeply concerned with the application of *ḥurriyyah* and has not neglected any of its four principal varieties, which are: political freedom, freedom of thought and expression, freedom of religion, and civic liberty.'[28] Muḥammad al-Ghazālī has observed that 'Islam sanctifies the liberty of man, just as it sanctifies his life. Liberty is natural and inherent in every man, as the Prophet ﷺ declared: "Every child is born in the natural state of freedom."'

ما من مولود إلا ويولد على الفطرة.

The normative and inherent validity of personal freedom may neither be disrupted, nor compromised, nor subjected to oppression except by the authority of the *Sharīᶜah*.'[29] Wahbah al-Zuḥāylī similarly wrote that 'freedom is the natural right of every human being'.[30]

III. Different Facets of Freedom in Islam

'The concept of freedom in Islam', according to Abdul Aziz Said, 'implies a conscious rejection of a purely liberal and individualistic philosophy of "doing one's own thing" as the meaning of life, or as the goal of society.' Said continues to add that Islam takes an egalitarian and communitarian approach to freedom. Freedom in Islam finds its meaning in 'belonging to the community and participating with the people'.[31] It is egalitarian in that freedom is not enjoyed at the expense of causing harm to others, and it is communitarian because in the event of a conflict between individual freedom and the social good, the latter is often given priority over the former. Freedom is basically a social concept in that it will have little meaning in a state of total isolation from society.

Western commentators have made similar observations. Montgomery-Watt has made the somewhat drastic observation that 'freedom has never had any place in Islamic thought. There is a word for freedom, namely *ḥurriyyah*, but this refers to the condition of the freeman (*ḥurr*) as contrasted with the slave (*ʿabd*).'[32] Part of the reason for the unimportance of the concept of freedom, Montgomery-Watt adds, was the theological view that man is always the slave (*ʿabd*) of God. There is also a reference to the 'great prominence' that Muslims gave to the virtue of patience (*ṣabr*) and how this might have meant the endurance of hardship and the acceptance of a servile status on the part of Muslim individuals. Having said this, Montgomery-Watt goes on to concede that 'despite such points, however, it seems likely that there is a combination of ideas somewhere in Islamic thought, which performs much the same function as the concept of freedom does in the West'.[33]

In a discussion of liberty and any safeguards that might have existed for it in Islamic law, Louis Gardet highlighted the metaphysical context of freedom in Islam. He came to the conclusion that freedom in the ideal Muslim state was, perhaps, not the freedom for which one dies and gives life. Its true meaning for Islam had to be found in the relationship of man to the divine.[34] Montgomery-Watt and Gardet have touched on only one of the many features of Islam's conception of freedom. The metaphysical and mystical meanings of freedom tend to precede, in the history of ideas on liberty, the social and political dimensions of freedom. Economic freedom appears to be the latest chapter on liberty that features in the relevant literature on the subject.[35] Abdul Aziz Said notes that 'personal freedom in Islam lies in surrendering to the Divine will and must be sought within oneself. It cannot be realised through liberation from external sources of restraint'.[36] Said adds that 'the goal of freedom is human creativity' through the liberation of the self'.[37]

Sayyid Quṭb is typical of Muslim writers in describing the Qur'ānic characterisation of the God-man relationship as the true liberator of the believer's conscience. Belief in the omnipotence of God, and submission to Him who alone has power over the destiny of His servants, liberates the believer from bondage to anyone else. Sayyid Quṭb thus wrote that 'the belief that no one but God Most High has any power over the life of the believer and that his fortune or misfortune, poverty and wealth, benefit and harm are all in the power solely of God, that there is no mediator or intercessor between man and his Creator [...] This belief and devotion only to God is a powerful liberator of the inner conscience of the believer from dependence on anyone but God'.[38] A number of Qur'ānic passages are quoted in support. To review only a few, it will be noted that in his five daily prayers, the Muslim worshipper recites the sūra al-Fātiḥah and the part thereof which reads, 'Thee alone we worship and Thee alone we ask for help' (al-Fātiḥah, 1:5)

إياك نعبد وإياك نستعين.

In another short sūra of the Qur'ān, namely al-Ikhlāṣ (Sincere Devotion) the believer is directed to:

> Say, He is One. God is One on whom all depend. He begets not, nor is He begotten, and none is like Him.

قل هو اللّه أحد اللّه الصمد، لم يلد ولم يولد ولم يكن له كفواً أحد.

The Prophet Muḥammad ﷺ was ordered to declare: 'My prayer and meditation, my life and death are all for God, the Lord of the universe. He has no associate; this is the order that I follow and I am the first and foremost among Muslims' (Al-Anʿām, 6:162-163).

قل إنّ صلاتي و نسكي و محياى و مماتي للّه رب العالمين، لا شريك له و بذلك أمرت و أنا أول المسلمين.

Elsewhere the Qur'ān reads in an address to the Prophet Muḥammad ﷺ: 'Say: I only call upon my Lord, and associate naught with Him. Say: I control neither evil nor good for you' (al-Jinn, 72:20-21).

قل إنما أدعو ربي ولا أشرك به أحدا، قل أنى لا أملك لكم ضراً ولا رشداً.

'Man's submission to God in Islam', according to Bāqir al-Ṣadr, 'is the tool whereby man breaks all other chains of submission or slavery [...] Therefore no power on earth has the right to fare with his destiny.'[39] Mutahhari drew a distinction between social freedom and spiritual freedom but explained that they are interdependent, so much so that the one cannot be realised without the other. Social freedom means having freedom in connection with other individuals in society so that others do not hinder one's growth, and nor do they exploit or enslave one. Social freedom may in turn be of several types.[40]

In the Holy Qur'ān, one of the explicit purposes of the Prophets was to offer mankind social liberty and deliver them from mutual enslavement. We note here the Qur'ānic call inviting mankind to unite on two things, as the *āyah* reads that, 'We worship none but God and we associate no partner with Him, and none of us must be slaves or masters of one another other than God' (Āl-ʿImrān, 3:64).

ألا نعبد إلا اللّه ولا نشرك به شيئا ولا يتخذ بعضنا بعضا أربابا من دون اللّه.

This means, as Mutahhari wrote, 'the abolition of the order of servitude, the system of exploitation of the exploiter and exploited, getting rid of inequality and enslavement'.[41] It is true then, Mutahhari adds, 'that social liberty is sacred'.[42]

Spiritual freedom is freedom from one's self, as opposed to social freedom, which is freedom from the bonds of others. Both social liberty and spiritual liberty are sacred, but unlike the school of the prophets that tried to achieve both, the humanist school tries 'to safeguard social liberty without seeking spiritual freedom'.[43]

Can human beings have social freedom without spiritual freedom? That is, can they be slaves to their own lust, anger and greed and at the same time respect the freedom of others? Only a person in whose heart and conscience there is a transcendent call can truly have respect for others' rights and liberties. But when a person becomes slave to wealth, he is in fact a slave to his or her own mental characteristics. For inanimate things like money and land have no power to enslave a person. The source of slavery therefore 'lies in one's own peculiarities such as greed, lust, anger and carnal desires'.[44]

The Qur'ān says, 'Have you noticed someone who has made his vain desires his god?' (al-Jāthiyah, 45:23).

أفرأيت من اتخذ إلهه هواه.

Thus if one liberates oneself from the bond of one's selfish desires, one will realise that one is not a slave to the temptations of the material world. It is only then that one is able to find one's own true worth, and understand the significance of God's declaration in the Qur'ān that 'All We have created on the earth is for you' (al-Baqarah, 2:29).

خلق لكم ما في الأرض جميعا.

The riches of the world are thus at the service of human beings and not vice versa. According to Mutahhari, if one's eyes, cars, stomach and carnal desires incite one to satisfy them by whatever means, then one is their slave. The human being is ruled by two types of ego: the animal ego and the human ego. Almighty God has granted the human being the ability to be his own judge. Many a time one can see people who judge fairly in respect of themselves and prefer the rights of others to their own. Spiritual freedom means that the higher human ego is free from the grips of the lower animal ego. The Qur'ān says, 'Nay, I swear by the self-reproaching soul' (al-Qiyāmah, 75:2).

و لا أقسم بالنفس اللّوامة.

And then again, with reference to the self, the Qur'ān declares, 'Prosperous is he who purifies it and failed is he who seduces it', meaning the ego (al-Shams, 91:9-10).

قد أفلح من زكّٰها و قد خاب من دسّٰها.

Self-purification is in fact spiritual freedom, and it is the single most significant programme of the prophets.[45]

The acknowledgement in Islamic theology and law that God alone is the absolute sovereign and arbiter of values has probably meant that Muslim jurists did not accentuate the concept of freedom in the manner that one finds in Western philosophy and jurisprudence. The juristic and political dimensions of freedom in any legal tradition necessarily regard the status of the individual vis-à-vis the sovereign authority of the state. But since the basic structure of moral and legal values in Islam, that is, the determination of moral values of good and evil, right and wrong, rights and duties, is made by reference to the will of God, and God, on the other hand, commits His illustrious self to justice, to mercy and to compassion, there thus remains little incentive for the Muslim jurist to expound on the individual's right to freedom and the latter's protection against arbitrariness within that framework.

Freedom of academic discourse too had its limitations for the Muslim theologian and *mujtahid*, who was not altogether at liberty to resort to independent reasoning, or *ijtihād*, in the face of a clear text. Outside the scope of decisive injunctions, the *mujtahid* was free to resort to *ijtihād* and was encouraged to do so at the expense even of taking some risk as to the veracity of his conclusions. This is the clear message of a *ḥadīth* in which the Prophet ﷺ promised the *mujtahīd* reward for his sincerity and effort even if he might have actually fallen into error.

Another factor that might explain the low priority that liberty has been given in the works of Muslim writers on constitutional law and politics has been the prevalence of despotic government throughout much of the history of government in the Muslim lands. This is particularly noted, as Mutawallī has pointed out, in relation to matters that had a bearing on the position of rulers and their policies.[46]

Although it is acknowledged that the *ᶜulamā'* and *mujtahids* were not hindered by the ruling authorities in their academic activities and writings on religious themes, this liberty was, however, curtailed when such activities presented a threat to the government in power. Noted in this connection is the fact that almost every one of the four leading Imāms have suffered ill-treatment at the hands of oppressive rulers of their times. The fact, for instance, that the Abbasid Caliph, Jaᶜfar al-Manṣūr (d. 775), punished Imām Mālik (with seventy lashes of the whip, as reports have it) was due to a *fatwā* in which the Imām declared invalid the pledge of allegiance (*bayᶜah*) that some of the Abbasid rulers obtained by recourse to dubious methods. Political oppression of this kind marked a departure from the valid precedent of the Rightly-Guided Caliphs.

The question of how much freedom could be vouchsafed to human beings in view of the omnipotence of God has occupied the theological discourse of the Muᶜtazilah, the Ashᶜariyyah and the Māturīdiyyah schools of thought. The Muᶜtazilah took the view that man is free and responsible for his own conduct. They also maintained that man is the creator of his own acts, and free therefore to change evil into good, and vice versa, in his personality and conduct. To acknowledge this, the Muᶜtazilah maintained, was a necessary conclusion of God's attribute of absolute justice. God is absolutely just and this is the basic premise and guarantee of human freedom. If God Most High were to create the acts and conduct of His servant, and then hold him accountable for it, this would be contrary to justice. Human freedom is thus a necessary concomitant of Divine justice.[47]

Theological schools generally concurred in the overriding authority of divine injunctions and the subservience therefore of the human will to them. But they differed on issues, whether human reason was a valid basis of judgement (*ḥukm*) and if so, to what extent. How did the human will relate to the will of God, and was the human will capable of determining values? Could human will and judgement be accepted as a valid determinant of responsibility and *ḥukm?* The Ashᶜariyyah expressed reservations about the basic liberty of the human will as well as the value of man's rational judgment vis-à-vis the Divine will and the clear injunctions of *Sharīᶜah*. The Māturīdiyyah took a middle position by agreeing with the Muᶜtazilah on the basic liberty of the human will and the capacity of human reason to discern good and evil and pass moral judgement, but tended to agree with the Ashᶜariyyah in holding that human will and reason could not determine responsibility (*taklīf*) and punishment without the aid and guidance of divine revelation.[48]

Fazlur Rahman has looked into the views of the Muʿtazilah, the Ashʿariyyah and others, and made the observation that the idea of an omnipotent God is not easy to reconcile with that of individual freedom, but added that this is not peculiar to Islam and is a problem for all religions, except a religion like Zoroastrianism, which patently believes in dualism. Fazlur Rahman maintained the view, nevertheless, that there is no arbitrary interference on the part of God with the exercise of freedom by man. Islam requires submission to God's will, but 'God's will, which operates both at the physical and moral level, has to be discovered by man'.[49] Man is, in other words, not here merely to surrender to a series of commands but must discover and understand the nature of God's message and command first before he can comply with it and fulfil his duty of submission to those commands.

Mutahhari draws attention to the reality of the law of causation as one of the most important of the universal norms that God has validated and upheld. It is within this context and also in relation to the equally important norms of accountability and justice that freedom acquires much of its meaning. Justice, like accountability, is linked with human freedom and choice. Therefore, 'belief in the principle of justice means belief in the principle of human freedom, human responsibility and human creativity'.[50] Mutahhari is critical of the advocates of predestination in saying that they have 'arrived at a belief regarding divine decree that was wholly inconsistent with human freedom'.[51] This is because of their denial of the law of causation, both in relationship to human conduct, and to natural phenomena—and also the belief that divine decree acts directly and without intermediation. According to this belief, 'fire does not cause to burn, but God causes to burn [...] Man does not cause the good or evil deed, but God directly carries out the good or evil deed through the human form'.[52]

Ismail Faruqi underscored the moral content of freedom in Islam when he wrote that man alone among other creatures is capable of action and is also free to act or not to act. This freedom vests him with a distinguishing quality, namely responsibility. It casts upon his action its moral character. An action is moral precisely when done freely, and it is this type of action that is the greater part of the Divine will.[53] Al-Kurdi has similarly noted that in Islam, 'freedom basically stands for the ultimate responsibility of man', and added that the Qur'ān has emphatically declared that 'every man is fully and discernibly responsible for deciding his own destiny'.[54]

Fatḥī ᶜUthmān has pointed out that Islam also advocates the independence of the Muslim community and state. The Islamic state is founded on its *Sharīᶜah* and is totally independent; its sovereignty may not be compromised, and nor must it allow aggression on or occupation of even an inch of its territory by hostile forces. The Islamic state knows no authority above the *Sharīᶜah* of God and the community of Muslims.[55] The Muslim Community (*ummah*) is the principal audience of the Qur'ān, God's vicegerent on earth and the custodian of the *Sharīᶜah*. The recognised sources of law in Islam include, next to the Qur'ān and *Sunnah*, the consensus (*ijmāᶜ*) of the Muslim community, their scholars and representatives. The will and consensus of the community thus stands in authority next to the will of God.

The *Sharīᶜah* also forbids violation of the liberty of others. Should there be an instance of aggression, the oppressed party is entitled to defend and regain its freedom through all possible means, as the Qur'ān directs: 'There is no blame on those who seek help after having become victims of injustice' (al-Shūrā, 42:41).

ولمن انتصر بعد ظلمه فأولئك ما عليهم من سبيل.

The international community too is under obligation, as Selim el-Awa has commented, to assist all those who struggle for their freedom; it is a Qur'ānic obligation of the Muslims to do so, as part of promoting a good cause. This is the purport of the following Qur'ānic *āyah*: 'Those who, if We establish them in the land, will keep up prayer and charity, enjoin good and forbid evil' (al-Ḥajj, 22:41).

الذين إن مكّنّهم في الأرض أقاموا الصلاة و آتو الزكاة و أمروا
بالمعروف ونهوا عن المنكر.

These are, in other words, people who use their power and influence to promote what is right and prevent what is wrong. To repel aggression and injustice undoubtedly falls within the ambit of this text.

IV. Affirmative Evidence

The Qur'ānic evidence that is reviewed in the following pages relates to a variety of themes, some of which are directly and others indirectly, related to freedom. It is relevant to examine, in addition to direct references on this subject, such other passages of the Qur'ān that occur on prophethood, and the manner in which the Prophet Muḥammad ﷺ was advised to observe the people's freedom of choice. It is worthwhile also to review the evidence on the dignity of mark, and the relevance in this connection of the principle of accountability, and the doctrine of *ḥisbah* (commanding good and forbidding evil). The following Qur'ānic *āyah* establishes freedom as an inherent attribute of all human beings:

> The nature ordained by God in which He has created mankind. Let there be no change in God's creation. (al-Rūm, 30:30)

فطرة اللّه التى فطر الناس عليها، لا تبديل لخلق اللّه.

To say that God has created man free by nature is an affirmation not only of freedom as the normative and original state but also of the abilities that man's nature is endowed with—and that the most distinctive of the natural abilities of man is his faculty of reason.[56] The often cited phrase that 'Islam is a natural religion' (*al-islām dīn al-fiṭrah*) implies that it stands for that which is upheld by common sense and reason. The natural freedom and reasonable propensities of man thus receive Islam's seal of approval.

To declare freedom a basic norm of the *Sharīᶜah* is tantamount to saying that everyone is presumed to be free in whatever they wish to do unless the law specifically provides otherwise. Freedom in this sense is the original state and the absence of freedom or restriction on it is exceptional to the norm. To recognise the normative validity of freedom also means that it is an inherent right of every human being, which is not amenable to abrogation or denial except under the law.

The substance of the above-mentioned *āyah* is also upheld in a *ḥadīth* wherein the Prophet ﷺ declares that 'every child is born in the natural state [of freedom]'.[57] .

ما من مولود إلا ويولد على الفطرة.

Furthermore, Islam has prohibited the primitive practice of capturing a free man and turning him into a slave or selling him into slavery—as in the following *ḥadīth qudsī* wherein God Most High said:

> There are three categories of people against whom I shall Myself be the opponent on the Day of Judgement. [Of these three], one is he who enslaves a free man, then sells him and devours the money.[58]

ثلاثة أنا خصمهم يوم القيامة [...] ورجل باع حرا فأكل ثمنه.

Thus it is concluded that freedom is a natural right, endowed in everyone from birth. It is inherent and incessant and no man has the authority to take what God has granted as a natural right. The essence of this message was conveyed by the Caliph ʿUmar ibn al-Khaṭṭāb in what he posed as a question that begged an obvious answer: 'Since when did you enslave the people whom their mothers gave birth to as free individuals?'[59]

متى استعبدتم الناس وقد ولدتهم أمهاتهم أحرارا.

One of the practical manifestations of the norm of liberty in the works of *fiqh* is the position of the foundling infant (*al-laqīṭ*), whose identity, whether born to a free man or a slave, is not known. The *laqīṭ* that is found in the street or at any place is presumed to be a free individual simply because the norm in regard to human beings is freedom. Moreover, it is a collective duty (*farḍ kifā'ī*) of the community as a whole, and a personal duty (*farḍ ʿaynī*) of the individual who finds the *laqīṭ* to bring it to safety and protect it.[60] Note also Imām Abū Ḥanīfah's ruling to the effect that an idiot (*safīh*) is not liable to interdiction for fear of squandering his own assets, simply because this would mean compromising his liberty and personal dignity for the sake of protecting his property.[61]

The Qur'ānic vision of the freedom of man is all-encompassing in that it makes the call to Islam, the mission of the Prophet Muḥammad ﷺ and the manner in which Islam is propagated, all subject to basic freedom of choice. The three most important objectives of the prophetic mission of Muḥammad ﷺ have thus been expounded as follows:

> He enjoins them [his followers] good and forbids them evil, and makes lawful to them the good things and prohibits them from that which is

impure, and removes from them the burdens and the shackles which were on them before (al-Aʿrāf, 7:157).

يأمرهم بالمعروف ويناههم عن المنكر ويحل لهم الطيبات ويحرم عليهم الخبائث ويضع عنهم إصرهم و الأغلال التى كانت عليهم.

The three paramount goals of Islam that are thus specified are to promote *ḥisbah*, that is commanding good and forbidding evil, to identify the *ḥalāl* and *ḥarām*, and to free people from restrictions that they suffered before. This characterisation of the prophethood of Muḥammad ﷺ can be extended to other prophets, all of whom were the champions of freedom and liberators of their people against oppression. Note, for example, the Qur'ānic passages where Pharaoh is quoted to have told Moses: 'Did we not cherish you as a child among us, and did you not stay in our midst many years of your life [...] and you are ungrateful.' (al-Shuʿarā', 26:18-19)

ألم نربك فينا وليدا ولبثت فينا من عمرك و أنت من الكافرين.

To this Moses replied: 'And is it a favour with which you reproach me that you have enslaved the Children of Israel?' (al-Shuʿarā', 26:22). Pharaoh evidently tried to ingratiate Moses but Moses replied that he could not remain silent at the enslavement of his people solely because he grew up in Pharaoh's household. Murtaza Mutahhari has drawn the following conclusion from this and other similar Qur'ānic passages: 'We definitely know that one of the aims of the prophetic mission [of all Prophets] has been to establish social freedom and fight against every form of enslavement and social depravation.'[62]

Further on the same theme, the Qur'ān described the Prophet Muḥammad ﷺ as a witness, a warner to the wrongdoers, and one who gave glad tidings to the righteous. His basic task was to inform the people and then leave them at liberty to make their own choices. They are, in other words, themselves responsible for the manner in which they exercise their freedom of choice. Whoever wished to follow correct guidance did so for their own benefit and whoever rejected it also did so at their own peril. This is, in fact, the theme of several declarations in the Qur'ān. To quote some:

O Prophet, surely We have sent thee as a witness, a bearer of good news and a warner. (al-Aḥzāb, 33:45)

يا أيها النبى إنا أرسلناك شاهداً و مبشراً و نذيرا.

Say, o people, the truth has indeed come to you from your Lord. So whoever follows guidance does so only for the good of his own soul, and whoever errs, errs only against it. I am not a custodian over you. (Yūnus, 10:108)

قل يا أيها الناس قد جاء كم الحقّ من ربّكم، فمن اهتدى فإنما يهتدى لنفسه ومن ضلّ فإنما يضلّ عليها، وما أنا عليكم بوكيل.

The Prophet ﷺ was neither a tyrant (*jabbār*) nor a controller (*musayṭir*), nor a wielder of power over the people. It was not within the terms of his reference to impinge on the people's liberty, but merely to alert them of the consequences of the choices they made:

And you are not one to compel them, so remind by means of the Qur'ān those who take heed. (Qāf, 50:45)

وما أنت عليهم بجبار، فذكر بالقرآن من يخاف وعيد.

So remind. You are only a reminder; you are not a warder over them. (al-Ghāshiyah, 88:21-22)

فذكر إنما أنت مذكر لست عليهم بمسيطر.

Islam rejects compulsion even if it is the only way to Islam itself, as the Qur'ān declares: 'There shall be no compulsion in religion. Guidance has been made clear from misguidance.' (al-Baqarah, 2:256)

لا إكراه في الدين قد تبين الرشد من الغى.

This affirmation of the freedom of religion finds even a more emphatic endorsement in the following address to the Prophet:

> Had thy Lord willed, all of the inhabitants of the earth would have professed the faith. Are you then forcing people to become believers? (Yūnus, 10:99)

ولو شاء ربك لآمن من في الأرض كلّهم جميعاً، أفأنت تكره الناس حتى يكونوا مؤمنين.

It is as if God Most High is telling the Prophet ﷺ: 'Are you doing what I chose not to do?' God has chosen to let the people make a free choice over the faith they embrace, and the Prophet was clearly alerted that there should be no compromise on this. This is a recurrent theme as the Qur'ān further elaborates: 'So let him who pleases believe, and let him who pleases disbelieve' (al-Kahf, 18:29).

ومن شاء فليؤمن ومن شاء فليكفر.

The Qur'ān also describes itself as a reminder (*al-dhikr*) to 'those among you who wish to be on the straight path' (al-Takwīr, 81:28).

إن هو إلا ذكر للعالمين لمن شاء منكم أن يستقيم.

Another Qur'ānic theme which has a bearing on freedom is the dignity of man and the various manifestations of that dignity that the text has elaborated in a number of places. The most explicit of all of these declarations is the one conveying God's affirmation that 'We have bestowed dignity on the progeny of Adam' (al-Isrā', 17:70).

ولقد كرمنا بنى آدم.

Man's freedom is, in the Qur'ānic order of values, a complementary part of his inherent dignity.

Another feature of Qur'ānic teaching that is affirmative of human freedom is man's accountability for his conduct. Four Qur'ānic *ayāt* may be quoted on this, the first of which speaks of an *amānah* (trust) that God Most High offered to His creatures. The text thus declares:

Verily We proposed to the heavens and the earth, and to the mountains to receive the 'trust' but they refused the burden and they feared to receive it. Man undertook to bear it. (al-Aḥzāb, 33:72)

إنا عرضنا الأمانة على السماوات والأرض والجبال فأبين أن يحملنها وأشفقن منها و حملها الإنسان.

Muhammad Iqbal's reading of this *amānah* is that 'man is the trustee of a free personality' and he therefore bears the responsibility that goes with it. 'Freedom, moreover, in this sense is a trust which man has accepted at his peril.'[63] Freedom is a trust with which God Most High has endowed mankind in the latter's capacity as God's vicegerent (*khalīfah*) on earth, a trust which necessitates man's ability to obey God or to disobey Him. God's endowment of this *amānah,* in other words, takes account of mankind's ability to carry it and with it goes the freedom of whether or not to comply with His trust, His religion and His *Sharīʿah*.[64] The other three passages quoted below elaborate some of the attributes of freedom versus accountability in Islam. Freedom is a prerequisite of accountability (*taklīf*):

Every soul is rewarded for what it does of good and held responsible for its evil deeds. (al-Baqarah, 2:286)

لها ما كسبت وعليها ما اكتسبت.

Every man is in pledge for what he has done. (al-Ṭūr, 52:21)

كل أمرئ بما كسب رهين.

No soul shall bear the burden of another soul. (al-Najm, 53:38)

ولا تزر وازرة وزر أخرى.

To be responsible for one's conduct, one must have the freedom to determine the course of that conduct.

Another feature of the Qur'ānic evidence on freedom is its frequent invitation to the exercise of rational judgement. In numerous places and in a wide variety of contexts, the Qur'ān praises those who observe and investigate (*yanẓurūn*), those who think (*yatafakkarūn*), those who reflect (*yatadabbarūn*), those who exercise rational judgment (*yaʿqilūn*), those who understand (*yatafaqqahūn*), and those who know (*yaʿlamūn*). Furthermore, the Qur'ān takes to task those who fail to investigate and think about God's messages and the world around them.[65] These are among the major themes of the Qur'ān, and occur regularly throughout the text. References to enquiry and observation (*al-naẓar*), for example, occur in fifty places, and to rational judgement (*taʿaqqul*) in fifty-two places, to knowledge (*al-ʿilm*) in over one hundred places, and to thinking (*tafakkur*) and understanding (*tafaqquh*) on about forty occasions.[66] It is partly due to the emphasis the Qur'ān lays on such themes that the *ʿulamā'* have considered the pursuit of knowledge a collective obligation of the Muslim community, and in some cases, as a personal obligation of every person. The Qur'ānic address in almost all of these verses is to free individuals who are under no compulsion to confirm or to deny unless they are convinced of the merit of the subject they investigate. Blind following of others, including that of one's own ancestors, and unquestioning conformity to, the legacy of the past is discouraged in the Qur'ān. The Qur'ān thus recounts with disapproval the disbelievers' assertion: 'It is sufficient for us to do what our forefathers did, even if their forefathers did not know and had no guidance' (al-Mā'idah, 5:104).[67]

قالوا حسبنا ما وجدنا عليه آباء نا أو لو كان أباؤهم لا يعلمون شيئا ولا يهتدون.

The Prophet ﷺ has basically endorsed the same message when he instructed the believers:

> Let none of you be turned into a tail who does good work or embark upon evil only when he sees others doing the same. Nay, make up your own minds. Let everyone join hands in good deeds and let no one follow others in evil conduct. [68]

لا تكونوا إمعة تقولون إن حسن الناس أحسنا و إن ظلموا ظلمنا، ولكن وطنوا أنفسكم إن أحسن الناس تحسنوا وإن أساء وا فلا تفعلوا.

On the subject of political freedom, one *ḥadīth* declares that 'there is no obedience in sin. Obedience is enjoined only in righteousness.'[69]

لا طاعة في معصية، إنما الطاعة في المعروف.

Thus when the ruling authorities give orders that violate the principles of Islam, the individual is not required to obey them. This *ḥadīth*, in effect, provides the basis of legitimacy for the citizens' uprising against lawlessness and despotism. In this sense, the *Sharīʿah* stands out as the only legal tradition to provide for what is seen as ultimate political freedom.[70]

The substance of this *ḥadīth* is upheld in another *ḥadīth* in which the Prophet ﷺ declares that 'the best form of *jihād* [struggle] is to tell a word of truth to an oppressive ruler'.[71]

أفضل الجهاد كلمة حق عند سلطان جائر.

The Prophet ﷺ also instructed his followers to 'tell the truth even if it be unpleasant'.[72]

قل الحق ولو كان مرا.

At the same time, silence that is inspired by fear of people is equated with humiliation of the self, as in the following *ḥadīth*:

> Let not anyone humiliate himself! To this the Companions responded: 'How does one do that, O Messenger of God?' Then the Prophet said: 'When someone sees an occasion in which he should speak out for the sake of God, but he does not, then God Most High will tell him on the Day of Judgement: "What stopped you from speaking on that issue?" And when the person answers: "For fear of people", then God says: "You should have feared Me and put Me above the fear of others."'[73]

لا يحقر أحدكم نفسه، قالوا يا رسول الله كيف يحقر أحدنا نفسه؟ قال يرى أمرا لله عليه مقال ثم لا يقول فيه، فيقول الله عز و جل يوم القيامة: ما منعك أن تقول في كذا و كذا؟ فيقول خشية الناس، فيقول فإياى كنت أحق أن تخشى.

Islam's emphasis on freedom of conscience and the moral autonomy of the individual is also evident in the following *ḥadīth*:

> When you see my community afraid of telling a tyrant, 'O tyrant', then it is not worth belonging to it anymore.[74]

إذا رأيت أمتى تهاب أن تقول للظالم يا ظالم، فقد تودع منها.

Political freedom in its affirmative sense is manifested in the citizen's right to elect and be elected to political office. To this effect it may be noted that the *Sharīᶜah* validates a representative system of government which comes into power through the citizen's pledge of allegiance (*bayᶜah*) and conducts its affairs by consultation (*shūrā*). Notwithstanding the long history of dynastic rule in the Muslim lands, such as those of the Umayyads, Abbasids, Ottomans etc., the Qur'ān associates monarchy with corruption (*fasād*) (al-Naml, 27:34) and speaks consistently of *ūlu al-amr* in the plural form (cf. al-Nisā', 4:59), which implies power-sharing and collective leadership. A government that refuses to abide by the Qur'ānic mandate of *shūrā*, according to some Qur'ān interpreters, thereby becomes illegitimate and may be deposed.[75]

The Rightly-Guided Caliphs were supportive of a consultative and participatory system of rule and encouraged the people to communicate freely with them. It is thus noted that the first Caliph, Abū Bakr, addressed the community in his inaugural sermon upon taking office with the following words: 'O people, I have been entrusted with authority over you, but I am not the best of you. Help me if I am right, and rectify me when I am wrong.'[76] Abū Bakr's successor, ᶜUmar ibn al-Khaṭṭāb, also asked the people in his inaugural speech to 'rectify any aberration' they might see in him. Upon hearing this a man rose from the audience and said, 'If we see deviation on your part, we shall rectify it by our swords.' In response to this, the Caliph graciously praised God for the fact that there were people who took such a rigorous stance in the cause of righteousness.[77] All of this was in adherence to the letter and spirit of the Prophet's directive and declaration that 'there is no obedience to the created in disobedience of the Creator'.[78]

لا طاعة لمخلوق في معصية الخالق.

This early period is consequently seen as exemplary in the political history of Islam. However, with the exception of a handful of rulers, such as the Umayyad ʿUmar ibn ʿAbd al-ʿAzīz, who followed the earlier precedent, caliphs and rulers of the dynastic periods generally departed from the early example. Despotism became the pattern of government. Abdul Aziz Said thus rightly notes that the form of government and freedom of political action 'from the Umayyad dynasty in the seventh century through the present, have been much more militaristic than they were Islamic'.[79]

The first step in the direction of constitutional government in recent Muslim history was taken in 1808 in Ottoman Turkey, when the Grand Vizier Bayrakdar Mustafa Pasha signed an agreement with the Sultan in Istanbul to convene a consultative assembly. This example was followed in 1829 when Muhammad Ali Pasha established a consultative assembly in Egypt. The first Ottoman constitution of 1876 declared that personal freedom was inviolable (Art. 10) and other articles dealt with freedom of worship, press, association, education etc., as well as freedom from arbitrary violation of the rights of person, residence and property.[80]

Any discussion of the Qur'ānic evidence on freedom would be deficient without mentioning the principle of *amr bi'l-maʿrūf wa nahy ʿan al-munkar*, that is, commanding good and forbidding evil (also known as *ḥisbah*) and also a brief reference to slavery. There are several *āyāt* in the Qur'ān on *ḥisbah*, just as it is also one of the major themes of the *Sunnah*. The jurists have similarly spoken at length on the conditions and valid application of *ḥisbah,* which need not, perhaps, be reviewed here.[81] In bare essence, *ḥisbah* entitles every individual to moral and political freedom to speak out and to act in pursuit of what he or she considers to be beneficial and good, or to discourage and forbid what he or she considers to be evil, provided that the person who does so is the direct observant and witness of the incident in question. *Ḥisbah* is a broad doctrine and provides the basic authority for many of the moral teachings and legal principles of the *Sharīʿah*. What we need to underscore here is its relevance to the moral autonomy of the individual and his liberty to take a stand on issues, and be an active participant in the affairs of the community to which he or she belongs. *Ḥisbah* can be applied and invoked by individuals who are not only free to form an opinion and judgement, but are also able to act on that basis in order to secure a benefit or prevent an evil which they know and believe they can achieve through personal initiative, advice or action. To quote only one of many *ḥadīth* on this, the Prophet has addressed one of the two aspects of *ḥisbah*, that is, the prevention of evil, in the following terms:

> If any of you sees something evil, he should set it right with his hand; if he is unable to do so, then with his tongue, and if he is unable to do even that, then [let him denounce it] in his heart. But this is the weakest form of faith.[82]

من رأى منكم منكراً فليغيره بيده، فإن لم يستطع فبلسانه، فان لم يستطع فبقلبه و ذلك أضعف الايمان.

The Qur'ān has strongly encouraged the manumission of slaves, which it has made an act of spiritual merit, and a form of expiation (*kaffārah*) for sins. Sinful conduct, such as taking a false oath, the deliberate breaking of the fast during the fasting month of Ramaḍān, and also erroneous killing may be atoned for by the charitable act of securing the release of a slave. The fact that the Qur'ān determines releasing a slave as an atonement for manslaughter has evoked the comment that granting freedom is here equated with the giving of life. When the killer destroys the life of a person, he is supposed to redeem himself by granting another person his freedom. It is as if slavery is equated with death and the slave is brought back to life by granting him his freedom.[83]

The fact that slavery has in principle survived in Islam may be explained by reference to two factors, one of which is the prevalence of this institution in Arab society, so much so that a total ban on it might not have been feasible. The other factor is warfare and the reciprocal treatment that warring parties accorded one another by turning war prisoners into slaves. Slavery, as a result, survived in a restricted form, under conditions, however, which envisaged its eventual termination. The fact that slavery is now outlawed and extinct is in harmony with the Qur'ān. But I propose to be brief on this issue as it is no longer of real significance.

It is not an exaggeration to conclude, as Ramadan wrote, that Islam's principles on moral virtue, human dignity and freedom are equally applicable to Muslims and non-Muslims. Justice, freedom of speech, freedom of belief, freedom of movement, and freedom of association 'are guaranteed for all people, Muslims and non-Muslims alike'. It is not permissible, therefore, to restrict the freedom of the individual in any way unless he or she transgresses the rights of others or harms the interests of the community.[84]

Other conclusions that commentators have drawn from the evidence of the Qur'ān and *Sunnah* on freedom may be summarised as follows: one commentator observes that Islam is a religion of freedom and liberation for both the individual and the community. It liberates the individual conscience and encourages individual accomplishment and growth through the freedom of choice.[85]

Freedom is also a manifestation of God's favour and grace on mankind. It is, as such, of divine origin, a gift of God to the whole of mankind, and not conferred from one man to another. It is therefore inherent in every human being and may not be denied to anyone; it is also irrevocable in that no one may terminate it or take it back, unless, of course, this is in the cause of justice and in conformity with the provisions of *Sharīᶜah*. Being God-given and sacrosanct, it commands respect and no one, including a ruler or judge, is authorised to overrule or derogate it without a valid cause. It is an obligation of the state to provide adequate guarantees for the protection of individual liberties.[86]

Since freedom is a manifestation of God's grace and originates in His will and command, it tends to acquire a religious dimension and finds a place in the conscience of the believer. Observance of the basic liberties of others is therefore not a matter only of compliance with formal rules but becomes a part of the piety and *taqwā* of a Muslim.[87]

Furthermore, to say that freedom is divinely ordained and authorised as an integral part of the dignity of man must also imply that it should, in principle, be immune to extremism and abuse.[88] Freedom should, in other words, be regulated in the light of the Qur'ānic conception of justice, which means a balanced implementation of divergent interests therein. Neither the community nor the individual is therefore authorised to disturb the balance between individual freedom and public interest at each other's expense in a way that violates the ideals of justice. Justice in the final analysis consists of a balanced implementation of rights and duties of both the individual and the community at large. Freedom, like other basic rights, cannot therefore be independent of justice in Islam.[89]

There is a fine balance between the claims of the community and its rights and those of individual rights and liberties, which is perceived under the twin concepts of the Rights of God (*ḥuqūq Allāh*), which consists mainly of community's rights, and the Right of Man (*ḥuqūq al-ᶜibād*), which relates to the rights and obligations of man vis-à-vis his fellow human beings. These rights also signify limits where individual freedom defers to the rights and liberties of others. The *Sharīʿah* basically aims to draw a regulatory framework for personal liberties, and the purpose is not to impinge upon them or restrict them. The purpose is not one of preconceived restriction, but of regulation, so as to facilitate benefit and fulfilment for both the individual and the community.[90]

A balanced implementation of individual freedom vis-à-vis the public interest also means that neither of these are absolute and both are susceptible to compromise. One individual's freedom may thus be restricted to the extent that its exercise does not inflict a harm (*ḍarar*) on other individuals, or the collective *maṣlaḥah* of the community. The detailed rules of *Sharīʿah* on the proper exercise of individual liberties go a long way to ensuring that they are not exercised in a manner that is prejudicial to others or unjust.[91]

The remainder of this chapter addresses the doctrine of permissibility (*ibāḥah*) and the principle of original non-liability (*al-barā'ah al-aṣliyyah*), which represent the juristic manifestations of *ḥurriyyah* in the works of Muslim jurists. The discussion on *ibāḥah* begins with a general characterisation of the relevant evidence in the Qur'ān relating to that subject.

V. The Doctrine of *Ibāḥah* (Permissibility)

The juristic expositions of the *fuqahā'* on rights and liberties and the terminology they have utilised are broadly reflective of the language and style of the Qur'ān and the *Sunnah* on the subject. As already noted, the Qur'ān does not speak of individual liberties either generally or in reference to its particular varieties. There are, on the other hand, numerous references to permissibility, comfort and the convenience that God has granted to mankind. When God avails man, of His grace, of the enjoyments of life and encourages His servants to utilise the resources of the earth, to travel in it and to explore, whether for pleasure or the pursuit of knowledge, to own property, to eat of the good food and enjoy the beauty of God's creation and so forth, these are in effect expressive of the liberty of man in regard to these activities.

The linguistic style of the Qur'ān in expounding the various aspects of human liberty is thus multifarious and diverse, including such declarations, as are often noted in the text, that such and such has been made lawful to you (*uḥillat lakum*) and expressions enjoining individuals 'not to forbid' (*lā tuḥarrimū*) such and such, or that 'there is blame on you' (*lā junāḥa ʿalaykum*) if you do such and such, or that 'you commit no sin' (*fa-lā ithma ʿalaykum*) if you act in a certain way, or that God will not take you to task (*lā-yu'ātkhidhukum*) if you acted in a certain way. Furthermore, the text may simply grant a permission (*idhn*) in regard to something, or indeed, speak in emphatic language regarding something, such as 'who has ever forbidden you?' (*man ḥarrama ʿalaykum*) from taking your share, for instance, of the beauty and good food that God has endowed the earth with (al-Aʿrāf, 7:32); or 'why do you forbid' (*lima tuḥarrim*) such and such, or the more general but negative statements that God only forbids what is indecent and sinful (cf. al-Aʿrāf, 7:33). The *Sunnah* adds to these such other expressions as *rufiʿ al-qalamu,* 'the pen has been lifted,' or that no hardship (*lā-ḥaraj*) or no liability (*lā-ḥanth*) is attached to such and such. At the root of all of these, and similar other expressions in the Qur'ān and the *Sunnah,* is the basic notion of permissibility and the liberty that is granted to the individual in these various contexts. This may be said to be a characteristic feature of the language and style of the Qur'ān on rights and liberties, which has in turn given rise to the doctrine of *ibāḥah.* God Most High has thus vouchsafed the basic liberty of the individual, not in the name specifically of *ḥurriyyah,* but by authoritative declarations of permissibility that are perhaps more befitting to the general pattern of God-man relationship in Islam. Taking their lead from the language of the Qur'ān and *Sunnah,* Muslim jurists have similarly remained reticent in their usage of the word '*ḥurriyyah*' in their juristic expositions and have spoken instead of permissibility, which is to all intents and purposes concurrent with, and equivalent to, *ḥurriyyah.* Thus according to one commentator, 'The notion of liberty [(*ibāḥah*) in Islamic juristic thought] lies at foundation of law. God has created all things for the benefit of man and man is hence free to acquire and dispose of them. Everyone is presumed to be free until the contrary be proved'.[92]

The renowned Mālikī jurist al-Shāṭibi (d. 1388), has moreover added a new dimension to '*ibāḥah*' by identifying it with the state of forgiveness (*martabat al-ʿafw*), an expression which strikes a note of agreement with the wording of a *ḥadīth* that al-Shāṭibi has quoted. The state of forgiveness, al-Shāṭibi tells us, falls between that which the *Sharīʿah* has declared forbidden and that which it has declared permissible. Thus it is provided in a *ḥadīth*:

> God has made certain things permissible and others forbidden. Whatever God has permitted is *ḥalāl* and whatever He has forbidden is *ḥarām*. As for that regarding which God has remained silent, this is forgiven.

أحل اللّه حلالا و حرم حراما، فما أحل اللّه فهو حلال، وما حرم اللّه فهو حرام، وما سكت عنه فهو عفو.

Ibn ᶜAbbās has been quoted to have said in this connection that things to which the Qur'ān has made no reference—these are the ones that God has forgiven.[93] The substance of the above *ḥadīth* is endorsed in another *ḥadīth* as follows:

> God has prescribed certain duties: do not neglect them; He has prohibited certain things, and laid down certain limits which you should not violate. He has also granted exemptions with regard to many things out of mercy, not out of oblivion, so do not scrutinise them [too much].[94]

إن اللّه فرض فرائض فلا تضيعوها، ونهى عن أشياء فلا تنتهكوها، وحد حدودا فلا تعتدوها، وعفا عن أشياء رحمة بكم لا عن نسيان فلا تبحثوا عنها.

Muslim jurists have also quoted three other Qur'ānic *āyāt* on the validity of *ibāḥah* as a normative principle of the *Sharīᶜah*, which are as follows:

> It is He who has created for you all that is on the earth (al-Baqarah, 2:29).

هو الذى خلق لكم ما في الأرض جميعا.

> God has subjugated to you all that is in the heavens and the earth. (al-Jāthiyah, 45:13)

وسخر لكم ما في السماوات وما في الأرض جميعاً.

> God has explained to you in detail what is forbidden to you excepting that to which you are compelled [without choice]. (al-Anᶜām, 6:119)

وقد فصل لكم ما حرم عليكم إلا ما اضطررتم إليه.

If the created world is for the benefit of human beings and is subjugated to their benefit and service, the underlying purpose of this is evidently to enable them to utilise the resources of the world. This is another way of saying that human beings are permitted to act so as to harness the resources of the earth to their advantage. Hence everything in the known world, including legal acts, contracts, exchange of goods and services and so forth, that is beneficial to human beings is lawful to them on the grounds of original *ibāḥah*.[95] The above-quoted *āyāt* are also self-explanatory on the point that God Most High has clearly explained what is prohibited, which means that a prohibition can only be established by a clear text. A mere presumption is therefore not enough to establish a prohibition. The position is precisely the reverse with regard to permissibility, which is presumed even in the absence of a clear text in respect to things that are not prohibited by a clear text. This is the precise purport of the legal maxim which declares that the norm, or the natural state of things, from the viewpoint of *Sharīᶜah* is permissibility (*al-aṣl fi'l-ashyā' al-ibāḥah*). The jurists have mentioned only two exceptions to this, namely devotional matters (*ᶜibādāt*) and relationships between members of the two sexes. The basic norm with regard to both of these is that they are prohibited unless there is evidence to the contrary. This is achieved, in the case of *ᶜibādāt,* by a clear text, and in the case of sexual relations between men and women, through marriage. It thus appears that the presumption of *ibāḥah* is concerned mainly with relations among human beings in the area of civil transactions and trade (*muᶜāmalāt*), which are all presumed to be permissible, and 'nothing in them is forbidden', as Ibn Taymiyyah has pointed out, 'unless God and His Messenger have decreed them to be forbidden'.[96]

The Qur'ānic passages quoted above also validate *ibāḥah* as a basis for commitment (*iltizām*), which means that people are free to commit themselves in regard to something that is permissible and deny themselves that permissibility, if they so wish, by means of a contractual commitment. This position is taken by the Ḥanbalīs, who have applied *ibāḥah* more widely than the other *madhāhib*. The Ḥanbalīs have thus validated stipulations in nominate contracts that may make *ibāḥah* the subject of a personal commitment. To give an example, under the Ḥanbalī doctrine of *ibāḥah,* the prospective spouses are allowed to stipulate, in their marriage contract, that the husband remain monogamous. The other leading schools have disagreed and held that the contracting parties may not circumvent the basic legality of polygamy in the *Sharīʿah* through contractual stipulations. To this the Ḥanbalīs have responded that polygamy is after all a permissibility, not a requirement. There being no text in the Qur'ān or the *Sunnah* to indicate that the spouses may not stipulate against polygamy, they are allowed to stipulate against it. For, after all, the norm of the *Sharīʿah* with regard to marriage is monogamy and those who wish to commit themselves to monogamy are only upholding what is the normal position in the *Sharīʿah*.[97]

The debate between the majority and the Ḥanbalī school on polygamy is part of a wider question that has arisen with regard to the freedom of contract, and the insertion into a contract of stipulations that are improvised by the contracting parties.

This issue has provoked divergent responses from the jurists. The Ẓāhirīs have taken the extreme position that the norm of the *Sharīʿah* in regard to contracts is prohibition (*ḥaẓar*) which means that every contract is unlawful unless it has been specifically declared otherwise. This basic presumption according to the Ẓāhirīs can only be overruled by a clear textual authority and not merely by the will of the parties. Hence a contract, or a stipulation for that matter, that the *Sharīʿah* has not validated is of no legal consequence. In Madkūr's assessment, the Ẓāhirī jurists have been 'exceedingly restrictive' in insisting that business activities and transactions among people should remain the way they used to be at the time of the advent of Islam. They have thus 'totally ignored the change of time and circumstance and their effects on the commercial life and activities of the people'.[98] Muṣṭafā al-Zarqā has held that *ibāḥah* is the normative principle of the *Sharīʿah* that applies to all contracts.[99] This may be said to be the purport of the *ḥadīth* that 'Muslims are bound by their stipulations unless it be a stipulation that permits what is forbidden, or forbids what is permissible.'[100]

المسلمون على شروطهم إلا شرطا أحل حراما أو حرم حلالا.

The Ẓāhiris have quoted in support the Qur'ānic *āyah* which declares: 'And to God belongs the kingdom of the heavens and the earth' (al-Jāthiyah, 45:27).

ولله ملك السماوات والأرض.

From this the conclusion has been drawn that only by God's permission can the people conclude transactions and contracts among themselves.[101] Two *ḥadīth* have also been quoted in this context, but it should promptly be noted that many *ʿulamā*, including al-Shawkānī (d. 1832), have disputed their authenticity. The *ḥadīth* thus provide:

> Whoever takes action on a matter which we have not authorised, it shall be void.

من عمل عملاليس عليه أمرنا فهورد.

> Stipulations that are not indicated in the Book of God shall be void, even if it be a hundred stipulations. The Book of God and His stipulation are most credible of all.

ماكان من شرط ليس في كتاب اللّه فهوباطل ولو كان مائة شرط'
كتاب اللّه أحق وشرط اللّه أوثق.

Imām Aḥmad ibn Ḥanbal has taken the opposite view, as discussed above, that the norm in regard to contracts and stipulations is *ibāḥah*. Ibn Taymiyyah has categorically stated that in validating contracts the Qur'ān (al-Mā'idah, 5:1; al-Nisā', 4:29) has spoken in the broadest of terms, and only laid down one basic requirement, namely the mutual consent of the contracting parties, as the essence of all contracts. This is also the basic criterion of validity for all contractual stipulations that do not otherwise violate the *Sharīʿah*.[102]

The majority of the leading schools, including the Ḥanafīs and the Shāfiʿīs, have taken an intermediate position between those of the Ẓāhirīs and the Ḥanbalīs by holding the view that the parties create the contract by their consent, but that the legal consequences of that contract, such as transfer of ownership in the case of sale, and the permissibility of sexual relations in the case of marriage, are determined by the *Sharīʿah*. The parties may not, in other words, impose stipulations that interfere with the legal consequences of contracts as determined by the *Sharīʿah*.[103]

Engaging the reader with further details of the scholastic positions on *ibāḥah* may not be necessary. Suffice it to say that the principle itself is firmly rooted in the *Sharīᶜah*. The basic tone and tenor of the Qur'ānic evidence on the normative validity of *ibāḥah* is endorsed in at least two other places where the text speaks disapprovingly of those who focus only on prohibitions but turn a blind eye to permissibilities:

> O believers, forbid not the clean things that God has made lawful to you. (al-Mā'idah, 5:87)

يا أيها الذين لا يحرموا طيبات ما أحل اللّه لكم.

The Prophet ﷺ has also been addressed in the following terms:

> Say, who has forbidden the adornments of life and the good provisions that God has brought for His servants? (al-Aᶜrāf, 7:32)

قل من حرم زينة اللّه التى أخرج لعباده والطيبات من الرزق.

Commentators have added the following conclusions to their understanding of the relevant evidence of the Qur'ān and *Sunnah* on the subject of *ibāḥah*.

First, in order to declare an act or transaction valid or permissible, there is no need to search for affirmative evidence in the sources. All that one needs to investigate is whether there is a clear and self-explanatory prohibition, and if none is found to exist, the act or transaction may be presumed to be valid. For *ibāḥah* is a basic presumption of the *Sharīᶜah* that applies in the absence of a prohibitory injunction. The prohibitory text which overrules the basic presumption of permissibility must also be decisive both in meaning and transmission (*naṣṣ qaṭᶜī al-thubūt wa'l-dalālah*). Al-Qaraḍāwī has suggested, rightly perhaps, that it is sufficient if the text in question is sound of authenticity and conveys a clear meaning (*ṣaḥīḥ al-thubūt ṣarīḥ al-dalālah*) because a text of this kind is generally sufficient to establish a practical ruling of the *Sharīᶜah*.[104]

Second, the forms of contract, acts and transactions that are explicitly validated in the Qur'ān and *Sunnah* are not exhaustive, and do not preclude new varieties on which the *Sharīᶜah* might have remained silent.[105]

Third, with regard to new transactions, contracts and unprecedented developments, there is in principle no need to search for supportive evidence in the views of the early jurists. For it is essentially incorrect to extend and apply a medieval juristic opinion to something that was not even known in those times. The correct approach in such instances would be to attempt independent *ijtihād*, that is, when the matter cannot be determined under the presumption of *ibāḥah*.

On the authority of a clear text in the Qur'ān (al-Nahl, 16:116), prohibiting what God Most High has permitted is no less a sin than permitting what is clearly prohibited. The main direction of the evidence of the Qur'ān and *Sunnah* on this is to narrow down and minimise the scope of prohibitions and try in this way to lighten the burden on people. To follow a trend in the opposite direction, that is, to expand the scope of prohibitions and to impose on people's freedom of choice is contrary to Qur'ānic directives. Some of the Qur'ānic principles that need not, perhaps, be elaborated here, including removal of hardship (*rafᶜ al-ḥaraj*), and the principle of *taysīr* (bringing ease and facilitating difficult situations) may also be added to the *Sharīᶜah* evidence in support of *ibāḥah*.

It should be briefly mentioned, however, that *ibāḥah* is a sub-topic of the *Sharīᶜah* doctrine of *istiṣḥāb*, that is the presumption of continuity, which is one of the subsidiary sources of the *Sharīᶜah*. *Istiṣḥāb* (lit. escorting or companionship) denotes that facts, custom, and rules of reason whose validity and existence had been known in the past are presumed to remain as they were before unless evidence shows that there is a change. The past thus escorts and accompanies the present without any interruption or change.[106] *Istiṣḥāb* is a rational doctrine, and a presumptive proof, much like *ibāḥah*, which derives its validity from the belief that Islam did not aim to establish a new life on earth, and nor did it aim to nullify or replace all the mores and customs of Arabian society at the time. Islam sought to overrule and replace only practices and customs that were deemed unacceptable. Thus with reference to social mores, and the cultural and commercial practices that society upheld then or at any other time, Islam takes a basic attitude of validation and permissibility towards them, unless there is evidence to the contrary. The *Sharīᶜah* has also left many things unregulated and when this is the case, human action may in regard to them be guided by good conscience and reason. *Ibāḥah* thus constitutes a major component of *istiṣḥāb*.

VI. The Principle of Original Non-Liability (*Barā'at al-Dhimmah al-Aṣliyyah*)

This too is a presumption that applies in the absence of evidence or when the evidence is doubtful. It is, like *ibāḥah*, an *istiṣḥāb*-related principle and presumes that everyone is free of liability and guilt unless the opposite is proven by lawful evidence. The basic presumption is that people are born innocent and remain in that state until there is proof to show otherwise. No one may therefore be punished for an offence, or his freedom violated, unless he or she is proved guilty. The word *'dhimmah'* denotes the legal capacity of the individual, that is, his or her capacity to incur rights and obligations. The *dhimmah*, in other words, is normally presumed to be free of obligation, liability or guilt. This is the purport of a legal maxim (*qāʿidah kulliyyah*), recorded in the *Mejelle,* declaring simply that 'freedom from liability is the norm [of the *Sharīʿah*].'[107] The principle of *barā'at al-dhimmah* is, to all intents and purposes, equivalent to what is known in modern law as the 'presumption of innocence'. The only difference that may be noted is that the presumption of innocence is basically applicable to crimes and punishment, whereas *barā'at al-dhimmah* applies equally to civil litigations and to crime. Like most other legal maxims, this has been derived from the totality of relevant evidence in the Qur'ān and the *Sunnah*. Some of the basic evidence that was reviewed under the principles of *ibāḥah* above can equally be brought in here.

The Qur'ān provides basic authority with regard to the claims that some people make against others, in that they must be investigated before any conclusion is drawn from them, even if the claimant happens to be a person of compromised integrity (al-Ḥujurāt, 49:6). Elsewhere, the Qur'ān proclaims that 'conjecture avails nothing against the truth' (Yūnus, 10:36).

إن الظن لا يغنى من الحق شيئا.

An unproven claim is tantamount to conjecture (*al-ẓann*) and therefore amounts to nothing. And then, according to the clear terms of a *ḥadīth-cum-legal maxim*, 'The burden of proof is on the claimant, but the defendant must take an oath'.[108]

البينة على المدعى واليمين على من أنكر.

The plaintiff may, in other words, ask the court to put the defendant on oath, in the event where the latter denies the claim, and there is no other evidence to confirm that he is telling the truth. This is the basic position, supported by the analysis that it would be extremely difficult for the defendant if he or she were in all cases required to prove his or her innocence. The claimant and prosecutor are therefore required, as in the above *ḥadīth*, to prove their allegations. If the claimant is in all cases required to prove his claim, then it follows that until he proves it, the defendant is presumed innocent. According to Ibn Qayyim al-Jawziyyah, if the claimant proves his claim, the court will adjudicate the dispute in his favour; otherwise, the last word is that of the defendant and the court shall credit what he says provided that he takes a solemn oath to affirm that he is telling the truth.[109] It is thus concluded that no one may be granted anything on the basis merely of a claim, suspicion or accusation alone, and that the claim must in all cases be supported by evidence. This conclusion is also upheld in another *ḥadīth*, as follows:

> If people were to be granted what they claim on the basis only of their claims, they would claim the blood and property of others, but the oath is on the shoulder of the defendant.[110]

لو يعطى الناس بِدَعْوَاهُم لادعى الناس دماء رجال وأموالهم
ولكن اليمين على المدعى عليه.

This *ḥadīth* clearly lays down the requirement that every claim must be proven by evidence and that nothing is proven by a claim which is not accompanied by proof. The basic liberty of the people and their original freedom from liability is, in other words, not affected by mere allegations, and the authorities are also not permitted to take any action on that basis alone. Both Bassiouni and Weeramantry drew from this *ḥadīth* the conclusion that 'Islamic criminal law consequently throws the onus of proof heavily upon the prosecution and in the absence of such proof the accused must be acquitted'.[111] The presumption of innocence is also upheld in the *ḥadīth* declaring that 'the whole of my community is innocent except for those who broadcast [and boast about] their sinful conduct'.[112]

كل أمتى معافى إلا المجاهرين.

If there is any doubt in the evidence presented by the prosecution, the defendant will be given the benefit of this doubt.[113] Doubt is to be resolved in favour of the accused. This is the purport of the following *ḥadīth*: 'Drop the prescribed punishments in cases of doubt as far as you can. For it is better to err in forgiveness than making an error in punishment.'[114]

ادرؤوا الحدود بالشبهات ما استطعتم، والخطاء في العفو خير من الخطاء في العقوبة.

Another legal maxim that supports the substance of the principle under consideration has it that 'the conduct of reasonable men [or reason alone] is of no consequence without the support of a legal text'. This evidently means that nothing may be declared forbidden (*ḥarām*) on grounds of reason, or by the verdict of reasonable people alone. A legal text is necessary, in other words, to overrule the original state of permissibility and establish that committing a particular act or transaction is unlawful. This is because declaring something *ḥarām* overrules the normal state of freedom, and this requires the authority of a clear legal text.[115]

The legal maxim, as reviewed above, that permissibility (*ibāḥah*) is the original norm in the *Sharīʿah* also lends support to the principle of original non-liability. For this too means that all things are permissible unless the law declares them to be otherwise. No one may therefore be accused of an offence, and his or her non-liability overruled, in the absence of a legal text.

According to another legal maxim, 'no one bears liability unless he is capable of understanding the law which imposes it'.[116] It is not enough, in other words, for there to be a legal text that creates the basis of a liability or obligation; in fact, the person remains in the original state of innocence unless he or she is capable of knowing the meaning of that text and also the nature of the obligation it has created.

The question of whether the original state of non-liability remains intact even after a claim has been made has led to some differences of opinion among the Shāfiʿī and Ḥanafī jurists. The disagreement here arises basically in regard to civil and financial claims. To illustrate this, suppose A claims that B owes him 1,000 dollars and B denies it. The question then arises of whether it is lawful at all for the parties to reach a settlement (*ṣulḥ*) after B has denied the claim. The

Ḥanafīs have answered this in the affirmative, but the Shāfiᶜīs have held that a settlement after the denial of a claim is not permissible on the analysis that when B denied the claim, the principle of original freedom from liability would apply to him, which means that he is not liable. As such, it would be unlawful for A to take anything from B by way of settlement. The settlement is therefore null and void and B's freedom from liability prevails. The Ḥanafīs have argued that B's non-liability after the claim is not inviolable. The claim, in other words, interferes with the operation of the principle under discussion. A certain doubt has arisen and B can no longer be definitely held to be free of liability. This being so, the settlement in question is permissible in the interest of preventing hostility between the parties.[117]

To this, one may add the rider that a settlement normally proceeds from some kind of agreement between the disputing parties, in which case B's agreement, however implicit, also interferes with the application of the non-liability principle to him. The Ḥanafī position on this issue cannot therefore be held as evidence against the normative validity of the principle of original non-liability.

Another brief illustration that is given in the *Mejelle* in support of the presumption of original non-liability is as follows: supposing A wastes or destroys the property of B and then they disagree over the amount of the loss. To apply the principle of original non-liability, that part of the claimed amount to which A is in agreement will be taken as right and therefore proven. But B will still need to prove the excess amount about which A is not in agreement.[118] This is to show that the presumption of original non-liability remains intact notwithstanding B's claim, and B's claim needs to be proven if it is to overrule that presumption.

Two other legal maxims that are usually quoted in conjunction with the principle of *barā'at al-dhimmah* are as follows: (1) 'Certainty may not be overruled by doubt'—(*al-yāqin lā-yazūlu bi'l-shakk*); and (2) 'The norm is the continuation of *status quo ante*'—(*al-aṣlu baqā' mā kāna ᶜalā mā-kān*).[119] Both of these have provoked a great deal of juristic detail which falls, however, beyond the immediate concern of this presentation. The first of these is a leading legal maxim, often quoted as one of the top six, in terms of overall significance within a range of about 1,000 legal maxims that Muslim jurists have compiled in the various branches of Islamic law. What it signifies in the present context is that original non-liability/innocence is a certainty in conjunction with a claim which is doubtful. A mere claim does not overrule the freedom from liability and guilt of the person against whom it is made. The second of the two maxims quoted here also endorses the principle of *barā'ah* in that every claim seeks to introduce a change in the *status quo ante*, which is, however, not upheld without proof. The law will presume that the *status quo* has not changed and it is held to prevail unless evidence shows otherwise.

To conclude this chapter, it may be said that the era of constitutionalism and government under the rule of law has marked a departure from the realities of law and government in medieval times. The source evidence of the Qur'ān and the *Sunnah* on freedom as a basic premise and foundational principle of the *Sharīᶜah* is affirmative beyond question. Muslim jurists of earlier times may not have found it necessary to project the reality of this principle in the kind of assertive language that is now commonplace in the constitutional law and literature of the twentieth century. The language of *fiqh* may now need to be adjusted to the requirements of the more challenging times that the *ummah* is experiencing.

The *fiqh* of earlier times in the field of *siyāsah sharᶜiyyah* and books that bore the general title *al-aḥkām al-sulṭāniyyah* were elaborate on the duties of the individual, but rarely devoted a section or a chapter to his basic rights and liberties. Note, for example, Abu'l Ḥasan al-Māwardī's renowned work, *al-Aḥkām al-Sulṭāniyyah,* which deals mainly with the institution of the caliphate and a variety of its other related themes, but has no section on the subject of the basic rights and liberties of the individual. This work is also silent, as would be expected, on citizenship as a concept, or the basic rights of citizens vis-à-vis the nation-state. This is merely to underscore the radical nature of the changes that have occurred over the course of history. This is, in the meantime, an area of Islamic law that has remained particularly underdeveloped thanks to the prevalence of imitation (*taqlīd*) that has dominated Muslim scholarship for many long centuries.

Some progress, however, has been made and Muslim jurists have in recent decades given attention, in their writings on the general subject of *niẓām al-ḥukm fi'l-islām* (principles of government in Islam), to fundamental rights and liberties. But we are still at an early stage of this endeavour. What I have presented here provides a general treatment of *ḥurriyyah.* I am currently engaged in writing a larger work on the subject where I plan to deal with the specific areas of fundamental rights and liberties in further detail. This is an area of the *Sharīᶜah* that merits attention and it is hoped that future contributions and research will further enrich the scope and calibre of existing information on the subject. The various areas of civil and constitutional liberties need to be individually addressed and explored in detail.

NOTES

1. A twentieth-century Western philosopher has, interestingly enough, taken the opposite view: 'Freedom in general may be defined as the absence of obstacles to the realisation of desires.' See B. Russell in R.N. Anshen (ed.), *Freedom, Its Meaning*, New York, Macmillan, 1941, p. 251. See also 'Ḥurriyya', *The Encyclopedia of Islam*, new edn., Leiden, E.J. Brill, 1965.
2. Rosenthal, *The Muslim Concept of Freedom*, Leiden, E.J. Brill, 1960, pp. 87-98.
3. Al-Badawī, *Daʿā'im al-Ḥukm fi'l-Sharīʿah al-Islamiyyah wa'l-Nuẓūm al-Dustūriyyah al-Muʿāṣirah*, Cairo, Dār al-Fikr al-Islāmī, 1984, p. 45.
4. Muḥsin al-ʿAbūdī, *al-Ḥurriyyāt al-Ijtimāʿiyyah bayn al-Nuẓūm al-Muʿāṣirah wa'l-Fikr al-Siyāsī al-Islāmī*, Cairo, Dār al-Nahḍah al-ʿArabiyyah, 1410/1990, p. 42.
5. Subḥī Maḥmaṣṣānī, *Arkān Ḥuqūq al-Insān fi'l-Islām*, Beirut, Dār al-ʿIlm li'l-Malāyīn, 1979, p. 71.
6. Muḥammad Kamīl Laylah, *al-Nuẓūm al-Siyāsiyyah*, Cairo, Dār al-Fikr al-ʿArabī, 1963, p. 1120.
7. ʿAbd al-Ḥamīd Mutawallī, *Mabādi' Niẓām al-Ḥukm fi'l-Islām*, Alexandria (Egypt), Mansha'āt al-Maʿārif, 1974, p. 278; 'Ḥurriyya', EI, new edn.
8. 'Ḥurriyya', EI, new edn.; Muṣṭafā al-Sibāʿī, *Ishtirākiyyāt al-Islām*, 2nd edn., Damascus, Dār al-Qawmiyyah li'l-Ṭibāh wa'l-Nashr, 1379/1960, p.44; Rosenthal, *The Muslim Concept of Freedom*, pp. 9-10; Muḥammad al-Quṭb Ṭubliyah, *al-Islām wa'l-Ḥuqūq al-Insān. Darāsah Muqārinah*, 2nd edn., Cairo, Dār al-Fikr al-ʿArabī, 1404/1984, p. 30.
9. Bernard Lewis, *The Middle East and the West*, London, Weidenfield & Nicholson, 1967, p. 47.
10. Muḥammad al-Ṭāhir ibn ʿĀshūr, *Maqāṣid al-Sharīʿah al-Islamiyyah*, Tunis, Maṭbaʿat al-Istiqamah, 1966, p. 133.
11. ʿAbd al-Wahhāb Khallāf, *al-Siyāsah al-Sharʿiyyah*, Cairo, al-Maṭbaʿah al-Salafiyyah, 1350AH, p. 30.
12. Mutawallī, *Mabādi'*, p. 279.
13. Khallāf, *al-Siyāsah al-Sharʿiyyah*, p. 30.
14. Maḥmaṣṣānī, *Arkān*, p. 72.
15. ʿAbd al-Karīm Zaydān, *al-Fard wa'l-Dawlah fi'l-Sharīʿah al-Islamiyyah*,

Gary, Indiana: al-Itthād al-ʿAlami li'l-Munaẓẓamāt al-Ṭullābiyyah, 1390/1970, pp. 55 and 61.

16. Laylah, *al-Nuẓūm al-Siyāsiyyah*, p. 1123.

17. Muḥammad Abū Zahrah, *Tanẓīm al-Islām li'l-Mujtamaʿ*, Cairo, Dār al-Fikr al-ʿArabī, 1385/1965, p. 190.

18. Fu'ād ʿAbd al-Munʿim Aḥmad, *Uṣūl al-Niẓām al-Ḥukm fi'l-Islām*, Alexandria (Egypt), Mu'assasat Shabāb al-Jāmiʿah, 1411/1991, p. 260; see also Badawī, *Daʿā'im*, p. 56.

19. ʿAbd al-Munʿim Aḥmad, *Uṣūl al-Niẓām*, pp. 260-284.

20. Sibāʿī, *Ishtirākiyyāt*, pp. 44ff; ʿAbd al-Wāḥid al-Wāfī, *Ḥuqūq al-Insān fi'l-Islām*, Cairo, Maṭbaʿat al-Risālah, n.d., p. 125; Badawī, *Daʿā'im* p. 43.

21. ʿAbd al-Razzāq al-Sanhūrī, *Fiqh al-Khilāfah wa Ṭatawwaruhā*, ed. Nādia al-Sanhūrī and Tawfīq Muḥammad al-Shāwī, Cairo, al-Hay'ah al-Miṣriyyah al-ʿĀmmah li'l-Kitāb, 1989, p. 182.

22. Al-Badawī, *Daʿā'im*, pp. 43-4.

23. Maḥmaṣṣānī, *Arkān*, pp. 70-71.

24. Ṭubliyah, *al-Islām wa Ḥuqūq al-Insān*, p. 269.

25. ʿAbd al-Ḥakīm al-ʿĪlī, *al-Ḥurriyyāt al-ʿĀmmah*, Cairo, Dār al-Fikr, 1403/1983, pp. 195 and 200.

26. ʿAbd al-Qādir ʿAwdah, *al-Tashrīʿ al-Jinā'ī al-Islāmī*, Beirut, Mu'assasat al-Risālah, 1403/1983, I, 29.

27. Fatḥī ʿUthmān, *al-Fard fi'l-Mujtamaʿ al-Islāmī: bayn al-Ḥuqūq wa'l-Wājibāt*, Cairo, al-Majlis al-Aʿlā li'l-Shu'ūn al-Islāmiyyah, 1382/1962, p. 27.

28. Al-Wāfī, *Ḥuqūq al-Insān*, p. 114.

29. Muḥammad al-Ghazālī, *Ḥuqūq al-Insān bayn Taʿalīm al-Islām al-Umam al-Muttaḥidah*, Alexandria (Egypt) Dār al-Daʿwah li'l-Nashr wa'l-Tawzīʿ, 1413/1993, p. 246; the *ḥadīth* appears in ʿAbd Allāh al-Khaṭīb al-Tabrīzī, *Mishkāt al-Maṣābīḥ*, ed. Muḥammad Nāṣir al-Dīn al-Albānī, 2nd edn., Beirut, al-Maktab al-Islāmī, 1399/1979, vol. I, *ḥadīth* no. 90.

30. Wahbah al-Zuḥailī, *al-Fiqh al-Islāmī wa Adillatuh*, 3rd edn., Damascus, Dār al-Fikr, 1409/1989, VI, 720.

31. Abdul Aziz Said, 'Precept and Practice of Human Rights in Islam', in *Universal Human Rights*, vol. I (Jan. 1979), p. 73.

32. W. Montgomery-Watt, *Islamic Political Thought. The Basic Concepts*, Edinburgh, Edinburgh University Press, 1968, p. 96.

33. Ibid., p. 97.

34. L. Gardet, *La Cité Musulmane*, p. 69, quoted in Rosenthal, *The Muslim Concept of Freedom* p. 121.

35. Ḥasan Ṣaʿb, 'al-Ḥurriyyah al-Falsafiyyah', in Jamīl Munayminah (ed), *Mushkilat al-Ḥurriyyah fi'l-Islām*, Beirut, Dār al-Kitāb al-Lubnānī, 1974, p. 97.

36. Said, 'Precept and Practice of Human Rights in Islam', p. 73; see also

for a similar analysis Muḥammad ʿAbduh, *al-Islām wa'l-Naṣrāniyyah maʿ al-ʿIlm wa'l-Madaniyyah*, 6th edn., Cairo, Maṭbaʿat al-Nahḍah, 1375/1956, pp. 155-6.

37. Ibid. p. 74.

38. Sayyd Quṭb, *al-ʿAdālah al-Ijtimāʿiyyah fi'l-Islām*, 4th edn., Cairo, ʿĪsā al-Bābī al-Ḥalabī, 1373/1954, p. 37; see also Sibāʿī, *Ishtirākiyyāt*, pp. 44-5, to the similar effect.

39. Muhammad Baqir al-Sadr, *Contemporary Man and the Social Problem*, Eng. trans. Yasin T.A. al-Jibouri, Teheran, World Organisation of Islamic Services, 1980, p. 141.

40. Ayatollah Murtaza Mutahhari, *Spiritual Discourses*, Eng. trans. Alauddin Pazargady, Albany (California), Muslim Students' Association in the US and Canada (PSG), 1986, p. 28.

41. Ibid., p. 30

42. Ibid., p. 30.

43. Ibid., p. 31.

44. Ibid., pp. 40-41.

45. Ibid., p. 46.

46. Mutawallī, *Mabādi*, p. 281.

47. Munayminah, *Mushkilat al-Ḥurriyyah*, pp. 100-101.

48. For further details see Mohammad H. Kamali, *Principles of Islamic Jurisprudence*, revised edn., Cambridge, The Islamic Texts Society, 1991, pp. 342ff.

49. Fazlur Rahman, 'The Status of the Individual in Islam', *Islamic Studies* 5 (1966), p. 327.

50. Ayatollah Murtaza Mutahhari, *Fundamentals of Islamic Thought: God, Man and Universe*, Eng. trans. R. Campbell, Berkeley (California), Mizan Press, 1985, p. 127.

51. Ibid., p. 126.

52. Ibid., p. 126.

53. Ismail al-Faruqi, 'Islam and Other Faiths', in Altaf Gauhar (ed.), *The Challenge of Islam*, London, The Islamic Council of Europe, 1978, p. 87.

54. Abdulrahman Abdulkadir al-Kurdi, *The Islamic State: A Study Based on the Islamic Holy Constitution*, London & New York, Mansell Publishing Ltd, 1984, p. 51.

55. ʿUthmān, *al-Fard fi'l-Mujtamaʿ al-Islāmī*, p. 27.

56. al-ʿĪlī, *al-Ḥurriyyāt*, p. 168.

57. Al-Tabrīzī, *Mishkāt*, vol.I, *ḥadīth* no. 90.

58. Muḥyi al-Dīn al-Nawawī, *Riyāḍ al-Ṣāliḥīn*, 2nd edn. by Muḥammad Nāṣir al-Dīn al-Albānī, Beirut, Dār al-Maktab al-Islāmī, 1404/1984, *ḥadīth* no. 1592: the other two categories concern those who cheat others, and those who refuse to give workers their due.

59. Cf. Abū Zahrah, *Tanẓīm al-Islām*, p. 28; Ṭubliyah, *al-Islām wa'l-Ḥuqūq*

al-Insān, p. 281; Mohamed Selim el-Awa, *Fi'l-Niẓām al-Siyāsī li'l Dawlah al-Islāmiyyah*, Cairo: al-Maktab al-Miṣrī al-Ḥadīth, 1983, p. 314.

60. Muḥammad Amīn ibn ʿĀbidīn, *Ḥāshiyah Radd al-Mukhtār ʿalā Durr al-Mukhtārī*, 2nd edn., Cairo, Muṣṭafā al-Bābī al-Ḥalabī, 1386/1966, IV, 139; Aḥmad Yusrī, *Ḥuqūq al-Insān wa Asbāb al-ʿUnf fi'l-Mujtamaʿ al-Islāmī fī Ḍaw' Aḥkām al-Sharīʿah,* Alexandria (Egypt), Mansha'at al-Maʿārif, 1993, p. 29; Zuḥaylī, *al-Fiqh al-Islāmī*, V, 766.

61. Cf. Abū Zahrah, *Tanẓīm al-Islām*, p. 135; al-ʿĪlī, *al-Ḥurriyyāt*, p. 362; Yusrī, *Ḥuqūq al-Insān*, p. 29.

62. Mutahhari, *Spiritual Discourses*, p. 30.

63. Muhammad Iqbal, *Reconstruction of Religious Thought in Islam*, Lahore, Shah Muhammad Ashraf Press, 1982, p. 95.

64. Ṣaʿb, 'al-Ḥurriyyah al-Falsafiyyah', p. 98.

65. For a review of the numerous *āyāt* on the authority of reason, see Muḥammad ʿAmmārah, *al-Islām wa Ḥuqūq al-Insān: Ḍarūrāt la Ḥuqūq*, Cairo, Dār al-Shurūq, 1409/1982, pp. 26-30.

66. Cf. Fu'ād ʿAbd al-Bāqī, *al-Muʿjam al-Mufahras li-Alfāẓ al-Qur'ān al-Karīm*, 2nd edn., Cairo, Dār al-Fikr, 1402/1981, under relevant entries.

67. See also al-Zukhruf (43:23) to the similar effect.

68. Al-Tabrīzī, *Mishkāt*, III, 1418, *ḥadīth* no. 5129.

69. Al-Tabrīzī, *Mishkāt*, II, *ḥadīth* no. 3665.

70. Ṣaʿb, 'al-Ḥurriyyah al-Falsafiyyah', p. 103.

71. Muḥammad al-Qawzīnī ibn Mājah, *Sunan Ibn Mājah*, Istanbul, Cagly Yayinlari, 1401/1981, *Kitāb al-Fitan, bāb al-amr bi'l-maʿrūf wa nahy ʿan al-munkar, ḥadīth* no. 4011.

72. Jalāl al-Dīn al-Suyūṭī, *al-Jāmiʿ al-Ṣaghīr*, 4th edn., Cairo, Muṣṭafā al-Bābī al-Ḥalabī, 1954, I, 111.

73. Ibn Mājah, *Sunan, Kitāb al-Fitan, b. al-amr bi'l-maʿrūf wa nahy ʿan al-munkar.*

74. Aḥmad Ibn Ḥanbal, *Musnad al-Imām Ibn Ḥanbal*, 6 vols, Beirut, Dār al-Fikr, n.d., II, 163; al-Suyūṭī, *al-Jāmiʿ al-Ṣaghīr*, I, 41.

75. Abū ʿAbd Allāh Muḥammad al-Qurṭubī, *al-Jāmiʿ li-Aḥkām al-Qur'ān* (also known as *Tafsīr al-Qurṭubī*), IV, 249 (see commentary on '*wa shāwirhum fi'l-amr*')

76. ʿAbd al-Mālik ibn Hishām, *al-Sīrah al-Nabawiyyah,* Cairo, Muṣṭafā al-Bābī al-Ḥalabī, 1936, IV, 262; Abū Ḥabīb, *Dirāsah fī Minhāj al-Islām al-Siyāsī*, Beirut, Mu'assasat al-Risālah, 1406/1985, p. 725; Sibāʿī, *Ishtirākiyyāt*, p. 45.

77. Muḥammad Abū Zahrah, *al-Jarīmah wa'l-ʿUqūbah fi'l-Fiqh al-Islāmī*, Cairo, Dār al-Fikr al-ʿArabī, n.d., p. 160; Sibāʿī, *Ishtirākiyyāt*, p. 50.

78. Al-Tabrīzī, *Mishkāt*, II, *ḥadīth* no. 3696.

79. Said, 'Precept and Practice of Human Rights in Islam', p. 75.

80. Cf. 'Ḥurriyya' in EI, new edn.; Lewis, *The Middle East and the West*, pp. 47ff.

81. A broad outline of *ḥisbah* can be found in Mohammad H. Kamali, *Freedom of Expression in Islam*, Cambridge, The Islamic Texts Society, 1997, pp. 28-33.

82. Muslim ibn Hajjāj al-Nishāpūrī, *Mukhtaṣar Ṣaḥīḥ Muslim*, ed. Muḥammad Nāṣir al-Dīn al-Albānī, 2nd edn., Beirut, Dār al-Maktab al-Islāmī, 1404/1984, p. 16, *ḥadīth* no. 34.

83. Cf. ᶜAmmārah, *al-Islām wa'l-Ḥuqūq al-Insān*, pp. 21-22.

84. Said Ramadan, *Islamic Law, Its Scope and Equity*, 2nd edn., Kuala Lumpur, Muslim Youth Movement of Malaysia, 1992, p. 147.

85. Ṣaᶜb, 'al-Ḥurriyyah al-Falsafiyyah', p. 96.

86. El-ᶜAwa, *Fi'l-Niẓām al-Siyāsī*, p. 314; Aḥmad, *Uṣūl Niẓām al-Ḥūkm*, pp. 256-7.

87. Yūsuf al-Qaraḍāwī, *al-Khaṣā'is al-ᶜĀmmah li'l-Islām*, Cairo, Maktabah Wahbah, 1409/1989, p. 48.

88. al-Qaraḍāwī, *al-Khaṣā'is*, p. 45; Aḥmad, *Uṣūl Niẓām al-Ḥūkm*, p. 257.

89. Munayminah, *Mushkilāt al-Ḥurriyyah fi'l-Islām*, pp. 51-3.

90. Ibid., 98.

91. al-Qaraḍāwī, *al-Khaṣā'is*, p. 45; Aḥmad, *Uṣūl Niẓām al-Ḥūkm*, p. 258.

92. J. Weeramantry, *Islamic Jurisprudence: An International Perspective*, Basingstoke (UK), Macmillan, 1988, p. 75.

93. Abū Isḥāq Ibrāhīm al-Shāṭibī, *al-Muwāfaqāt fī Uṣūl al-Sharīᶜah*, ed. Shaykh ᶜAbd Allāh Dirāz, Cairo, Maktabat al-Tijāriyyah al-Kubrā, n.d., I, 100; Ṭubliyah, *Ḥuqūq al-Insān*, p. 279.

94. Al-Tabrīzī, *Mishkāt*, I, *ḥadīth* no. 197.

95. Muḥammad Abū Zahrah, *Uṣūl al-Fiqh*, Cairo, Dār al-Fikr al-ᶜArabī, 1377/1958, p. 236; ᶜAbd al-Wahhāb Khallāf, *ᶜIlm Uṣūl al-Fiqh,* 12th edn., Kuwait, Dār al-Qalam, p. 92; Abū al-ᶜAynayn Badrān, *Uṣūl al-Fiqh al-Islāmī*, Alexandria (Egypt), Mu'assasat Shabāb al-Jāmiᶜah, 1404/1984, p. 219.

96. Taqī al-Dīn Aḥmad Ibn Taymiyyah, *Naẓariyyāt al-ᶜAqd*, Beirut, Dār al-Maᶜrifah, 1317AH, p. 266; Ibn Qayyim Al-Jawziyyah, *Iᶜlām al-Muwaqqiᶜīn ᶜan Rabb al-ᶜĀlamīn*, ed. Muḥammad Munīr al-Dimashqī, Cairo, Idārah al-Ṭibāᶜah al-Munīriyyah, n.d., I, 344.

97. Kamali, *Principles of Islamic Jusripsrudence*, p. 306.

98. Muḥammad Salām Madkūr, *al-Fiqh al-Islāmī*, 2nd edn., Cairo, Maṭbaᶜat al-Fajālah, 1955, p. 421; Zuḥaylī, *al-Fiqh al-Islāmī*, IV, 202ff.

99. Muṣṭafā al-Zarqā, *al-Madkhal al-Fiqhī al-ᶜĀm*, 3 vols, Damascus, Dār al-Fikr, 1967, I, 215.

100. Abū Dāwūd, *Sunan Abū Dāwūd*, Eng. trans. Ahmad Hasan, Lahore, Ashraf Press, 1984, II, 120.

101. Yaḥyā ibn ᶜAlī al-Shawkānī, *Irshād al-Fuḥūl min Taḥqīq al-Ḥaqq ilā ᶜIlm al-Uṣūl*, Cairo, Dār al-Fikr, n.d., p. 251; Sayf al-Dīn al-Āmidī, *al-Iḥkām fī Uṣūl*

al-Aḥkām, ed. ʿAbd al-Razzāq ʿAfifi, 2nd edn., 4 vols, Beirut, al-Maktab al-Islāmī, 1402/1982, V, 32.

102. Taqī al-Dīn ibn Taymiyyah, *Majmūʿ Fatāwā Shaykh al-Islām Aḥmad Ibn Taymiyyah*, ed. ʿAbd al-Raḥmān b. Qāsim, Beirut, Mu'assasat al-Risālah, 1398AH, III, 239; see also Zuḥaylī, *al-Fiqh al-Islāmī*, IV, 206.

103. Zuḥaiy, *al-Fiqh al-Islāmī*, IV, 201.

104. Yūsuf al-Qaraḍāwī, *Bayʿ al-Murābaḥah li'l-Āmir bi'l-Shirā'*, 2nd edn., Cairo, Maktabah Wahbah, 1409/1982, p. 13.

105. Ibid., p. 125.

106. There is a chapter on *istiṣḥāb* in Kamali, *Principles of Islamic Jurisprudence*, pp. 297-310.

107. Cf. *The Mejelle: being an English Translation of el-Ahkam el-Adliya*, trans. C.R. Tyser, Lahore, Law Publishing Co., 1967, art. 8. The Arabic version of the maxim simply reads, '*al-aṣlu barā'at al-dhimmah*'. See also Shaykh Aḥmad ibn Muḥammad al-Zarqā, *Sharḥ al-Qawāʿid al-Fiqhiyyah*, ed. Muṣṭafā al-Zarqā, 3rd edn., Damascus, Dār al-Qalam, 1414/1993, pp. 105ff.

108. Aḥmad ibn Ḥusayn al-Bayḥaqī, *al-Sunan al-Kubrā*, Beirut, Dār al-Fikr, n.d, *Kitāb al-daʿwā wa'l-bayyināt bāb al-bayyina ʿala'l-muddaʿi*; Ibn Qayyim al-Jawziyyah, *al-Ṭuruq al-Ḥukmiyyah fi'l-Siyāsah al-Sharʿiyyah*, ed. Muḥammad Jamīl Ghāzī, Jeddah, Maṭbaʿat al-Madanī, n.d., p. 94. This is also a legal maxim recorded in the *Mejelle* (art. 76); Zarqā, *Sharḥ al-Qawāʿid*, p. 369

109. Ibn Qayyim, *al-Ṭuruq*, p. 28.

110. Muslim, *Mukhtaṣar Ṣaḥīḥ Muslim*, p. 280, *ḥadīth* no. 1053.

111. Weeramantry, *Islamic Jurisprudence*, p. 78; Cherif. M. Bassiouni (ed.), *The Islamic Criminal Justice System*, London & New York, Oceana Publications, 1982, p. 67.

112. Muslim, *Mukhtaṣar Ṣaḥīḥ Muslim*, p. 215, *ḥadīth* no. 832.

113. Maḥmaṣṣānī, *Arkān*, p. 106.

114. Yaʿqūb ibn Ibrāhīm Abū Yūsuf, *Kitāb al-Kharāj*, 5th edn., Cairo, al-Maṭbaʿah al-Salafiyyah, 1396AH, p. 164; Abū ʿĪsā Muḥammad al-Tirmidhī, *Sunan al-Tirmidhī*, Beirut, Dār al-Fikr, 1400/1980, II, 439.

115. Cf. ʿAwdah, *al-Tashrīʿ al-Jinā'i*, I, 115. The Arabic version of the maxim reads: '*lā ḥukma li-afʿāl al-ʿuqalā' qabla wurūd al-naṣṣ*'. Cf. A. Kevin Reinhart, *Before Revelation*, Albany, State University of New York Press, 1995.

116. Khallāf, *ʿIlm*, p. 173; see also Mohammad H. Kamali, 'The Limits of Power in an Islamic State', *Islamic Studies* 28 (1989) p. 334.

117. Al-Zarqā, *Sharḥ al-Qawāʿid*, p. 114; Muḥammad Abū al-Nūr Zuhayr, *Uṣūl al-Fiqh*, Cairo, Dār al-Ṭibāʿah Muḥammadiyyah, c. 1372/1952, IV, 180-81; Kamali, *Principles of Islamic Jurisprudence*, p. 305.

118. Cf. *The Mejelle* (art. 8), p. 3; Zarqā, *Sharḥ al-Qawāʿid*, p. 114.

119. Al-Zarqā, *Sharḥ al-Qawāʿid*, p. 105.

CHAPTER TWO

Equality (*Musāwāt*)

I. Introductory Remarks

The *Sharīʿah* stands firmly for equality and justice. These are the two major areas of human rights that are pivotal to the value structure of Islam. Islam has often been characterised as a social uprising against the oppressive and discriminatory practices of Arabian society, and it took a rigorous stand on equality at a point in history when this was far from a commonly accepted norm. Given the historical setting of Arab society fourteen centuries ago, the Islamic vision of creating an egalitarian society was nothing less than a social revolution. Since Islam's social agenda and reforms originated in the normative principles of the Qur'ān and *Sunnah*, there was no room for a class struggle or confrontation of the kind that has often characterised the human struggle for equality and justice. The Qur'ānic declarations on the essential principles of the equality of man, as reviewed in the following pages, remain to this day a source of inspiration for the vast majority of contemporary Muslims. They remain a source of inspiration partly also because they have yet to be translated into reality.

The discussion in this chapter begins with a general introduction to equality as a principle of constitutional law and then addresses the status specifically of non-Muslims and women. The discussion in these parts also reviews scholastic differences among the leading schools of Islamic law on some of the divergent conclusions they have drawn from the source materials of the Qur'ān and *Sunnah*.

In Western constitutional law, equality is generally associated with the French Revolution of 1789, which enunciated the equality of citizens before the law as an integral part and pillar of democracy.

Political democracy was thus conceived by its early founders as government of the people, from the people and by the people, which was evidently predicated on the recognition of equality as a basic right of all citizens.

Equality is basically a relative concept in that no absolute equality can be said to exist either in nature or in society. People are naturally different in talents and skills and their usefulness to society. Nor has there ever existed, in recorded history, a society that availed all its members of equal opportunities for self-development and growth. The following Qur'ānic passage may be cited to confirm this:

> He it is who has made you successors in the land and elevated some of you in rank above others—that He may try you by what He has given you. (al-Anᶜām, 61:166)

وهوالذى جعلكم خلائف الأرض ورفع بعضكم فوق بعض درجات ليبلوكم فيما آتاكم.

Whereas this *āyah* refers to differences in wealth and also in spiritual rank, elsewhere the Qur'ān distinguishes men of piety and knowledge from those who lack these qualities (al-Ḥujurāt, 49:13 and al-Mujādilah, 58:11). There is further confirmation of this to the effect that 'God has favoured some of you over others in the provision of means' (al-Naḥl, 16:71)

والله فضل بعضكم على بعض في الرزق.

and that 'to all are [assigned] ranks according to their deeds. God will recompense their deeds, and no injustice will be done to them' (al-Aḥqāf, 46:19).

ولكل درجات مما عملوا وليوفيهم أعمالهم وهم لا يظلمون.

This *āyah*, interestingly enough, confirms that these differences will still not interfere with the ideals of justice, and if anything, justice can be better served when these differences are acknowledged. No one will be subjected to any discrimination in regard to the merit of their deeds: 'Anyone who has done an atom's weight of good shall see its reward, and anyone who has done an atom's weight of evil shall see its recompense' (al-Zilzāl, 99:7-8).

ومن يعمل مثقال ذرة خيرا يره ومن يعمل مثقال ذرة شرا يره.

God Most High has thus conveyed the message that His plan for mankind, of making life on this earth a testing ground and a preliminary for the hereafter, does not fit in well with the notion of total equality. This is the purport of the phrase in the above-quoted text that 'He may try you by what He has given you'. Yet the differences in rank that the Qur'ān has indicated are a part, generally, of the relationship of man with God Most High, which is indicative mainly of spiritual distinction in the realm of *ᶜibādah*. As for the sphere of transactions (*muᶜāmalāt*) and men's relations among themselves, the *Sharīᶜah* is affirmative on equality in basic rights, and the spiritual distinction that some individuals may have over others are not taken into account. The Qur'ān has, for instance, laid down the law of retaliation for murder as consisting of 'life for life', and enacted certain punishments for adultery and theft, on the premise that these are applicable equally to all. Thus if a pious man kills an impious person, or a man of ill-repute for that matter, the killer's predicament before a court of justice will not be any different merely because of his piety, or indeed because of what religion he or she follows.

As a principle of constitution, equality is basically understood to mean four things.

(1) Equality before the law, which means that all citizens are treated as a single unity without discrimination in the enforcement of the law on grounds of race, language or religion and the like. It also means that all citizens enjoy equal civil and political rights, most important among which are immunity of life and property, freedom of belief, movement and expression, and the right to education and work. All civil rights are in principle subject to equality, which is a corollary of the belief that people are born equal and must therefore be accorded equal treatment.

(2) Equality before the courts of justice, and this implies not only equal access to judicial relief but also a uniform judiciary that applies uniform standards to all citizens. This also precludes disparities in the form of specialised tribunals for different classes of citizens and different treatment on grounds of social status.

(3) Equality in employment opportunities, which basically means

that all citizens are equally treated if they meet the required conditions for employment to government offices and other public sector opportunities.

(4) Equality in general duties and obligations such as in the areas of taxation and military service.[1]

II. Affirmative Evidence

The Qur'ānic evidence on equality can be related to two major themes. One of these is the fraternity of the believers, their unity in faith and equality before the law, and the other is the wider fraternity of the human race, which implies equality of all individuals in basic rights and duties. There is conclusive evidence on the first, and also affirmative, yet somewhat inconclusive, evidence on the second, which may explain some of the juristic differences that have arisen among the *ʿulamā'*. There are also areas of special interest in both categories, such as women and non-Muslims, which need to be separately addressed.

The discussion here begins with a review of the salient evidence in support of general equality in the Qur'ān and *Sunnah*. This is followed by a summary of the divergent views that are found both for and against the equality of non-Muslims and women. The two trends of opinion are then digested and examined in conjunction with modern opinion proffered by *ʿulama'* and scholars who refer the issues back to the source evidence and the overriding objectives of the Qur'ān and *Sunnah*.

The following Qur'ānic *āyāt* and *ḥadīth* are frequently cited in support of the general equality of all human beings regardless of divisions of races, language, religion or social status:

> O mankind, surely We have created you from a male and a female, and made you tribes and nations that you may know each other. Surely the noblest of you in the eyes of God is the most pious among you. (al-Ḥujurāt, 49:13)

يأيها الناس إنا خلقناكم من ذكر وأنثى وجعلناكم شعوبا وقبائل
لتعارفوا، إن أكرمكم عند الله أتقاكم.

In a commentary on this *āyah* Ibn Kathīr has stated that the address here is to mankind in general and not to Muslims in particular. The main purpose of the division of mankind into groups, tribes and nations is to facilitate recognition, which in turn invites familiarity, co-operation and friendship among people. God Most High has informed mankind that they are all alike in ancestry and descent. 'On the Day of Judgement you will not be asked about your lineage or social status. Only the most righteous of you will be honoured on the merit of their conduct.'[2] Al-Bahī has noted, concerning the meaning of *taqwā* in this *āyah*, that people often expect *taqwā* to mean the observance of religious duties. The Qur'ān rejects this and stresses that *taqwā* is not necessarily attained through prayer and worship but through genuine belief, and that the moral excellence of an individual is really in his good intention and not entirely in his ritual performance. The other indicators of *taqwā* that are given in the Qur'ān itself include the giving of material help to those in need, honesty, fulfilment of one's pledges, and patience in the face of adversity.[3]

On man's unity of origin and the essence of human fraternity, the Qur'ān provides:

> O mankind, keep your duty to your Lord who created you from a single soul and created its mate of the same [kind] and created from them multitudes of men and women. And keep your duty to your Lord by whom you demand your rights from one another, and [observe] the ties of kinship. (al-Nisā', 4:1)

يا أيها الناس اتقوا ربكم الذى خلقكم من نفس واحدة وخلق منها زوجها وبثّ منهما رجالا كثيرا ونساء‘ واتقوا اللّه الذى تساءلون به والارحام.

This *āyah* is explicit on the unity of origin, and equality in creation, of the entire human race. Their descent from a common ancestor places them all in a position where they bear a certain obligation towards one another: they are to be mindful of the ties of fraternity and kinship and treat one another as members of a single unity. It is only then that they will have a legitimate claim to a set of basic rights.

It is significant that the *āyah* above accentuates the bond of unity among human beings with the expression '*al-arḥām*' (ties of kinship), a term usually employed in the Qur'ān in the context of family relations and inheritance (i.e. *dhawū'l-arḥām*). The text thus begins by identifying man's unity of origin and then advises all members of the human race to be mindful of their ties of kinship. This wider fraternity of man in Islam has then been reinforced, as al-Qaraḍāwī points out, in the case of Muslims, 'by their fraternity in religion [*al-ikhā' al-dīnī*]'. The latter does not weaken the former, rather it substantiates and endorses the wider fraternity of mankind. There is no conflict between this and the other Qur'ānic declaration to the effect that 'the believers are brethren'.[4] The children of Adam are all brethren, but the believers are also brethren in their common belief in Islam.

The text under discussion further implies that rights and duties that people have in relation to one another emanate from God's will and are sanctified by Him. To recapitulate, the text begins with a reminder to 'keep your duty to your Lord' and ends by another reminder that 'through Him you demand your mutual rights' from one another. Every human being is a sparkle of light splintered from the same source and he or she relates to others through that source. Rights and duties in Islam thus emanate in God and manifest His grace. Furthermore, when the right-bearer demands his or her right from another, it is manifested in an obligation on the part of the latter. Both rights and obligations thus become an integral part of the equality that originates in divine grace.

The following *ḥadīth* also provide evidence in support of the fraternity of man and general equality for all:

> O people! Your Creator is one, and you are all descendants of the same ancestor. There is no superiority of an Arab over a non-Arab, or of the black over the red, except on the basis of righteous conduct.[5]

يا أيها الناس إن ربكم واحد وإن أباكم واحد، لا فضل لعربي على عجمى ولا لأسود على أحمر إلا بالتقوى.

The Prophet has also declared, in the broadest of terms, that 'people are as equal as the teeth of a comb'.

الناس سواسية كأسنان المشط.

The main thrust of the foregoing evidence is not so much on religious unity and equality among Muslims but on the equality of all human beings. Equality itself, it may be added, is not the only goal and purpose; rather it is equality with an awareness of the basic bonds of fraternity in creation and descent, and awareness also of the reciprocal rights and duties that ensue from that. Islam's conception of equality may not therefore be read in isolation from the ties of fraternity and the unity of destiny and origin of mankind.

The second of the two major themes of the evidence under discussion is moral excellence, or *taqwā*, which is the only recognised criterion of superiority in the eyes of God. This is once again indicative of the notion that mankind cannot not pursue different codes of morality and values and yet seek to remain loyal to a common bond of fraternity. The need, in other words, to subscribe to a universal code of moral values and seek to excel only in that context is a corollary of the unity and brotherhood that the Qur'ān envisages. *Taqwā* is grounded in God-consciousness, of course, but the Qur'ān itself gives *taqwā* a wider meaning, as already noted, which is essentially humanitarian and does not confine its scope to any particular religion. Since Islam recognises the validity of other revealed religions and contains detailed provisions on that subject, the scope of *taqwā* and God-consciousness would thus extend to them all. For if one were to read *taqwā* as an attribute of only the Muslims, one would run the risk of reading discrepancies into the Qur'ānic *āyāt* reviewed above. The *āyāt* which begin with an address to the whole of mankind would then be deemed to end by addressing the Muslims only, a meaning that the text itself cannot be said to sustain.

It is proclaimed in a *ḥadīth* that, 'Through Islam, verily God has eradicated the egoism and arrogance of the Time of Ignorance, and the [false] pride that people took in their ancestry. For all men are descended from Adam and Adam was made from clay.'[6]

إن اللّه قد أذهب بالإسلام نخوة الجاهلية وتفاخرهم بأبائهم، لأن
الناس من آدم و آدم من تراب.

The same message is conveyed, somewhat more emphatically perhaps, in another *ḥadīth*, which declares that 'those who promote tribal fanaticism [*ᶜaṣabiyyah*] do not belong to us, nor do the ones who fight for *ᶜaṣabiyyah*, nor those who die for *ᶜaṣabiyyah*'.[7]

ليس منا من دعا إلى عصبية، وليس منا من قاتل على عصبية،
وليس منا من مات على عصبية.

It is reported that a group of Qurayshite dignitaries paid a visit to the Prophet ﷺ and told him: 'How can we sit with you, O Muhammad, while you keep the company of such people as Bilāl al-Ḥabshī, Salman al-Fārsī, Suhayb al-Rūmi, ʿAmmār and slaves and commoners of their type? Exclude them from your company and we will sit with you and listen to your invitation.' The Prophet ﷺ refused to comply but they still requested him to 'assign a day for them and one for us'. At this point, the following Qur'ānic passage was revealed:

> And drive not away those that call upon their Lord, morning and evening, desiring only His pleasure; you are not accountable for them in aught, nor are they accountable for thee in the least. You shall be among the wrongdoers if you shun them. (al-Anʿām, 6:52)

ولا تطرد الذين يدعون ربهم بالغداة والعشى يريدون وجهه ما
عليك من حسابهم من شئ، وما من حسابك عليهم من شئ،
فتطردهم فتكون من الظالمين.

This was a resolute rejection of tribal and ethnic superiorities of the type that the Qurayshite leaders had in mind. The Prophet ﷺ was clearly advised to pay more attention to those who possessed the qualities of *taqwā*, regardless of their origin or descent.

On a similar note, it is reported that the Prophet ﷺ was explaining the tenets of Islam to an assembly of the leaders of the Quraysh tribe whom he had invited to embrace Islam, but at this point Ibn Umm Maktūm, who was blind, interrupted and asked the Prophet ﷺ a question on a religious matter. The Prophet ﷺ virtually ignored him while attending to the Qurayshite dignitaries. A Qur'ānic sūra was subsequently revealed concerning this incident to remind the Prophet ﷺ of Islam's commitment to equality. This was not just a simple reminder, as the text has it:

> He frowned and turned away, because the blind man came to him. And what makes thee know that he might purify himself [...] and would benefit by a reminder. As for him who considers himself free of need, you attend to him [...] As for him who came to you striving hard and God-fearing you pay no attention. (ʿAbasa, 80:1-10)

عبس وتولى أن جاء ه الأعمى، وما يدريك لعله يزكى [...] فتنفعه الذكرى، أما من استغنى، فأنت له تصدى [...] وأما من جاءك يسعى وهو يخشى فانت عنه تلهى.

The whole of this short sūra, bearing the title ʿ*Abasa* (He Frowned), is devoted to the incident, and it served to remind the Prophet ﷺ of the equality of all men. Later when the Prophet ﷺ met Ibn Umm Maktūm, he greeted him in these words: 'Greetings to the one concerning whom my Lord reprimanded me.'[8]

مرحبا بمن عاتبنى فيه ربي.

Equality before the law means that all men are equally subject to the rule of law without any discrimination, and there is no recognition of any privileges in this regard for anyone, including government leaders and the heads of state. The Prophet-cum-head of state clearly spoke about this in his last sermon:

> O people! If I have flogged anyone [wrongly], let him retaliate here and now. If I have insulted anyone, let him reciprocate. If I have taken anyone's property, let him claim it and take it from me. Let no one fear any rancour on my part, for that would not be becoming of me. Be aware that one who takes back his right from me is most dear to me, for I wish to meet my Lord with a clear conscience.[9]

يا أيها الناس، من كنت جلدت له ظهرا فهذا ظهرى فليستقد منه، ومن كنت شتمت له عرضا فهذا عرضي فليستقد منه، ومن أخذت له مالا فهذا مالي فليأخذ منه، ولا يخش الشحناء من قبلي فإنها ليست من شأني، ألا أن أحبكم الي من أخذ منى حقا إن كان له أو حللنى فلقيت ربي وأنا أطيب النفس.

In yet another *ḥadīth*, the Prophet ﷺ went on record to confirm that he would enforce the law on his own family if there were occasion for him to do so. He stated this in response to the attempted intercession by a number of Companions, including Usāmah bin Zayd, who approached the Prophet ﷺ to grant pardon to a woman who had committed theft, as she was, so the reports say, newly converted to Islam. The Prophet ﷺ showed annoyance and said:

> People before you perished because they did not punish a noble man among them if he committed theft, but enforced the punishment only on the weak. By God, if Muḥammad's daughter, Faṭimah, committed theft, I shall [not hesitate to] cut her hand.[10]

إنما هلك الذين قبلكم أنهم كانوا اذا سرق فيهم الشريف تركوه
و اذا سرق فيهم الضعيف أقاموا عليه الحد، وأيم اللّه لو أن فاطمة
بنت محمد سرقت لقطعت يدها.

The Rightly-Guided Caliphs followed the Prophet's example and claimed no privilege vis-à-vis the rule of law and equal treatment before the courts of justice. They are known to have advised others not to obey them if they transgressed the limits themselves. The substance of this message was conveyed by the first Caliph Abū Bakr, and also by his successor, ʿUmar ibn al-Khaṭṭāb, both of whom addressed the people in their inaugural speeches upon taking office and asked that they withhold their assistance and obedience to their leaders if the leaders themselves deviated from the right path.[11]

It is reported that on one occasion, the Caliph ʿUmar struck a man and the man said to him: 'You are one of the two types: a man who did not know and then gained knowledge or one who fell in error and was forgiven.' The Caliph replied: 'You are right, here I am ready for you to retaliate.'[12]

In another incident, when Jubla ibn al-Ayham, the leader of al-Jufna, embraced Islam, he and his five hundred followers came to visit the Caliph ʿUmar in Medina. The Caliph was overjoyed and went out with Jubla to perform the Ḥajj together. There was an incident in the Kaʿbah in which Jubla's garment fell when he bumped into a man from the tribe of Banū Fazara. Jubla beat the man and broke his nose, at which point the Caliph intervened, and asked Jubla either to ask the man for forgiveness or let him retaliate. Jubla protested and said: 'He is a commoner and I am a King.' The Caliph replied: 'Islam has made the two of you equal [...].' Jubla said: 'I thought that I would be honoured in Islam.' The Caliph reiterated his earlier statement. Jubla fled that night to Constantinople and embraced Christianity.[13]

As for equality before courts of justice, once again no one, including the head of state, enjoys any exceptional privileges, and everyone is to be treated equally before the law. Here too the precedent of the Pious Caliphs provides vivid illustrations of the normative validity of this principle. Thus it is reported that the Caliph ᶜUmar ibn al-Khaṭṭāb took a horse that a man had offered for sale and rode it, but the horse suffered an illness. The man disputed with the Caliph and they agreed to appoint an arbitrator, and nominated Shurayḥ al-ᶜIrāqī for the purpose. Shurayḥ then told the Caliph: you took it when it was fit and you bear responsibility to return it in the same condition. The Caliph then paid the price of the horse to the owner and also appointed Shurayḥ to a judicial post.[14] In a renowned letter that the Caliph ᶜUmar addressed to his judges, he wrote that it was not permissible for a judge to treat the disputing parties differently, in their presence, in the courtroom or in their judgement. The parties to a dispute must both be assured of impartial treatment.[15]

According to yet another report, a group of people brought a claim against the Abbasid Caliph al-Manṣūr to the judge Muḥammad ibn ᶜUmar al-Ṭalḥī. The latter summoned the Caliph to attend the court and when the parties were both present, the judge treated them with total impartiality. After hearing the parties' arguments, the judge gave a judgement against the Caliph. The Caliph later met with the judge and complimented him for his exemplary decision.[16] The general principle of equality before the court is recorded in the *Mejelle* (Art. 1799) in the following terms:

> The judge is under duty to treat the litigants equally both in regard to the application of the basic principles of justice and in the conduct of trial, such as in the matter of seating, and the manner of address, even if one of them be a man of nobility and the other a commoner.

Evidence thus suggests that Muslim rulers and judges have shown respect for the principle of equality before the law, and the equal treatment of litigants in court proceedings. They have done so not only by way of conformity to a set of rules but as pious individuals who perceive equality and justice as of central value to Islam and an inalienable ingredient of *taqwā*.

The Federal Sharīᶜah Court of Pakistan judgement in *N.W.F.P. Provincial Assembly (Powers, Immunities and Privileges) Act 1988*[17] addressed the issue of official privileges and the question of whether such privileges were in conflict with the injunctions of Islam on equality. The Act itself was also disputed and considered to be contrary to Muslim principles and therefore unconstitutional. In this case, a member of the Northwest Frontier Provincial Assembly pleaded that he should be granted exemption for failure to attend a civil court hearing in a revenue-related matter due to official engagements, and claimed special privilege under the Immunities and Privileges Act 1988. The trial court dismissed the case and the case was appealed before the Federal Sharīʿah Court.

The presiding judge, Tanzil-ur-Rahman, too, dismissed the appeal for grant of special privilege and held that in Islam everyone is equal before a court of justice, and everyone has a right to equal treatment, irrespective of official status or position. The Court referred to several Qur'ānic *āyāt* (including al-Ḥujurāt, 49:13, and al-Nisā', 4:135) and also cited *ḥadīth* on equality, and reached the conclusion that no one, including the head of state, could be granted any special privileges before the Court. The Caliph ʿUmar's famous letter addressed to the judges was also quoted in support of the court decision that no exemption or privileges would be given to any of the disputing parties, and that the court proceedings could not necessarily be stayed for or against a party because he was a member of a Provincial Assembly, or for that matter of National Assembly or Senate.

Equality in regard to employment opportunities is also recognised. This evidently means that people are entitled to equal treatment when they are equally qualified for the employment they seek regardless of race, language or religion. The early precedent on this speaks for itself when it is noted, for example, that the Prophet ﷺ appointed former slaves like Bilāl al-Ḥabshī and Zayd ibn al-Ḥārithah as governors of Medina in his absence on military expeditions and paid no attention to the fact that they were not even Arabs by origin. And then Usāmah ibn Zayd, who was a capable young man of seventeen, was appointed as military commander. Note also the statement the Caliph ʿUmar made on his death-bed at the time when he was nominating a council of elders to deliberate on the choice of a new leader. He said: 'I would have chosen Sālim, the freedman of Ḥudhayfa, had he been alive', for he had heard the Prophet ﷺ speaking in praise of Ḥudhayfa. The fact that Ḥudhayfa was a former slave did not come into it.

With regard to Imāmate, that is, the office of the head of state, al-Māwardi and the majority of jurists have stipulated Qurayshite descent as one of the required qualifications of the candidate for this office. Yet the opposing view that challenges the validity of this stipulation is based mainly on the principle of equality. This view relies on source evidence showing that tribe, race and social class are not to be given credibility in candidacy for public office. The only valid criteria on which eligibility for employment to public office should be determined, as the Qur'ān indicates, are strength and trustworthiness (cf. al-Qaṣaṣ, 28:26). Government positions partake of trusts (*al-amānāt*) which are to be entrusted only to those who are best qualified (cf. al-Nisā', 4:58). The only piece of evidence that is quoted in support of the majority position is the *ḥadīth* declaring that 'the leaders shall be from the Quraysh—*al-a'immatu min quraysh*.' This is, however, of doubted authenticity not only because of its discordance with the rest of the evidence in both the Qur'ān and *Sunnah* on equality, but also because no one referred to this *ḥadīth* at the meeting of Saqīfah bani Sāᶜidah, which was held between the Emigrants and Helpers (*muhājirīn wa anṣār*) for the very purpose of electing a successor to leadership following the Prophet's ﷺ demise. Abū Bakr and ᶜUmar were both present at this meeting and they did not mention this *ḥadīth*. This would have been crucially relevant in view of the fact that the Saqīfah meeting was actually convened by Helpers with the purpose of electing Saᶜd bin ᶜUbādah, himself a non-Qurayshite, for leadership. Had this been known to the Anṣār or to Saᶜd, they would most likely not have nominated Saᶜd. It was on this basis that the Kharijites and the Muᶜtazilah maintained that every Muslim is entitled to become the Imām regardless of his ancestry or tribe. For the Prophet ﷺ had clearly declared that 'there is no superiority of an Arab over a non-Arab, except on the ground of *taqwā*.' Eligibility for leadership is therefore determined by reference to personal qualities and conduct. Among the early scholars, Abū Bakr al-Baqillāni and ᶜAbd al-Raḥmān ibn Khaldūn omitted, in their writings, the requirement of being a Qurayshite from the qualifications that the candidate for caliphate must possess. More recently, Abu'l Aᶜlā Mawdūdī, Muḥammad Yūsuf Mūsā, ᶜAbd al-Wahhāb Khallāf, Maḥmūd al-ᶜAqqād, ᶜAbd Allāh Basyūnī, Saᶜdī Abū Ḥabīb and Muḥammad al-Ṣādiq ᶜAfifi, among others, have supported the view that being a Qurayshite is not a requirement of candidacy for leadership.[18]

The Qur'ānic *āyah* on the subject of trusts (*al-amānāt*) was specifically revealed in reference to government positions. This was, as the

Qur'ān commentators have noted, the theme and occasion for the revelation of the *āyah* which provides that 'God commands you to hand over the trusts to whom they belong, and when you judge among people, judge with justice' (al-Nisā', 4:58). The Prophet ﷺ clarified the substance of this Qur'ānic address in a *ḥadīth* in which he said: 'Whoever employs a man to a task while knowing the existence of a more qualified person for the same task, truly betrays God and His Messenger and the believers.'[19]

من استعمل رجلا في مسألة وهو يعلم بوجود من هو أفضل منه فقد خان اللّه ورسوله والمؤمنين.

The Caliph ʿUmar ibn al-Khaṭṭāb stipulated that the necessary conditions for public office should include, in addition to knowledge and piety, such other qualities as strength, authority, humility and kindness towards others.[20] It is thus concluded that anyone who employs another for public office in exchange for a bribe or a benefit, because of friendship, ethnicity, or association with a *madhhab,* locality or group, or sacks a qualified person because of hostility and personal inclination, betrays God and His Messenger by the abuse of trust.[21]

The *Sharīʿah* also recognises the principle of equality in meeting people's welfare needs. In this regard, the *Sharīʿah* may be said to be the earliest legal tradition in history to entitle every individual to financial assistance from the public treasury (*bayt al-māl*), not just on the basis of his or her contribution to the public wealth but as a right of everyone independent of contribution. There can be no discrimination in entitlement to welfare assistance on grounds of race, gender, language and religion.[22] A difference of opinion is known to have arisen between the first two caliphs, Abū Bakr and ʿUmar, as to whether the individual record of service and contribution should be taken into account in the allocation of financial assistance from the *bayt al-māl.* Abū Bakr applied the principle of equal distribution to all alike, including women, children and slaves. His successor, ʿUmar ibn al-Khaṭṭāb, and many leading Companions were of the view that personal record of service and loyalty to Islam should be reflected in these allocations. Abū Bakr disagreed and responded that persons who had served Islam would have their reward from God Most High; as for dealing with the people's needs, they should be treated equally without any reference to their past record. Later, ʿUmar ibn al-Khaṭṭāb changed the criterion of distribution on the analysis, as he put it, that 'we cannot treat equally those who fought with the Messenger of God and those who fought against him'.[23] Although the caliph ʿUmar introduced a certain order of priority and distinction in entitlement to assistance, these were in the nature of specific formulae that reflected a certain viewpoint and rationale, but were not, however, meant to affect the basic principle of equality, in that recipients in each category were equally treated regardless of race, language or religion.[24]

The principle of equality is also observed in the area of taxation. All Muslims are liable, for example, to the payment of legal aims (*zakāh*), which is a religious duty, and both Muslim and non-Muslim citizens are liable to the payment of land tax (*kharāj*), and the quantities involved are on the whole determined not by reference to race or religion, but to the assets themselves and the fulfilment of certain criteria that are objectively applied to all individuals alike. The basic objective of taxation and *zakāh*, as enunciated in Qur'ān, is 'so that wealth does not circulate in the hands only of the rich among you' (al-Ḥashr, 59:7).

كي لا يكون دولة بين الأغنياء منكم.

This is eminently egalitarian and predicated on the just distribution of wealth in the community. Since *zakāh* is a religious duty, non-Muslim citizens are not liable to pay it; they are instead required to pay a poll tax (*jizyah*) which is equivalent to *zakāh*. This subject will be further elaborated later.

III. The Status of Women

Men and women are equal in Islam in regard to the essence of human dignity, reward and accountability for personal conduct, and matters pertaining to property rights, morality and religion. There is disagreement, however, about whether women enjoy equality in political rights and participation in government. There are also some differences between the sexes in the area of family law, including marriage, divorce and inheritance. Commentators have differed, however, on the question of whether these differences do actually amount to inequality. An analysis of these issues is attempted in the following pages, beginning with a review of the evidence in favour of equality in the Qur'ān, followed by an examination of the political rights of women and their status within the family.

The Qur'ānic evidence on the fundamental equality of the sexes refers, in the first place, to their equality in their essential humanity. One reference to this in the following *āyah* is posed as a question, for added emphasis perhaps: 'Was he not a small life-germ in sperm emitted? Then he was a clot. So He created him and made him of two kinds, the male and the female.' (al-Qiyāmah, 75:37-39)

ألم يك نطفة من مني يمنى ثم كان علقة فخلق فسوّى فجعل منه الزوجين الذكر والأنثى.

Then comes the affirmation: 'We have bestowed dignity on the progeny of Adam.' (al-Isrā',17:70)

ولقد كرمنا بني آدم.

The 'progeny of Adam' includes both men and women, who are equal in the way they are created and in their inherent dignity. The divine grace from which they emanated does not discriminate between the male and the female. The egalitarian call of the Qur'ān is confirmed in several other places, in reference, for instance, to personal accountability and reward for good work.

> Every soul is pledged for what he [or she] has done. (al-Ṭūr, 52:21)

كل أمرى بما كسب رهين.

> Then their Lord accepted their prayer and answered them: Never will I suffer the work of any worker among you to be lost, whether male or female, the one of you being from the other. (Āl ʿImrān, 3:195)

فاستجاب لهم ربهم أني لا أضيع عمل عامل منكم من ذكر أو أنثى بعضكم من بعض.

> Whoever does good, whether male or female, and is a believer, We shall

> certainly make them live a good life, and We shall certainly give them their reward for the best of what they have done. (al-Naḥl, 16:97)

> من عمل صالحاً من ذكر أو أنثى وهو مؤمن فلنحيينه حياة طيبة ولنجزينهم أجرهم بأحسن ما كانوا يعملون.

The Qur'ān is especially emphatic on equality in regard to the various aspects of human conduct that transcend the requirements of the law. The text thus provides:

> Surely those who submit [to God], men and women, those who believe, men and women, those who obey, men and women, those who are truthful, men and women, those who are patient, men and women, those who are modest, men and women, those who are charitable, men and women, those who fast, men and women, those who guard their modesty, men and women, and those who remember their Creator, men and women—God has prepared for them forgiveness and great reward. (al-Aḥzāb, 33:35)

> إن المسلمين والمسلمات والمؤمنين والمؤمنات والقانتين والقانتات والصادقين والصادقات والصابرين والصابرات والخاشعين والخاشعات والمتصدقين والمتصدقات والصائمين والصائمات والحافظين فروجهم والحافظات والذاكرين الله كثيرا والذاكرات أعد الله لهم مغفرةً وأجراً عظيما.

These are some of the most cherished of human values, and the most important attributes, one might say, of the cultural outlook of Islam, and are evidently not gender-specific, and cover aspects of both people's relations with God and with fellow human beings. In all of this, men and women are declared equal.

When these passages are read together with those reviewed earlier on the unity of the creation and origin of the human race, the equal ranking in the Qur'ān of men and women in the essence of human dignity, spiritual attainment, *taqwā*, accountability and reward is established beyond doubt.[25]

As for women's equality in matters of employment and eligibility to public office, there are those who maintain that men and women are equal only in regard to what is known as the domain of private authority (*wilāyah khāṣṣah*) but not in respect of public authority (*wilāyah ʿāmmah*). The word '*wilāyah*' generally implies authority of one person over another person/s, which renders the latter bound by the decision of the former without any need for prior agreement.[26] Private *wilāya* primarily refers to guardianship over the person and property of another because of some deficiency in the legal capacity of the latter. It is thus stated that women can be legal guardians, and may be employed as nurses and teachers or supervisors of *waqf*, but not as ministers, judges and Imāms.[27]

As for women's eligibility to public office, which partakes of *wilāyah ʿāmmah*, such as the office of the head of state, prime minister (*wazīr al-tafwīḍ*), judges, governors, officers in charge of *ḥisbah* (commanding good and forbidding evil) and the head of the public grievances tribunal (*wālī al-maẓālim*), which partake of both religious and temporal authority, commentators have held that only the first two are reserved for men but the rest are subject to disagreement. Al-Māwardī spoke in support of the prevailing juristic opinion, which precluded women from the post of Caliph and Prime Minister as both of these entailed military leadership for which women were not eligible. The main textual authority quoted in support of this view is the Qur'ānic *āyah* that 'men are the maintainers of women because God has made some of them excel others, and because of what they spend of their wealth'. (al-Nisā', 4:34)

الرجال قوّامون على النساء، بما فضل اللّه بعضهم على بعض، وبما أنفقوا من أموالهم.

Another *āyah* often quoted in this context states that 'women have rights similar to those that men have over them, in a just manner, and men are a degree above them. (al-Baqarah, 2:228)

ولهن مثل الذي عليهنّ بالمعروف وللرجال عليهنّ درجة.

There is also a *ḥadīth* declaring that, 'A nation whose affairs are led by a woman shall not succeed.'[28]

لن يفلح قوم ولوا أمرهم امرأة.

Both these *āyāt* have come under scrutiny by the Supreme Court of Pakistan, and have generated debate about the meaning of '*qawwāmūn*' in the first *āyah*, a summary of which is as follows.

In *Ansar Burney v. Federation of Pakistan*[29] the petitioner Ansar Burney filed a suit to challenge the appointment of women judges, and argued before the Federal Sharīʿah Court that Islam required the seclusion of women; their appointment as judges was therefore repugnant to the injunctions of Islam, and was in violation also of Article (203 D) of the Constitution of Pakistan. The counsel for the petitioner argued that since the testimony of two women is equivalent to that of one man, at least two female judges would be required to decide a case. The court rejected this proposition and held that acceptance of the counsel's argument would mean that no *qāḍī* sitting alone could decide a civil or criminal case. According to *fiqh* rules, in cases other than that of adultery, in which four eye-witnesses are required to prove the offence, at least two male witnesses are required to prove disputes about property, as well as the crimes of *ḥudūd* and *qāḍīs*. If the argument of the counsel were taken to its logical conclusion, it would follow that the number of *qāḍis* to decide a case would have to correspond with the number of witnesses required to prove it.

The court then examined in detail passages in the Qur'ān and *ḥadīth* relating to the issue and held that there is 'no express or even implied restriction on the appointment of a female *qāḍī* in the Qur'ān and *Sunnah*', and the matter therefore fell within the ambit of *ibāḥah* and the legal maxim that 'what is not prohibited by the Holy Qur'ān and *Sunnah* is permitted, and the burden of proof that anything is prohibited is on the person who claims it to be so'.

The court also reviewed a number of Qur'ān commentaries on the precise meaning of '*qawwāmūn*' in the Qur'ānic *āyah* quoted above, which declares that 'men are *qawwāmūn* [maintainers, protectors] over women' (al-Nisā', 4:34). Various translations had been recorded for this word, including 'rulers', 'masters', 'holders of sovereign power', 'persons having authority', 'guardian or head of the family', and so on, but the court held that many of them were inaccurate. '*Qawwām*' in Arabic is a derivative of '*qawamah*', which means a provider, supporter or furnisher for another with the means of subsistence. It also means manager, care-taker, custodian or guardian. Abdullah Yusuf Ali's translation of the word '*qawwām*' as 'protector', and that of Arberry as 'one who manages the affairs of women' were considered to accord with the subsequent part of the text to the effect that men spend of their property to support women. The superiority, if any, is not about the natural proficiency of one and the deficiency of another, but is only on account of the responsibility for maintenance. It must follow then that one who does not maintain his wife cannot be *qawwām*. 'To call a male sovereign', the Court observed, 'or one who exercises full dominion over the life and property of a woman [...] cannot be in accordance with the Qur'ānic injunctions.'

The Court also cited some of the Qur'ānic *āyat* on justice, such as that which directs the believers as follows: 'When you judge among people, judge with justice' (al-Nisā', 4:58), and stated that this and similar other Qur'ānic directives on justice are addressed to both sexes.

The Court then made several references to the *Sunnah* of the Prophet ﷺ and how the Prophet ﷺ himself solicited counsel from his wives on issues of public concern. The Prophet's widow ʿĀ'ishah, for instance, corrected Abū Hurayrah in respect of the transmission of *ḥadīth* that she found to be repugnant to the Qur'ān. It was also stated that on many occasions when the Companions differed on a matter, they referred the case to ʿĀ'ishah. The Court also cited the incident where a woman corrected the Caliph ʿUmar ibn al-Khaṭṭāb in regard to his proposal to fix a quantitative limit on dower, and cited a Qur'ānic *āyah* in support of her argument, with which the Caliph agreed. The source evidence of the *Sharīʿah* therefore does not lend support to the assertions on any inherent superiority in men.

With regard to the testimony of women, the main Qur'ānic reference on this occurs in the *āyah al-mudāyana*, that is, the *āyah* concerning period loans and financial obligations that are deferred to a future date. The text thus begins with an address to the believers:

> When you enter into transactions involving a debt for a fixed period [in the future], reduce it to writing. And let a scribe write it down between you in fairness [...] And bring two witnesses from among your men. Should there not be two men, then a man and two women of the women that you choose to be witnesses; if the one of the two errs, the one may remind the other. (al-Baqara, 2:282)

اذا تداينتم بدين الى أجل مسمى فاكتبوه، وليكتب بينكم كاتب بالعدل [...] واستشهدوا شهيدين من رجالكم، فإن لم يكونا رجلين فرجل وأمرأتان ممن ترضون من الشهداء أن تضّل إحداهما فتذكر إحداهُما الأخرى.

This is a long *āyah* (the longest single *āyah* in the Qur'ān) and provides additional relevant details relating to documentation and testimony. It should be noted at the outset that the text here is concerned exclusively with financial obligations that are deferred to a future date. Notwithstanding the general wording of the text, that applies to all sale transactions that proceed from the giving or taking of credits, Ibn ʿAbbās and other Qur'ān commentators have stated that this *āyah* was revealed concerning the *salam* sale only. *Salam* is a sale in which the price is paid at the time of contract but delivery is postponed to a future date, sometimes for two or even three years, as the *ḥadīth* of *salam* itself indicates. This is not the place to discuss the accuracy of confining the wider scope of this *āyah* to *salam* only. What is of concern here is to note the then prevailing illiteracy in the Arab society of the prophetic period. Illiteracy was common among both men and women, but especially among women, and there was a scarcity of people who were able to write.

This concern about the scarcity of writers and scribes, and also of witnesses, is clearly expressed in the subsequent portion of the text, which contains such phrases as, 'Nor should the scribe refuse to write [...] And the witnesses must not refuse when they are summoned, and let them not be averse to writing.' Note also that two concessions are granted in the same *āyah*, one of which is when the parties to a proposed transaction trust one another, and the other when the transaction itself does not involve any deferment of obligations but is one that is completed on the spot. In both cases, the parties may choose not to document or witness the transaction they conclude.

It may be noted that the text under review does not preclude the possibility of a deferred transaction that is documented after the event, that is, when the deal is done but its documentation is delayed for practical reasons of difficulty in having the scribe and witnesses readily available. If there is such a time lag, or when a subsequent dispute arises about any details of the recorded transaction, then the possibility of one of the two witnesses making an error or forgetting may arise or (note that this includes male witnesses too), and he or she may need to be reminded by the other. The Arabic dual pronoun '*humā*' in the phrase '*fa-tudhakkir iḥdāhumā*' can refer either to two male witnesses or to two females. Bearing in mind the nature of the deferred transactions with which the text is exclusively concerned, and the practicalities of finding scribes and witnesses, it is not surprising that the Qur'ān lays down first that there must be two witnesses to testify, so that one may remind the other, and that if the witnesses are female, there should be a minimum of two.

The stipulation that two women take the place of one man in testimony is explained, as Ibn Qayyim has commented, by the fact that women customarily did not attend to commercial transactions or judicial disputes, and hence their retentiveness was deemed to be weaker than that of men.[30] The other point that Ibn Qayyim and Maḥmūd Shaltūt have both emphasised is that the Qur'ānic text here speaks in a language of persuasion and preference, and not in the manner of laying down a decisive injunction. The text, in other words, does not preclude the possibility of one woman acting as a witness, or women being witnesses in a case without there being any male witnesses. Ibn Qayyim thus wrote: 'God Most High did not say, "Adjudicate on the testimony of two men, but if there are not two men, then one man and two women."'[31] The one man-two women equation in the text does not therefore preclude women's testimony on their own. Commenting on the same subject Maḥmūd Shaltūt wrote that 'the testimony of one woman alone, or of women not accompanied by men, is acceptable in order to establish the truth and serve the cause of justice. The reference to two female witnesses does not mean that a judge cannot adjudicate a case on the basis of the testimony of women.'[32] Shaltūt also refers to Ibn Qayyim's analysis elsewhere that the *Sharīʿah* requires evidence (*bayyinah*) for the resolution of disputes. *Bayyinah* is a derivative of *bayān* (clarification), and can be anything that exposes the truth. The judge may rely on circumstantial evidence, on the testimony of non-Muslims, or that of women, if this will serve the cause of justice. Shaltūt also refers to Muḥammad ʿAbduh, who confirmed that the Qur'ānic reference to two women being equivalent to one man in testimony only envisages the prevailing conditions of society at the time; the fact, that is, that women did not engage in commercial transactions and in market activities.[33] To this, one may add the point that both Ibn Qayyim and Shaltūt have recorded that the *Sharīʿah* permits the testimony of one woman, and credits it as a full proof, in matters in which women's familiarity and understanding is considered to be superior to that of men—such as family matters, pregnancy, child birth and so on.[34]

Elsewhere, the Qur'ān itself, as Shaltūt notes, equates the testimony of men with that of women in the context of divorce by *liʿān* (imprecation). The Qur'ānic text here is as follows:

> And those who accuse their wives and have no witnesses except them-

selves, let one of them testify four times, bearing God to witness [...] and the chastisement shall be averted from her if she testifies four times, bearing God to witness, that he is of those who lied' (al-Nūr, 24:6-8).

والذين يرمون أزواجهم ولم يكن لهم شهداء إلا أنفسهم فشهادة أحدهم أربع شهادات بالله [...] ويدرأ عنها العذاب أن تشهد أربع شهادات بالله إنه لمن الكاذبين.

'Four testimonials by a man [...] are rebutted by four similar testimonials by a woman who affirms that she is telling the truth and that the man has lied.' In writing this, Shaltūt explained that in the matter of human dignity and justice, Islam does not discriminate between the sexes.[35] Since the Qur'ān does not impose a prohibition on female testimony, and because the circumstances of female literacy and familiarity with business and commerce have changed, female testimony may be admitted in any combination. For giving testimony is an act of merit because it advances the cause of justice and the discovery of truth, and no unnecessary restrictions should be imposed on it.

General consensus (*ijmāʿ*) is said to have been reached that only men are eligible for the offices of the head of state and prime minister. This ruling has then been extended by analogy to a number of other public offices, as mentioned above, which are also reserved for men.[36] Imām Abū Ḥanīfah has, on the other hand, held that women may become judges in matters in which they are admissible as witnesses, which means practically all matters except the prescribed penalties (*ḥudūd*) and retaliation (*qiṣāṣ*).[37] Ibn Ḥazm has held that except for the caliphate itself, women are eligible for all other offices of government. In support of this view, he has referred to the Qur'ānic text on this very subject (of government office), quoted above, that 'God commands you to hand over the trusts to whom they belong' (al-Nisā', 4:58).

إن الله يأمركم أن تؤدوا الأمانات إلى أهلها.

This basically addresses everyone, men and women alike, and should be followed as such, unless the text provides otherwise.[38] With reference to judicial office, Ibn Jarīr al-Ṭabarī has held that women may become judges in all types of disputes, including those of *ḥudūd* and *qiṣāṣ*. Al-Ṭabarī has regarded the analogy drawn between the office of the head of state and that of the judge as superfluous. For the head of state is the commander-in-chief of the army, whereas a judge is not. The most important qualification for a judicial post, al-Ṭabarī points out, is knowledge of the *Sharīᶜah* and the ability of a person to conduct *ijtihād*, in regard to which men and women stand on exactly the same footing.[39] As for the rank that men are given above women in the two *āyāt* above, this is on account of men's responsibility for maintenance, which is why men enjoy leadership of the family unit.[40]

As for the *ḥadīth* noted above, which the majority have quoted in support of their verdict that women are not qualified to become judges or Imām, it is evidently inconclusive, as it was, in fact, uttered in a particular context, that is, when the Prophet ﷺ was informed that the daughter of the Chosroe of Persia had taken charge of the affairs of that country. One should also note that the *ḥadīth* in question only speaks of prosperity/success and does not, as such, impose a prohibition. Ibn Ḥazm has said, concerning this *ḥadīth*, that it refers to only one position, namely that of the head of state, and it therefore does not apply to other public offices (*wilāyāt*) to which women are generally eligible.[41] Recent writers on Islamic principles of government have added that unlike earlier times, power in a modern state is diffused between its various organs under a set of checks and balances that have become a familiar feature of constitutional law in almost all Muslim countries.[42] The *ḥadīth* at issue actually envisages one woman who wields total power over government affairs, which can no longer be the case.

The question of whether there has, in fact, been *ijmāᶜ* in reserving the top leadership position for men only has been raised by one commentator, who states that almost everyone refers to *ijmāᶜ* on this and yet hardly anyone has questioned its real existence.[43] It thus appears that if there is *ijmāᶜ* on this, it is a presumptive *ijmāᶜ* that may be reflective of the realities of the medieval era, but not of the normative guidance of the Qur'ān and *Sunnah*. A presumptive *ijmāᶜ* does not establish a binding *ḥukm*. The minority view, which is supported by a wide spectrum of modern scholarship, maintains that a woman is qualified to be a witness, a representative (*wakīl*) in parliament, and a judge, all of which partake of public authority (*wilāyah ᶜāmmah*). Hence the view that confined women's participation in public life to *wilāyah khāṣṣah* (private authority) was unwarranted.[44]

It may be noted in passing that a group of the Kharijites, namely the Shuhaybiyyah, have held that women are eligible for the office of the head of state.[45] The majority (*jumhūr*) have also held it permissible, as a matter of necessity, for a woman to become Imām, if she assumes office by military force in order to prevent bloodshed. But this is tolerated as a caliphate of necessity, which may only last as long as it has effective power at its disposal.[46]

The pro-equality view advocated by al-Ṭabarī, Ibn Ḥazm and a number of modern scholars including Rashīd Riḍā, Mahmūd Shaltūt and Muḥammad Yūsuf Mūsā, maintains that women are eligible for public offices that partake of *wilāyah ᶜāmmah*, with the exception, however, of the two top positions. The proponents of this view have quoted in support the following passages from the Qur'ān:

> And women have rights similar to those that men have over them in a just manner. (al-Baqarah, 2:228)
>
> ولهنّ مثل الذى عليهنّ بالمعروف.

The implication of all this is clearly the equality of the sexes, and it sustains the conclusion therefore that the Qur'ān rejects the inherent inferiority or superiority of one sex over the other.

> And the believers, men and women, are protectors of one another. They enjoin good and forbid evil, and keep up prayer and pay the *zakāh*. (al-Tawbah, 9:71)
>
> والمؤمنون والمؤمنات بعضهم أولياء بعض، يأمرون بالمعروف
> وينهون عن المنكر ويقيمون الصلاة ويؤتون الزكاة.

Men and women are not only declared protectors (*awliyā'*) of one another, but they partake equally in the conduct of *ḥisbah*, that is enjoining good and forbidding evil. The text here uses the word *awliyā'* which is a derivative of *wilāyah* (to have authority, to befriend, to protect) in reference to both sexes, and this obviously does not leave room for inequality on account of *wilāyah*. Similarly, government as a whole, that is, all its major branches, namely the legislative, judicial, and executive, partakes of *ḥisbah*. If the text declares both men and women to be the custodians of *ḥisbah*, this implies their equality in respect of participation in government generally, including membership of representative assemblies. The advocates of this view have further cited in support the fact that the Prophet ﷺ received the pledge of allegiance (*bayʿah*) from both men and women on at least two of three occasions, the first two of which are known as the First ʿAqabah and the Second ʿAqabah, and the third as *Bayʿat al-Riḍwān*. This last of the three events is also confirmed in the Qur'ān (al-Mumtaḥina, 60:12) in a context where God Most High speaks approvingly of the advice that the daughter of the prophet Shuʿayb offered to her father (al-Qaṣāṣ, 28:26).

Reports also show that the Prophet Muḥammad ﷺ consulted his wife, Umm Salamah, on a public issue and acted on her counsel on the day of Ḥudaybiyyah.[47] It is also well-known from the relevant literature that a woman by the name of Umm Hāni' granted safe conduct (*amān*) to an unbeliever who had shown hostility toward ʿAli ibn Abī Ṭālib, and hired him for a task, but when the Prophet heard of this, he said that her pledge would be honoured and said, 'We have hired the person whom you have hired, O Umm Hānī'!'[48] Furthermore, the Prophet's widow ʿĀ'ishah demanded punishment for the assassins of the slain Caliph ʿUthmān, and led a military contingent in the Battle of the Camel.[49] Women's eligibility for public office is also endorsed by the fact that the Caliph ʿUmar ibn al-Khaṭṭāb appointed a woman by the name of Shifā' bint ʿAbd Allāh as the officer in charge of *ḥisbah* (market inspection) in Medina.[50] Evidence thus shows that women were not excluded from public life, and any restrictions that were subsequently imposed on them were partly due to circumstantial developments that did not command normative and undisputed validity in the *Sharīʿah*. 'There is no textual ruling in the Qur'ān, or in the *Sunnah* of the Prophet, or in *ijmāʿ*', wrote al-ʿĪlī, 'to deprive women of their political rights.'[51] Muḥammad ʿAbduh has drawn attention to the Qur'ānic declaration, quoted above, that women have rights similar to the obligations that they bear, and stated that this is a general norm that must regulate the pattern of social relations and equality of rights not only in the family but also in public life and in participation in government. Equality must in turn be moderated, ʿAbduh adds, by considerations of propriety and justice.[52]

It may be concluded therefore that equality remains the overriding principle and norm of the *Sharīʿah* in gender-related matters, but it remains in the meantime open to considerations of justice, public interest (*maṣlaḥah*) and the prevailing realities of society. This is true, of course, of most other rights also, and is not peculiar to this particular context, as these considerations could equally apply to men. The point is that arithmetical equality is not always desirable. Total equality in respect of public office may not necessarily correspond with the ideals of *maṣlaḥah* and the proper allocation of tasks. Women may, for instance, still have a bigger role in the family, and men outside the home, and a certain situational disparity may well be considered to be in harmony with the realities of a given community and its prevailing circumstances. These are all acceptable so long as they do not conflict with the dictates of equality and justice. In the event of a conflict between *ad hoc* provision or circumstantial reality, and the basic norms of equality and justice, the latter must naturally prevail. To take a parochial view of equality and subjugate it to stipulations that compromise its basic concept is neither tenable nor necessarily Islamic. This has happened in the past, and people have tried to read into equality a meaning that the word cannot sustain, or else tried to justify practical situations by giving them a veneer of normality by means of a tenuous interpretation of the text.

Women enjoy full legal capacity in the *Sharīʿah* in the areas of civil transactions and finance. They are thus qualified to conclude contracts and transactions, buy or sell property and dispose of it by means of gifts and bequests, provided, of course, that they are in possession of their normal legal capacity. This is a general rule and its basic validity is not affected by marriage. The husband of a married woman has no right to interfere with her property, nor is she required to obtain permission from him when dealing with her own assets. She may appoint her husband as her representative (*wakīl*), if she wishes and may terminate his representation as and when she pleases.

The wife's freedom in regard to financial transactions is indicated in the Qur'ānic *āyah* declaring that 'men are entitled to what they have earned and women are entitled to what they have earned' (al-Nisā', 4:32).

للرّجال نصيب مما اكتسبوا وللنّساء نصيب مما أكتسبن.

The Qur'ān also provides, in an address to the husband, that 'it is not permissible for you to take back what you may have given them [as dower]' (al-Baqarah, 2:229).

ولا يحلّ لكم أن تأخذوا مما آتيتموهن شيئا.

Another *āyah* on the same subject states, 'And give women their dower as a free gift. If they then wish to give you anything back of their own good pleasure, you may take it with pleasure' (al-Nisā', 4:4).

وآتوا النّساء صدقاتهنّ نحلة، فإن طبن لكم عن شئ منه نفسا فكلوه هنيئا مريئا.

The source evidence thus speaks affirmatively of the basic liberty of married women to do as they please with what belongs to them, independently of their husbands. Islamic law also applies the regime of the separation of property between spouses, unless they wish to opt for joint ownership of assets.

Pursuit of knowledge and education is a right that Islam recognises for men and women alike, both in regard to religious and secular knowledge. It is correct to identify education as a right of both men and women, but it is actually even more than that: it is a requirement, indeed, an obligation, founded in the clear terms of the *ḥadīth* declaring that the 'pursuit of knowledge is a duty of every Muslim'.[53]

طلب العلم فريضة على كل مسلم.

'Every Muslim' includes women, of course. Another version of the same *ḥadīth* actually continues with the words 'man and women.' The Prophet's widow, ʿĀ'ishah, is widely acclaimed as a leading scholar among the Companions, and features prominently in scholarship because of her knowledge of the Qur'ān and *ḥadīth*. The Prophet ﷺ also employed a woman, Shifā' al-ʿAdawiyyah, to teach his other wife, Ḥafṣah, basic literacy and writing. Ibn Ḥazm has rightly observed that Islam imposes a number of religious duties, such as the daily prayers, fasting, the pilgrimage of Ḥajj and so forth, which necessitate a certain degree of knowledge of the essentials of the faith. Everyone is therefore expected to have a basic knowledge of the *ḥalāl* and *ḥarām*. There is no difference at all in this regard between men and women, who are equally entitled to, and indeed under an obligation to, seek knowledge.[54]

IV. Towards an Egalitarian Regime of Family Law

In the area of matrimonial law, the rules of *fiqh* pertaining especially to polygamy and divorce, as developed by the various *madhāhib*, have come under scrutiny in modern times. Legislative reforms that have been introduced in many countries since the early decades of the twentieth century have brought about changes in the equality of spouses. With regard to women's eligibility to conclude their own marriage contracts, it may be noted that this has clearly been recognised by the Ḥanafī school. The other leading schools of Islamic law require the consent of a woman's guardian (*walī*) to validate the marriage contract of even an adult woman. The *fuqahā'* have had their reasons for this, but these rules are the product mainly of *fiqh* on which evidence in the sources is open to interpretation. This is why the *madhāhib* have interpreted the source materials differently. Modern law reform on this subject is generally in line with the Ḥanafī position, and recognises the right of an adult female to conclude her own marriage contract. Women are entitled, according to all the leading schools of Islamic law, to the custody and guardianship of young children, and they are also entitled to seek judicial divorce in circumstances that are specified in the law, such as a husband's insanity, incurable disease, failure to maintain, and cruelty. The *fiqh* rules also provide for divorce by mutual consent (*mubārāt*), and divorce in which the wife initiates the divorce proceedings (i.e. *khul*ᶜ), and also delegated divorce (*ṭalāq al-tafwīḍ*) in which the husband delegates his power of unilateral *ṭalāq* to the wife, which she may exercise at her own initiative. The husband is regarded as the head of the household, who is responsible for supporting his immediate family. The basic outlook of Islam on divorce is embodied in the *ḥadīth* which identified it as 'the worse of all permissible things in the eyes of God'.[55] Yet the spirit of this teaching was not observed in the early days of Islam, as we know that the Caliph ᶜUmar ibn al-Khaṭṭāb tightened the rules of divorce because of frequent abuse of them. The same concern has more recently been the motivating factor behind legal reforms which either restricted or totally removed the husband's unilateral power of *ṭalāq*. As a result of these reforms, divorce has generally become a judicial matter determined by a court of justice, and no longer by the unilateral will of the husband.

The Syrian Law of Personal Status 1953 was the first in a series of Middle Eastern legal codes which introduced important reforms in the *Sharīʿah* laws of marriage and divorce. In its preamble on the section on divorce, this law stated that 'the true purposes and conditions of divorce in Islam have sadly been misconstrued and perverted by the jurists of the past, whose doctrine has led to a lack of security in married life', and that their exercise of excessive care in order to avoid any breaking the law had often produced the opposite results. In this situation, the proper policy was to 'open the door of mercy' from the provisions of the *Sharīʿah* itself, to 'return to the origins of the law of divorce in Islam and adopt from outside the four [Sunni] schools provisions which will be conducive to public welfare'. The actual reforms of divorce law that were introduced in Syrian legislation were not as ambitious as might have been expected. But it was nevertheless an important impetus for the reform that followed in other countries in the Middle East and Asia.[56] The Tunisian Law of Personal Status 1959 went as far as to abolish all forms of extra-judicial divorce, whether by *ṭalāq* or by mutual agreement of the spouses, by enacting that 'any divorce outside the court of law is devoid of legal effect' (art. 30). In support of this major innovation, Tunisian jurists attempted a novel interpretation of the Qur'ānic passages on the subject (i.e. al-Baqarah, 2:229 and al-Nisā', 4:35), especially that which validate *khulʿ* divorce at the initiative of the wife (i.e. al-Nisā', 4:35). Without entering into details, this *āyah* provides: 'If you fear discord between the spouses, appoint an arbitrator [*ḥakam*] from his side, and one from hers.'

وإن خفتم شقاق بينهما فابعثوا حكما من أهله وحكما من أهلها.

The Tunisian jurists reasoned that the very nature of divorce is such that it must be preceded by some degree of discord, yet in most cases no opportunity has been provided for arbitration. The obvious solution to this was to provide that no divorce would be effective except by the consent of court. The Qur'ānic provisions above were also utilised, on a more limited scale, by Egyptian law (No. 25) of 1929, and later in 1967 by the Supreme Court of Pakistan. In *Khurshid Bibi v. Muhammad Amin*[57] the Supreme Court of Pakistan reinterpreted the relevant Qur'ānic passages and concluded that the court had authority to enforce *khulʿ* even against the will of the husband whenever the judge apprehended that a harmonious married state as envisaged by the Qur'ān would not be possible.

The second of the two-pronged legislative reforms that were

mainly introduced in the latter part of the twentieth century were concerned with polygamy, which has become, like divorce, dependent on a judicial order. The intending polygamist is consequently required to fulfil a number of conditions and satisfy the court as to his personal and financial capabilities before a decree can be granted in his favour. Such conditions include the infertility of the existing wife, attainment of 'a lawful benefit', the just character of the husband and his financial ability to maintain a second wife. Some countries have also stipulated the consent of the existing wife to the proposed marriage, which must be given before the court.[58] At the one extreme of the reformist legislation on polygamy stands the Tunisian Law of 1957, which tersely states that 'polygamy is prohibited'. At the other is the Moroccan Law of 1958 which stipulates that 'if any injustice is to be feared between co-wives, polygamy is not permitted'. Syria, Iraq, Pakistan and Malaysia have adopted the middle course by making polygamy subject to court permission, which is granted only when certain conditions, as noted above, are satisfied. These reforms are also based on a novel interpretation of the Qur'ānic verses of polygamy (i.e. al-Nisā', 4:3 and 129) which permit polygamy but stipulate at the same time that 'if you fear that you cannot be just, then marry only one' (al-Nisā', 4:3).

وان خفتم ألا تعدلوا فواحدة.

It is then declared that 'you cannot do justice between co-wives, even though you wish it' (al-Nisā', 4:129).

ولن تستطيعوا أن تعدلوا بين النساء ولو حرصتم.

Modern reformers have argued that since the fear of injustice is bound to be present in almost all cases of polygamy, the Qur'ān has in effect closed the door on it, which either means a total ban, or the imposition of heavy restrictions on it. They have thus given the Qur'ānic provisions on polygamy the force of law, contrary to the traditional approach, which considers these verses as mere moral exhortations addressed to the good conscience of the husband.[59]

Broadly speaking, the Qur'ānic provisions on marriage and divorce consist of proclamations that leave scope for interpretation. It is, in other words, possible to take a restrictive approach, as was taken by the *ᶜulamā'* of the past, or an egalitarian approach that seeks to establish a balance between the rights and obligations of the spouses. The latter approach has to a large extent been taken in the reformist legislation of the twentieth century in Muslim countries. Many prominent *ᶜulamā'* in recent times, including Muḥammad ᶜAbduh, Sayyid Quṭb, Muṣṭafā al-Marāghī and Maḥmūd Shaltūt have advocated the balanced approach, and advised a departure from the exceedingly restrictive attitudes that were generally adopted in the past.[60]

I venture to conclude this discussion by repeating a remark that I made in 1984, when I published an article on 'Divorce and Women's Rights', where I stated that 'Islamic law must grow abreast of the needs of Muslim society and be responsive to its problems. To achieve this is far more meaningful than conformity to the traditional demand for unquestioning loyalty to the authorities of the past'.[61]

V. The Status of Non-Muslims

Broadly speaking, the *Sharīᶜah* applies equally to both Muslim and non-Muslim citizens in the sphere of public law and secular affairs, but non-Muslims are free to follow their own laws and traditions in religious and customary matters that may be said to be closely associated with religion, such as marriage and divorce.

Muslim jurists have drawn a distinction between two categories of non-Muslims, namely non-Muslims who are permanent residents of Muslim-dominated territory, known as *dhimmīs* (also *al-muwāṭinūn*), and aliens who are granted safe conduct (i.e. *amān*) and reside there temporarily for a particular purpose, known as *musta'mīn*. This discussion is concerned mainly with the first category. As for the *musta'mīn*, it may be stated briefly that during their stay in Muslim territories, they too are entitled to safe conduct and the protection of their lives and properties in the same way as the *muwāṭinūn*. Whereas the latter are required to pay the poll-tax (*jizyah*), the *musta'mīn* are exempt from *jizyah* for an initial period of four months, and according to some, one year. Should they remain for a longer period, they too have to pay the poll-tax, and they are entitled to become *muwāṭinūn* if they plan to become permanent residents.[62]

Before examining the detailed evidence relating to the status of non-Muslims, a word needs to be said concerning the manner in which this evidence is treated. For there are passages in the Qur'ān that can be quoted in support of both equality and inequality. Many have in fact quoted them in support of inequality, but those who have done so tend to adopt a somewhat atomistic approach by reading the various passages of the text in isolation. These interpreters have divided the world into the so-called abode of Islam and the abode of war (*dār al-Islām, dār al-ḥarb*) and see the doctrine of *jihād* (struggle) as an institutionalised expression of Islam's hostile attitude toward non-Muslims. Then there are those who base their conclusions on the balance of evidence in the Qur'ān, and are consequently able to advocate a different perspective, which is incidentally critical of the method that is applied by the first group.

There is general agreement among Muslim scholars that Islam recognises equality in the essential dignity of human beings, but there is disagreement about whether Islam guarantees equality before the law to all alike. Mutawallī has thus observed that complete equality before the law is not the norm in the *Sharīᶜah*. Despite the variable meanings of equality in different periods of history and in different cultural settings, if one takes equality before the law in the sense in which it now features in the constitutions of many Muslim countries, it evidently does not admit of any discrimination between citizens on account of religion, nor does it accept slavery, or the superiority of men over women. Mutawallī has thus recorded one of the two opposing views outlined above that the *Sharīᶜah* recognises these distinctions. The legal status of *dhimmīs* and non-Muslims is not equal to that of Muslim citizens, slavery is permitted, and women do not enjoy equal rights. This last point has been further elaborated by him in that the *Sharīᶜah* permits a Muslim male to marry a Jewish or Christian woman, but the marriage of a Muslim woman to a non-Muslim man is not permitted.[63]

Two Qur'ānic *āyāt* have been quoted by the advocates of this view, which are as follow:

> You are the best community evolved for mankind, enjoining what is right, forbidding what is wrong and you believe in God. If only the People of the Scripture had believed, it would have been better for them. Some of them are believers but most of them are transgressors. (Āl ᶜImrān, 3:110)

كنتم خير أمة أخرجت للناس تأمرون بالمعروف وتنهون عن المنكر وتؤمنون بالله، ولو آمن أهل الكتاب لكان خيرا لهم، منهم المؤمنون وأكثرهم الفاسقون.

> Fight those who believe neither in God nor the Last Day nor forbid that which God and His Messenger have forbidden, nor acknowledge the religion of truth [even if they are] of the People of the Book until they pay the tribute [*jizyah*] and pay it in subjugation. (al-Tawbah, 9:29)

قاتلوا الذين لا يؤمنون بالله ولا باليوم الآخر ولا يحرمون ما حرم الله ورسوله ولا يدينون دين الحق من الذين أوتوا الكتاب حتى يعطوا الجزية عن يد وهم صاغرون.

Two basic conclusions have been drawn from these passages. First, Muslims are superior to members of all other religious groups, as they are designated 'the best community.' Second, Christians and Jews who have not accepted Islam should be conquered, brought down and subjected to the payment of the tribute (*jizyah*).[64] The advocates of this view have also made reference to another *āyah*, which addresses the Muslims as follows:

> O you who believe, take not the Jews and the Christians for friends and protectors. They are but friends and protectors to each other. He among you who turns to them for friendship is [one] of them. (al-Mā'idah, 5:51)

يا أيها الذين آمنوا لا تتخذوا اليهود والنصارى أولياء، بعضهم أولياء بعض ومن يتولّهم منكم فإنه منهم.

This is basically the sum-total of the evidence that is quoted in support of Muslim/non-Muslim inequality. The evidence in the *Sunnah* is, on the whole, supportive of general equality and contains little that can be quoted to support the opposite argument.

The second view, which maintains that Islam is fundamentally egalitarian, looks at the preponderance of evidence in the sources, and maintains that some of the instances of inequality between Muslims and non-Muslims, and also between men and women, are justified, and do not therefore alter the basic position of general equality between them.

Several passages in the Qur'ān and numerous *ḥadīth* have been quoted by the advocates of this view. Many prominent scholars of recent times, including Abū Zahrah, Maḥmūd Shaltūt, Qaraḍāwī and Maḥmaṣṣānī have also responded and developed a fresh perspective on these issues often in contrast to the rulings of the leading schools of *fiqh*. These are summarised in the following pages. The discussion begins with a review of the basic evidence on the *ahl al-dhimma*.

V.I. A Review of the Source Evidence

This section reviews the source evidence in support of equality for non-Muslim residents of territories under Muslim domination. These are known as *dhimmīs*, or covenanted people, simply because the Muslim authorities have committed themselves to their protection against hostility and abuse. The evidence in favour of equality in the Qur'ān, the *Sunnah* and the precedent of the Rightly-Guided Caliphs that features prominently in the works of Muslim jurists includes three passages in the Qur'ān and three *ḥadīth*, which are as follows:

> Surely those who believe, and those who are Jews, and the Christians and the Sabians, whoever believes in God and the Last Day and does good, they have their reward with their Lord, and there is no fear for them, nor shall they grieve. (al-Baqarah, 2:62)

> إن الذين آمنوا والذين هادوا والنصارى والصابئين من آمن بالله وعمل صالحاً فلهم أجرهم عند ربهم ولا خوف عليهم ولا هم يحزنون.

This is clearly a far-reaching proclamation on equality that draws a parallel between Muslims and followers of other revealed scriptures, the Jews, Christians and Sabians, in terms of reward for good deeds and faith in God. It is the conduct itself, in other words, that is the criterion of judgment and reward, regardless of which of the revealed religions is being followed. Virtue and moral rectitude are thus seen as the criteria for excellence on a wider level, that is, within or outside of Islam specifically. The next Qur'ānic *āyah* quoted below refers to social interaction and friendship between Muslims, Jews and Christians:

> This day [all] things good and pure are made lawful to you. The food of

> the People of the Book is lawful to you and your food is lawful to them. And so are the chaste from among the believing women and the chaste women from among those who have been given the Scriptures before you. (al-Mā'idah, 5:5)

اليوم أحل لكم الطيبات وطعام الذين أوتوا الكتاب حل لكم وطعامكم حل لهم والمحصنات من المؤمنات والمحصنات من الذين أوتوا الكتاب.

The text here permits beneficial exchange, hospitality and intermarriage between Muslims, Jews and Christians. The Qur'ān, in other words, encourages good relations and friendship with people of other faiths. Of the enjoyments of life and worldly benefits, everything that is lawful for Muslims is also lawful for the followers of other faiths. There is an even more explicit reference to this in another Qur'ānic *āyah*, which is as follows:

> God forbids you not to be good and just to those who have not fought you over your religion, nor have they evicted you from your homeland. For God loves those who are just. (al-Mumtaḥinah, 60:8)

لا ينهاكم اللّه عن الذين لم يقاتلوكم في الدين ولم يخرجوكم من دياركم أن تبروهم وتقسطوا إليهم، إن اللّه يحب المقسطين.

Provided there is no hostility and abuse between Muslims and their fellow non-Muslim citizens, they should be fair and good to one another. Equal treatment thus becomes a necessary component of being fair and good to the non-Muslims. For it is unlikely that one could be 'good and just' to others and at the same time apply a regime of discrimination against them.

The following *ḥadīth* are also quoted in support of the equality of the rights and obligations of non-Muslim citizens:

> They have the same rights as we do and the same obligations as we have.[65]

لهم ما لنا وعليهم ما علينا.

> Beware that I myself shall be the opponent, on the Day of Judgment, of anyone who is unjust to a covenanted person, or burdens him with something he cannot bear, or takes something from him, or makes him suffer a loss without his valid consent.[66]

ألا من ظلم معاهدا أو كلفه فوق طاقته أو أخذ منه شيئا أو انتقصه
أو أخذ منه شيئا بغير طيب نفسه فأنا حجيجه يوم القيامة.

> Whoever annoys a *dhimmī,* I shall be a litigant against him on the Day of Judgment.[67]

من آذى ذميا فأنا خصمه ومن كنت خصمه خصمته يوم القيامة.

According to another report, the Prophet ﷺ said: 'I am the bearer of a trust to impose just retaliation in favour of the *dhimmīs'*. With these words, as reported by ᶜAbd al-Raḥmān al-Baylamānī, the Prophet ﷺ ordered the execution of a Muslim who had murdered a *dhimmī*.[68] There are additional *ḥadīth* that reiterate the same theme, wherein the Prophet ﷺ has recommended fair dealing with and kindness to non-Muslims.

The Caliph ᶜUmar ibn al-Khaṭṭāb is also reported to have advised his successors to fulfil their covenant and be good to the *dhimmīs*, to defend them against aggression and not to cause them hardship. The Caliph ᶜAlī is similarly quoted to have said concerning the *dhimmīs* that 'they only entered the covenant so that their lives and properties would be [protected] like our lives and properties'.[69]

V.II. The *Fiqh* Discourse on *Dhimmīs*

This discussion briefly reviews the juristic views of the *madhāhib* on issues such as just retaliation (*qiṣāṣ*) in cases of homicide when the victim is a non-Muslim, and the testimony of non-Muslims before the *Sharīᶜah* Court. Other questions to be discussed are whether non-Muslim citizens enjoy equal rights to participation in government offices, and also whether they enjoy equality in economic and financial matters. The *fiqh* discourse on non-Muslim citizens also extends to their personal matters such as marriage, divorce and inheritance.

In the areas of crime and punishment, including just retaliation (*qiṣāṣ*), blood money (*diyyah*) in unintentional homicide, or *diyyah* for personal injuries, the most preferred (*arjaḥ*) position is that the *Sharīᶜah* does not differentiate between Muslim and non-Muslim citizens of the Islamic state. Thus it is held that the Qur'ānic text on just retaliation, which explicitly proclaims 'life for life' (*al-nafsa bi'l-nafs*) as its basic formula (al-Mā'idah, 5:45), applies equally to all. This position is endorsed in another *āyah* declaring that 'retaliation has been prescribed for you in all cases of murder' (al-Baqarah, 2:178).

كتب عليكم القصاص في القتلى.

The reference is again to the crime itself, without any consideration of the religious following of its perpetrator. This is endorsed further in a *ḥadīth* which simply declares that '[all] intentional crime calls for retaliation—*al-ᶜamdu qawad*'. These are all general (*ᶜāmm*) rulings and worded so as to apply equally to all the cases to which they could apply. A Muslim who deliberately kills a non-Muslim and vice versa will generally be liable to just retaliation. This is the Ḥanafī position, which also finds support in the practical *Sunnah* of the Prophet ﷺ. Quoted also in support of this position is the precedent of the Caliphs ᶜAlī ibn Abī Ṭālib and ᶜUmar ibn ᶜAbd al-ᶜAzīz, who are reported to have approved of retaliation in cases involving the murder of *dhimmīs* by Muslims.[70] It is thus reported that when the Prophet approved of retaliation against a Muslim for killing a *dhimmī*, he said, 'I am committed, more than anyone else, to fulfilling my covenant.'[71]

أنا أحق وفى بذمته.

The Caliph ᶜAlī also made the statement that 'we give them what they give us, for their blood is like our blood and their *diyyah* [blood money] is like our *diyyah*'.[72]

The majority of jurists in the leading schools have, however, held that a Muslim may not be killed for killing a *dhimmī*, and have referred in support of this view to a *ḥadīth* where it is stated that 'a Muslim is not killed for killing an unbeliever'.[73]

لا يقتل مسلم بكافر.

Reference is also made in this connection, to another *ḥadīth* that is inconclusive but is still quoted, which reads that 'the blood of one Muslim is equal to that of another'

المسلمون تتكافأ دماء هم.

implying therefore that the blood of a non-Muslim is not of the same value. The proponents of this view have also quoted, inconclusively once again, the Qur'ānic *āyah* that 'the companions of Fire are not equal of the companions of Paradise' (al-Ḥashr, 59:20)

لا يستوى أصحاب النار و أصحاب الجنة.

and have drawn the conclusion therefore that the two are not equal.

The third view on the subject, which is held by Imām Mālik and the Shīʿah Imāmiyyah, has it that a Muslim is retaliated for killing a *dhimmī* if the killing is with the purpose of taking his property and in cases where the killer is a habitual criminal. This view also refers to cases that were accordingly disposed in this way during the time of the Caliphs ʿUmar and ʿUthmān, but many have disputed the accuracy and details of the reports concerning them.[74]

Of the three views discussed above, the Ḥanafī ruling tends to have greater harmony with Qur'ānic provisions on justice, and specially the *āyah* that provides that 'God does not forbid you from being good and just to those who have not waged war against you over your religion' (al-Mumtaḥinah, 60:8).

لا ينهاكم الله عن الذين لم يقاتلوكم في الدين

To be just to the followers of other faiths must mean giving them equal rights and protection in all respects. This is also the essence of the covenant (*dhimmah*) that the Muslim state has offered them, and the Prophet clearly entitled them to equal rights. As for the *ḥadīth* that 'a Muslim is not killed for killing a *kāfir*', Imām Abū Ḥanifah has interpreted this by saying that '*kāfir*' here means a *ḥarbī*, that is, the belligerent non-Muslim who is not protected under the covenant of *dhimmah*.[75]

The jurists have also differed on the *diyyah* (blood money) of a *dhimmī* in unintentional homicide (*qatl al-khaṭā'*), which is payable to the next of kin of the deceased. There are three views on this, one of which is that the *diyyah* of a *dhimmī* is half that of a Muslim. This is the view of Imām Mālik and the Caliph ʿUmar ibn ʿAbd al-ʿAzīz. This view is apparently based on a *ḥadīth* on the authority of one ʿAmr ibn Shuʿayb, who reported from his father, and from his father's father, that the Prophet ﷺ said, 'The *diyyah* of an unbeliever is half that of the Muslim.'[76]

دية الكافر عن نصف من دية المسلم.

The second view quantifies the *diyyah* of a *dhimmī* at one third that of a Muslim. This view, held by Imām Shāfiʿī, is attributed to the Caliphs ʿUmar and ʿUthmān and a number of *ʿulamā'* among the followers (*tābiʿūn*). The third view has it that the *diyyah* of a Muslim and non-Muslim is the same, and this is held by Imām Abū Ḥanifah and Sufyān al-Thawrī, and is also attributed to the Caliphs ʿUmar, ʿUthmān and a number of scholars among the *tābiʿūn*. Ibn Rushd, who has recorded these views, considers the Ḥanafī position to be preferable, and he cites the following Qur'ānic *āyah* in support: 'If the deceased is from people with whom you have a covenant, then compensation [*diyyah*] is to be paid to his family and a believing slave is to be freed.' (al-Nisā', 4:92).

وإن كان من قوم بينكم وبينهم ميثاق فدية مسلمة إلى أهله
وتحرير رقبة مؤمنة.

This ruling applies equally to Muslims and to those who are in a treaty of alliance with them. Abū Ḥanifah has also referred to a *ḥadīth* in its support, related on the authority of al-Zuhrī, in which the Prophet said that 'the *diyyah* of a Jew, a Christian and every *dhimmī* is like the *diyyah* of a Muslim.'

دية اليهودي والنصراني وكل ذمى مثل دية المسلم.

This is also said to have been the practice of the four Rightly-Guided Caliphs until the first Umayyad Caliph Muᶜāwiyah, who began to pay half to the public treasury (*bayt al-māl*) and the other half to the relatives of the deceased. Then the Caliph ᶜUmar ibn ᶜAbd al-ᶜAzīz passed judgment in favour of the reduced *diyyah,* but he stopped payment to the public treasury and only made one-half of the *diyyah* of a non-Muslim payable to the heirs of the deceased.[77] Thus it can be seen that the quantitative change in the *diyyah* of non-Muslims represents a later development that does not find clear support in the sources.

Commenting on the different views of the *madhāhib* on this issue, the late Shaykh of al-Azhar, Maḥmūd Shaltūt, has drawn attention to the basic principle of the *Sharīᶜah* that endorses the equality of all people in respect of the right to life. No one's blood is more precious than anyone else's, and the law does not recognise any distinction between people in this regard. Shaltūt adds that differences of opinion among jurists are known to exist on the subject of *diyyah* and retaliation (*qiṣāṣ*), not only with reference to non-Muslims but also with regard to certain other categories of individuals, such as father and son, master and slave, and even men and women. But these are, as he put it, 'matters of personal understanding concerning only the *fuqahā'* who have expressed the views in question and not necessarily a statement of the general principles of the *Sharīᶜah*'.[78] Shaltūt further comments that the *fuqahā'* may have deduced these exceptional rules by bearing in mind the prevailing circumstances of their times. They are often in agreement on basic principles but tend to vary in other respects: with reference to the same subjects, that is, blood-money and retaliation, it may be noted that the *fuqahā'* are all in agreement on the criminal responsibility of the perpetrator in crimes of violence, regardless of the religion of the victim, but they differ in their approach to the determination of punishment.

ᶜAwdah has looked into some of these scholastic differences and reached the conclusion that the Ḥanafī position, which subscribes to equality among individuals regardless of their religion, is more acceptable to and bears more harmony with the applied law of the present-day in Muslim countries, and is therefore generally considered to be preferable.[79] Mawdūdī has in turn drawn attention to the point that the *Sharīᶜah* does not differentiate, in regard to the application of penalties, especially the prescribed (*ḥudūd*) penalties, between Muslims and non-Muslims, and these penalties are applied equally to all. Whether one talks of the punishment for adultery, or theft, or slanderous accusation, etc., no distinction is made on the grounds of the religious affiliation of the perpetrator. This should also be the case in regard to retaliation and *diyyah*.[80]

As for the question of equality before courts of justice, the evidence in the *Sunnah* and the early precedent of the Rightly-Guided Caliphs is supportive of the equality of non-Muslims, and there is no disagreement on this. The Prophet ﷺ has emphasised in more than one *ḥadīth* the equal rights of litigants to a fair hearing and trial. Thus according to one *ḥadīth*, the Prophet ﷺ said to ʿAlī ibn Abī Ṭālib, on the latter's departure as judge to the Yemen, 'When the litigants appear before you, do not decide for one until you hear the other. It is more likely that by doing so, the reasons for a judgment will become clear to you.'[81]

اذا جلس بين يديك الخصمان فلا تقضى حتى تسمع من الآخر
كما سمعت من الأول.

In a widely known incident involving the two leading Companions, ʿUmar ibn al-Khaṭṭāb and ʿAlī ibn Abī Ṭālib, it is reported that the latter had a dispute with a Jew whom he took to court where ʿUmar ibn al-Khaṭṭāb was presiding. ʿUmar addressed the Jew by his name but called ʿAlī, out of respect, by his appellation Abū al-Ḥasan. This invoked ʿAlī's displeasure, and when ʿUmar asked ʿAlī whether he was unhappy because he had to attend the court with a Jew, ʿAlī replied that on the contrary he was unhappy because ʿUmar had not accorded equal treatment since there was a discrepancy in the tone of the address and the choice of the litigants' titles used. ʿUmar is reported to have accepted the explanation and was appreciative of it.[82] This incident was the beginning of a series of reform measures that the Caliph ʿUmar took regarding court procedure. The Caliph later issued a letter to his judges in which he laid special emphasis on the equal treatment of litigants before the court. This renowned letter of ʿUmar contained the following exhortation:

> Treat the people equally in your presence, in your judgment, and in the way you speak to them, so that the strong does not entertain the thought of your being partial, and nor does the weak despair in your sense of commitment to justice.[83]

The *Sharīᶜah* protects the property of non-Muslim citizens and defends them against unfair treatment and discrimination. It is reported in this connection that during the time of the Caliph ᶜUmar, a poor non-Muslim woman refused to sell her house to the local governor who had taken it in order to enlarge a mosque. She complained to the Caliph, who then ordered the house to be returned to her, and he also reprimanded the governor for putting her under pressure.[84]

In the area of adjudication and the testimony of witnesses, the *Sharīᶜah* court jurisdiction in civil litigation does not extend to disputes in which both parties are non-Muslim, unless the parties themselves make a request for it. But when one of the disputing parties is a Muslim, the case falls under the *Sharīᶜah* court jurisdiction. This is, however, not the position in criminal prosecution, as in principle criminal law applies equally to all the parties involved. The only exception here is with regard to offences of a religious type, such as wine-drinking and apostasy, which only apply to Muslims and preclude non-Muslim citizens altogether.[85]

Muslim jurists have recorded certain restrictions in regard to the admissibility of non-Muslims as witnesses in a court of *Sharīᶜah*. As a general rule, non-Muslim citizens are admissible as witnesses without restriction in the cases of other non-Muslims. Their testimony is also generally admissible in disputes concerning acts and transactions in which they usually participate and interact freely with their partners and clients, Muslim or non-Muslim. In certain other disputes, such as those concerning marriage and divorce, religious offences and matters of Muslim worship, the testimony of non-Muslims is not admissible in disputes involving Muslims.[86] The ruling here is based on the analysis that a difference of religion is grounds for doubt. According to a general rule of the law of evidence concerning the enforcement of penalties, the charge must be proved beyond doubt, and this is why the testimony of non-Muslims is precluded.

The rules of inheritance are generally based on equality, although not necessarily on amicability or friendship. A difference of religion is a bar to inheritance, which means that neither side is entitled to inherit from relatives if they belong to different religions. Thus a non-Muslim does not inherit from a Muslim relative, or vice versa.[87] It is permissible, however, according to the Ḥanafīs at least, to make a bequest in favour of a non-Muslim, a ruling that can to some extent be used to remedy the difficult situation of disinheritance between relatives who subscribe to different religions. Non-Muslim citizens of the Islamic state are, however, free to practice their own laws and customs in the areas of marriage, divorce, inheritance, bequests, religious rituals and customary matters. This also includes non-Muslim practices that may conflict with the *Sharīᶜah* such as in the case of wine-drinking or the consumption of pork. Non-Muslims are free to follow their own rules on these matters provided they do not promote them among Muslims. Non-Muslim citizens also enjoy total equality in areas of trade and transactions, as well as ownership of property, and are free to take part in other economic and industrial activities, or interact as partners and associates with their fellow Muslims without restriction. They may reside in any locality they wish and conduct their customary, religious and cultural affairs as they wish.

Muslim jurists are generally in agreement that Muslims may accept and extend hospitality to non-Muslims, and nurture good neighbourly relations with them. As noted previously, the Qur'ān clearly permits Muslims to eat food prepared by non-Muslims, including meat that is slaughtered by Jews and Christians, and in this way contribute to an atmosphere of friendship and amicable social relations with them.[88]

With regard to employment to government offices, there is historical precedent to show that non-Muslim citizens were employed in government posts during the time of the Rightly-Guided Caliphs, and in later periods to ministerial positions, as army commanders and chiefs of religious schools.[89] Al-Māwardī translated that precedent into a specific formula that the *dhimmīs* may be appointed to a ministerial portfolio (i.e. *wazīr al-tanfīdh*) but not to the post of prime minister (*wazīr al-tafwīḍ*), and they are not included in the *ahl al-ḥall wa'l-ᶜaqd*, or those who loosen and bind, that is, the electoral college of elders who nominate the prospective Imām. This is because, according to Māwardī, the prime minister enjoys wide political powers over governors, the army and the treasury.[90] Historical evidence shows that non-Muslims were employed in large numbers and in high government positions under the Umayyads and the Abbasids, and they are known to have become particularly influential due to their economic power and wealth.[91] Juristic manuals further specify that the *dhimmīs* may be appointed as judges, but only when their jurisdiction is confined to their own community. This rule is an extension of the same restrictions imposed on the admissibility of non-Muslims as witnesses in the *Sharīʿah* courts.[92] There is general consensus, however, that a non-Muslim may not become the head of state of a Muslim land.

Yet there is some support for the view that a non-Muslim may adjudicate disputes among Muslims. Since the testimony of a non-Muslim concerning a Muslim is admissible in civil/non-religious matters, and since eligibility for judgeship is analogous, according to the Ḥanafīs, to eligibility as a witness, it follows that non-Muslims may be appointed as judges regardless of the religious affiliation of litigants. This analysis seems to have persuaded the committee of Turkish *ʿulamāʾ* who drafted the *Mejelle,* as there is no reference to the religious affiliation of the judge in its relevant articles on this subject. Article 1794, which spells out the qualifications of the judge, mainly specifies erudition in the *Sharīʿah* and the applied law of the land, but does not stipulate that the judge must be a Muslim. This is also the case in the provision of the *Mejelle* (art. 1705) pertaining to testimony. Witnesses must accordingly be upright individuals of good record and reputation, but there is no stipulation that they must also be Muslims.[93]

With regard to taxation, non-Muslim citizens are liable to pay a poll-tax (*jizyah*), which is at about the same rate as that of *zakāh,* but since *zakāh* is a religious duty in Islam, and one of the five pillars of the faith, non-Muslims are not required to pay it. *Jizyah* is not a substitute for *zakāh* either; it is a contribution to the costs of protection and security that the state incurs. Non-Muslim citizens are, on the other hand, exempted from military service as this too is a religious duty that tends to partake of *jihād.* But if non-Muslim citizens themselves wish to serve in the army, they may do so, in which case they will be exempted from the payment of *jizyah.* In the event where an Islamic state fails to defend its non-Muslim citizens against aggression, it must return the *jizyah* taken from them.[94] Only those who are capable of paying are required to pay the *jizyah,* and this has meant that the sick and disabled, the elderly, children, women and monks are not required to pay.[95]

There is evidence, on the other hand, to suggest that the *dhimmīs* are entitled to equal support from the funds of the *bayt al-māl* which may include revenues from *zakāh.* The precedent of the Caliph ʿUmar, who entitled the Jews to assistance from *bayt al-māl,* is often quoted as supportive evidence for this practice. ʿUmar himself justified his position by reference to the Qurʾānic *āyah* which specifies the recipient of *zakāh* as the 'poor and the needy' (al-Tawbah, 9:60) without any reference to their religious affiliation.[96]

It may be said in conclusion that due to drastic changes in circumstances, and the fact that taxation and military service laws are today applied equally to all citizens, there remains no basis for the imposition of *jizyah* as a separate tax on non-Muslim citizens. To take a technical approach to the imposition of *jizyah* in disregard of the prevailing circumstances may well amount to injustice, which the Qur'ān has clearly proscribed.

And lastly, it is interesting to note al-Qaraḍāwī's observation that there is basically no objection to the elimination of the *zakāh-jizyah* duality and making the *zakāh* equally applicable to both Muslim and non-Muslim citizens alike. The latter will pay it, not as a religious duty but as a special welfare tax that applied equally to all, provided that those in authority, that is, the *ᶜūlu al-amr,* deemed this appropriate. For the Muslims, *zakāh* will, of course, remain a religious duty. But a uniform application of *zakah* in this way will have the advantage, in addition to meeting the objectives of equality, of easier administration of tax.[97]

VI. A Survey of Modern Opinion

In addition to the views of Maḥmūd Shaltūt and Yūsuf al-Qaraḍāwī that were previously cited on retaliation and *jizyah* respectively, many prominent Muslim scholars and *ᶜulamā'* have in recent decades supported the egalitarian interpretation of the *Sharīᶜah* in regard to the treatment of non-Muslim citizens. These views merit attention as they are refreshingly different and partake of sound *ijtihād,* often attempted with the purpose of bridging the gap between the changed conditions of society and the basic tenets of the *Sharīᶜah* on the issues concerned. These views may be summarised as follows.

In a reference to the Qur'ānic *āyah*: 'O mankind! Surely We have created you from a male and a female, and made you tribes and nations that you may know each other. Surely the noblest of you in the eyes of God is the most pious among you' (al-Ḥujurāt, 49:13), Abū Zahrah has highlighted the egalitarian spirit of this Qur'ānic declaration and observed that this verse has laid down the foundation of the equality of all citizens before the law without discrimination on the basis of wealth colour, race or religion. The only criterion of superiority that Islam accepts is moral excellence (*taqwā*) and righteous conduct.[98]

Referring to the same *āyah* (i.e. 49:13) Maḥmūd Shaltūt has observed that 'Islam has declared mankind a single unity and a requirement of that unity is the equality of all human beings in respect of their rights and obligations, which is also the only way for the establishment of justice. Justice, being the overriding objective of Islam, cannot be achieved without equality.'[99]

Further stressing the normative value of justice and the prominence it has been given in the Qur'ān (there are about twenty-eight *āyāt* in the Qur'ān on justice—*ʿadl* and *qiṣt*),[100] Rashīd al-Ghannushī observed that 'Islam did not command justice only for Muslims but for mankind generally, and this is perfectly clear in the Qur'ān, where justice is an obligation that must be observed even when one is dealing with one's enemy.'[101]

Maḥmaṣṣānī has similarly observed that 'the brotherhood of man is one of the fundamental postulates of Islam, which contemplates the whole of mankind as a single great nation—*ummah kabīrah wāḥidah*'.[102] In support of this statement Maḥmaṣṣānī elaborates that Islam subscribes to monotheism (*tawḥīd*) and through it to the realisation of the unity of the human race. Muhammad's ﷺ mission was for humanity as a whole, which is borne out by numerous affirmations in the Qur'ān, such as 'we did not send you save as a bringer of good tidings and a warner to mankind (Sabā, 34:28; two other *āyāt* cited are al-Shūrā, 42:15 and Sabā, 34:26). Moreover, on the subject of unity and equality, Fazlur Rahman has drawn attention to the tone of Qur'ānic language, in particular, the 'short, forceful and indeed explosive' sūras of the Qur'ān which in the standard arrangement of the Qur'ān appear at the very end. The reader finds that only two themes are insistently preached. One is the unity of God, and the other an essential egalitarianism. Fazlur Rahman then identifies a positive link between the moral-spiritual ideal of *tawḥīd* and the idea of an egalitarian society in the Qur'ān: 'The Qur'ān seems to say that if there is one God, then essentially there must be one humanity.'[103]

Commenting on the *āyah* in sūra al-Ḥujurāt (49:13), Maḥmaṣṣānī wrote further that Islam abolished the tribalism and social discriminations based on lineage and nobility of descent that were so common in pre-Islamic Arabia. Islam invited people to unite on the basis of *tawḥīd*. The Prophet ﷺ endorsed this unitarian message, and called for the social transformation of Arab society when he said unequivocally in a *ḥadīth*:[104]

> He is not one of us who promotes tribal kinship [*ʿaṣabiyyah*], who fights for *ʿaṣabiyyah,* and who dies for *ʿasabiyyah.*[105]

ليس منا من دعا الى عصبية، وليس منا من قاتل على عصبية،
وليس منا من مات على عصبية.

Al-Qaraḍāwī has distinguished two types of fraternity in Islam, namely the fraternity of man (*al-ikhā' al-insānī*) and religious fraternity (*al-ikhā' al-dīnī*), both of which are recognised in the Qur'ān. 'The believers are brethren' (al-Ḥujurāt, 49:10) is a clear and unequivocal affirmation of the religious fraternity of Muslims. Al-Qaraḍāwī then adds that this level of fraternity is not in conflict with the wider fraternity of man, and the two should in fact be seen as complementary, and not contradictory, to one another.

Al-Qaraḍāwī has based his analysis on his understanding of the Qur'ānic text (al-Nisā', 4:1) that has already been discussed. Both levels of fraternity, al-Qaraḍāwī adds, find support in the Qur'ān. Hence the two are complementary and co-extensive.[106]

ʿAbd al-Qādir ʿAwdah has observed that Islam advocates 'equality absolutely, without any restrictions or exceptions, for the whole of mankind, and without recognition whatsoever of any distinction or superiority of one man over another, or of one group over another, or of one race over another, and that includes equality between men and women, the ruler and ruled'.[107] ʿAwdah has referred to supportive evidence in the sources for his conclusion, including the following two *ḥadīth*:

> People are as equal as the teeth of a comb.

الناس سواسية كأسنان المشط.

> God Most High has released you from the burdens of the Days of Ignorance and the pride that was taken over ancestry. You are all the descendants of Adam and Adam was created from clay.[108]

إن الله عز وجل قد أذهب عنكم عبية الجاهلية وفخرها بالآباء.
أنتم بنوا آدم و آدم من تراب.

Muḥammad Salām Madkūr has commented that nationality and religion are now separate matters, and are treated as such under the prevailing laws of contemporary Muslim states. People belonging to different religions enjoy equal rights, just as they also share equally in the duties of military service and taxation. It would thus be quite reasonable to depart from the earlier criteria of religion-based distinctions, and treat the issue from the wider perspectives of equality and justice.[109]

Al-Ghannushī has further observed that Islam's basic commitment to equality is not at all in doubt either generally or in respect of the rights and obligations of non-Muslims. There are, however, differences of detail among jurists concerning the status of non-Muslims, which have largely been due to differences of religious belief, and it is not unreasonable that some of these should be accepted. To attempt to establish total equality among people who subscribe to different values, al-Ghannushī adds, might amount to injustice. To impose on non-Muslims, in other words, something that is disagreeable to their religion is likely to go against the essence of equality and justice.[110]

Murtaza Mutahhari has characterised the Qur'ānic vision of equality as one of positive, rather than negative, equality. Whereas negative equality takes 'no account of natural distinctions among individuals' and denies their acquired distinctions in order to establish equality, positive equality means the 'creation of equal opportunities for all [...] and denial of imaginary and unjust distinctions'.[111] Furthermore, the Qur'ān envisages a 'natural society' as opposed to a discriminatory society. Mutahhari elaborates that a natural society is one in which every possible means by which one person lives by exploiting another is condemned. Islam envisages a society in which the basic framework of the relationship among individuals is 'one of mutual taming'. What this means is that all strive freely according to their abilities and 'all are tamed by one another' in accordance with their abilities. This analysis is based on Mutahhari's understanding of the following Qur'ānic text:

> It is We who portion out among them their livelihood in the life of this world, and We raise some of them above others in degrees, so that they might obtain labour from one another [or benefit from the fruit of each other's labour] (al-Zukhruf, 43:32).

نحن قسمنا بينهم معيشتهم في الحياة الدنيا ورفعنا بعضهم فوق
بعض درجات ليتخذ بعضهم بعضا سخريا.

The Qur'ān has thus envisaged employment and 'mutual benefit' (*sukhriyyah*) in socio-economic relations. This is based on cognisance of natural differences among individuals; whoever has the greater ability will attract a greater number of forces to himself. For instance, an individual who has the greater ability in science will attract a greater number of prospective students in science to himself and tame them to a greater extent, and one who is more capable in arts will do likewise. Yet the discrepancy in merits is not one-sided; that is, people do not fall into one of the two classes of naturally superior and naturally inferior. For according to the text before us, all enjoy some superiority and all tame each other in certain ways. This is the purport of the portion of the text that reads 'so they might obtain labour from each other', and not that one class will obtain labour or service exclusively from another. This notion of 'mutual taming' is understood from the Arabic word '*sukriyyah*', which connotes mutual power and influence in a way that overrules the unilateral domination of one group of people over another.[112]

Tawfīq al-Shāwī has reached the conclusion that the different rulings of the *madhāhib* on some of the basic rights and liberties of non-Muslim citizens are on the whole the outcome of circumstantial *ijtihād* (*ijtihādāt ẓarfiyyah*), reflective, on the whole, of the state of hostility and war that prevailed between Muslim and non-Muslim powers at the time. Bearing in mind the changes that have taken place since, and the fact that the prevailing pattern is now one of treaty relations that require reciprocal treatment (*al-muʿāmalah bi'l-mithl*), this should be acknowledged and adopted as a guideline in regulating relations among nations at the present time. Hence it becomes necessary to abandon all that is disagreeable to the general regime of equality between Muslim and non-Muslim citizens, whether it is the *jizyah*, military service or employment to government positions, except for the office of the head of state, which should be reserved for Muslims. Al-Shāwī is also supportive of al-Qaraḍāwī's conclusion, discussed above, that there is basically no objection to the idea that non-Muslim citizens could pay the *zakāh* alongside Muslims.[113]

It may be said in conclusion that the evidence in the Qur'ān and the *Sunnah* is supportive of equality and justice for all, including women and non-Muslims. It would indeed be disagreeable to the essence of equality to read forced meanings into the language of the text in support of inequality and discrimination. Equality, like freedom and justice, is basically indivisible, hence any interpretation that departs from its essence is bound to be questionable and weak. Some of the divergent interpretations of jurists of different ages, which assigned a different status to women and to non-Muslims, should thus be seen as circumstantial developments that may have been prompted by the pressure of prevailing conditions. The prevailing conditions at the end of the twentieth century are now strongly supportive of universal equality that is in harmony with the spirit of fraternity and promotes cooperation between the various strata of society. Many *ᶜulamā'* and scholars of the twentieth century have advocated a fresh and uncompromising approach to the understanding of the Qur'ān and *Sunnah* on equality, and the inherent strength of this message is beyond question.

NOTES

1. Qāḍ, Samīr ᶜĀliyah, *Naẓariyyah al-Dawlah fi'l-Islām*, Beirut, Mu'assasah al-Jāmiᶜiyyah, 1408/1980, p. 86.
2. Ḥāfiẓ Abū'l-Fida Ismāᶜīl ibn Kathīr, *Tafsīr al-Qur'ān al-ᶜAẓīm* (also known as *Tafsīr Ibn Kathīr*), Cairo: Dār al-Shaᶜb, 1393/1973, IV, 218.
3. Muḥammad al-Bahī, *al-Dīn wa'l-Dawlah min Tawjīhāt al-Qur'ān al-Karīm*, Beirut, Dār al-Fikr, 1391/1971, p. 350.
4. Al-Qaraḍāwī, *al-Khaṣā'iṣ,* p. 84.
5. Extract from the Prophet's sermon on the occasion of the Farewell Pilgrimage. Aḥmad Ibn Rabbih, *al-ᶜIqd al-Farīd li'l-Malik al-Saᶜīd*, 3rd edn., Cairo: Maṭbaᶜah Lajnat al-Ta'līf, 1384/1965, II, 357; Maḥmaṣṣānī, Arkān, p. 266.
6. Zakī al-Dīn al-Mundhirī, *al-Targhīb wa'l-Tarhīb*, Cairo, Muṣṭafā al-Bābī al-Ḥalabī, 1373/1954, IV, 23; al-ᶜĪlī, *Ḥurriyyāt*, p. 271.
7. al-Suyūṭī, *al-Jāmiᶜ al-Ṣaghīr,* II, *ḥadīth* no. 7684.
8. al-ᶜĪlī, *Ḥurriyyāt*, p. 271.
9. ᶜAlī ibn Aḥmad ibn al-Athīr, *al-Kamil fi'l-Tārikh*, Cairo, Maṭbaᶜat al-Shaykh Aḥmad al-Bābī al-Ḥalabī, 1303 AH, II, 154; al-ᶜĪlī, *Ḥurriyyāt*, p. 272.
10. Abū Yūsuf, *al-Kharāj*, p. 166.
11. Abū Zahrah, *Jarīmah*, p. 160; Sibāᶜī, *Ishtirākiyyāt*, p. 50.
12. Abū Yūsuf, *al-Kharāj*, p. 65.

13. Sulaymān Muḥammad al-Ṭamāwī, *ᶜUmar ibn al-Khaṭṭāb wa Uṣūl al-Siyāsah wa'l-Idārah al-Ḥadhīthah*, Cairo, Dār al-Fikr al-ᶜArabī, 1969, p. 337; al-ᶜĪlī, *Ḥurriyyāt*, p. 273; Maḥmaṣṣānī, *Arkān*, p. 266.

14. Muḥammad ibn Idrīs al-Shāfiᶜī, *Kitāb al-Umm*, ed. Muḥammad Sayyd Kaylāni, 2nd edn., Cairo, Muṣṭafā al-Bābī al-Ḥalabī, 1403/1983, VI, 268.

15. Al-Mawardī, *Kitāb al-Aḥkām*, pp. 59-60; Ibn Qayyim al-Jawziyyah, *Iᶜlām*, I, 85. An English translation of this letter appears in M. Ishaque, 'al-Ahkam al-Sultaniyya: Laws of Government in Islam', *Islamic Studies*, 4 (1965), p. 289.

16. Cf. Muḥammad Salām Madkūr, *al-Qaḍā' fi'l-Islām*, Cairo, Dār al-Nahḍah al-ᶜArabiyyah, 1964. p. 34.

17. All Pakistan Legal Decision (1988), Federal Sharīᶜah Court 283.

18. See for details el-Awa, *The Political System*, pp. 34-39; Muḥammad al-Ṣadīq ᶜAfīfī, *al-Mujtamaᶜ al-Islāmī wa-Uṣūl al-Ḥukm*, Cairo, Dār al-Iᶜtiṣām, 1400/1980, p. 115; Khallāf, *al-Siyāsah*, p. 55; ᶜAbd al-Ghanī al-Basyūnī ᶜAbd Allāh, *Naẓariyyat al-Dawlah fi'l-Islām*, Beirut, Dār al-Jāmiᶜiyyah, 1986, p. 241.

19. al-ᶜĪlī, *Ḥurriyyāt*, p. 275.

20. al-Badawī, *Daᶜā'im*, p. 400.

21. Al-Ṭamāwī, *ᶜUmar ibn al-Khaṭṭāb*, p. 273.

22. Ibn Taymiyyah, *al-Siyāsah*, pp. 4-11.

23. Ibid., p. 97. For further details, see the section on distributive justice which appears under the chapter on justice below.

24. Abū Yūsuf, *al-Kharāj*, p. 42.

25. al-ᶜĪlī, *Ḥurriyāt*, p. 280.

26. Cf. al-Sanhūrī, *Fiqh al-Khilāfah*, p. 187.

27. This was the conclusion of the *Fatwā* Committe of the Ahzar University of Egypt issued in 1952 during the Premiership of Najīb al-Hilālī, when Egyptian women had stepped up their demand for equal rights in elections and candidacy for elected assemblies. See for detail, Mutawallī, *Mabādi'*, pp. 417ff.

28. Al-Bukhārī, *Ṣaḥīḥ al-Bukhārī*, IX, *ḥadīth* no. 219.

29. All Pakistan Legal Decisions (1983), Federal Sharīᶜah Court 73.

30. Ibn Qayyim al-Jawziyyah, *Ṭuruq*, p. 149.

31. Ibid.

32. Maḥmūd Shaltūt, *al-Islām ᶜAqīdah wa Sharīᶜah*, Kuwait, Maṭābiᶜ Dār al-Qalam, n.d., pp. 251-2.

33. Ibid., p. 252.

34. Ibn Qayyim al-Jawziyyah, *Ṭuruq*, p. 152; Shaltūt, *al-Islām*, p. 252.

35. Shaltūt, *al-Islām*, p. 253.

36. Abu'l-Ḥasan al-Māwardī, *Kitāb al-Aḥkām al-Sulṭāniyyah*, 2nd edn., Cairo, Muṣṭafā al-Bābī al-Ḥalabī, 1386AH, p. 27; Abū Yaᶜlā Muḥammad

al-Farrā', *al-Aḥkām al-Sulṭāniyyah*, Cairo, Muṣṭafā al-Bābī al-Ḥalabī, 1357AH, p. 25.

37. Al-Māwardī, *Kitāb al-Aḥkām*, p. 65.

38. Abū Muḥammad ʿAlī Ibn Ḥazm, *al-Muḥallā*, ed. Aḥmad M. Shākir, Cairo, Dār al-Fikr, n.d., ; Aḥmad, *Uṣūl Niẓām*, p. 183.

39. al-Mawardī, *Kitāb al-Aḥkām*, p. 64.

40. Cf. Rashīd Riḍā, *Tafsīr al-Qur'ān al-Ḥakīm* (also know as *Tafsīr al-Manār*), Beirut, Dār al-Maʿrifah, 1328AH, II, 375; Qāḍ, *Naẓariyyat al-Dawlah*, p. 69.

41. Ibn Ḥazm, *al-Muḥallā* (ed. Hasan Zaydan), X, 632.

42. ʿAbd al-Ḥamīd al-Anṣārī, *al-Shūrā wa Āthāruhu fi'l-Dimuqrātiyyah al-Ḥadīthah*, 2nd edn., Cairo, al-Maktabah al-ʿAṣriyyah, 1400/1980, p. 294.

43. Ibid.

44. Cf. Mutawallī, *Mabādī'*, p. 422.

45. Abū Muḥammad ʿAlī ibn Ḥazm, *al-Fiṣal fi'l-Milal wa'l-Ahwā' wa'l-Nihal*, Cairo, Maktabat al-Salām al-ʿĀlamiyyah, n.d, IV, 167.

46. al-ʿĪlī, *Ḥurriyyāt*, p. 288.

47. Cf. Mahmūd ʿAbd al-Majīd Khālidī, *Qawāʿid Niẓām al-Ḥukm fi'l-Islām*, Kuwait, Dār al-Buḥūth al-ʿIlmiyyah, 1980, p. 168; al-ʿĪlī, *Ḥurriyyāt*, p. 292.

48. Yaḥyā ibn ʿAlī al-Shawkānī, *Nayl al-Awṭār: Sharḥ Muntaqā al-Akhbār*, Cairo, Muṣṭafā al-Bābī al-Ḥalabī, n.d., VIII, p. 17; al-ʿĪlī, *Ḥurriyyāt*, p. 292; Zuḥaylī, *al-Fiqh*, VI, 429.

49. Abū Jaʿfar Muḥammad al-Ṭabarī, *Ta'rīkh al-Rusul wa'l-Muluk*, Cairo, al-Maṭbaʿah al-Tijariyyah, 1358/1939, III, 479.

50. Ibn Qudāmah, *al-Mughnī*, Cairo, Maṭbaʿah al-Manār, 1367AH, II, 375.

51. al-ʿĪlī, *Ḥurriyyāt*, p. 296.

52. Muḥammad ʿAbduh, *Risālat al-Tawḥīd*, 6th edn., Cairo, Dār al-Manār, 1973, II, 375.

53. al-Suyūṭī, *al-Jāmiʿ al-Ṣaghīr*, II, 97, *ḥadīth* no. 5264.

54. Abū Muḥammad ʿAlī ibn Ḥazm, *al-Iḥkām fī Uṣūl al-Aḥkām*, ed. Aḥmad Shākir, Beirut, Dār al-Āfāq al-Jadīdah, 1400/1980, V, 121.

55. Al-Tabrīzī, *Mishkāt*, II, *ḥadīth* no. 3280.

56. Qānūn Ḥuqūq al-ʿĀ'ilah, Decree Law no. 59, 1953; for further information in Syrian Law see J.N.D. Anderson, 'The Syrian Law of Personal Status', BSOAS, XVII (1955), pp. 34-39.

57. All Pakistan Legal Decision (1967), Sharīʿah Court 97.

58. In the case of Malaysia, The Islamic Family (Federal Territories) Act 1984 contained wide-ranging reforms of the law of polygamy and divorce, some of which have, however, been overruled by The Islamic Family Law (Federal Territories) Amendment Act 1994. For a general summary of Islamic family law reform in the Middle East and Asia, including Afghanistan, see

Mohammad H. Kamali, *Law in Afghanistan: A Study of the Constitutions, Matrimonial Law and the Judiciary*, Leiden, E.J. Brill, 1989, pp. 154ff and pp.189ff. For developments in Malaysia, see Mohammad H. Kamali, 'Islamic Law in Malaysia: Issue and Developments', *Yearbook of Islamic and Middle Eastern Law*, vol. 4 (1997-98), pp. 153-80.

59. See for further details, Kamali, *Law in Afghanistan*, pp. 130-158.

60. For a summary of their views, see Kamali, 'Divorce and Women's Rights', pp. 89ff.

61. Ibid., p. 99.

62. For a discussion of the disagreement on whether the tax exemption period should be four months or one year, see al-Mawardī, *Aḥkām*, p. 130; al-Sanhūrī, *Fiqh al-Khilāfah*, p. 185 and Muḥammad Salām Madkūr, *Ma^cālim al-Dawlah al-Islamiyyah*, Maktabat al-Falāḥ, 1403/1983, p. 101.

63. Mutawallī, *Mabādī'*, p. 391.

64. See for a discussion Costa Luca, 'Discrimination in the Arab Middle East' in Willem A. Veenhoven (ed.), *Case Studies on Human Rights and Fundamental Freedoms*, vol. 1, The Hague, 1975, pp. 211-40.

65. al-Kāsānī, *Badā'i^c al-Ṣanā'i^c*, Cairo, Maṭba^cah al-Istiqāmah, 1956, vol. VII, p. 100; al-Shawkānī, *Nayl al-Awṭār*, vol. VII, p. 13.

66. Abū Dāwūd, *Sunan*, vol. II, p. 265.

67. Al-Suyūṭī, *al-Jāmi^c al-Ṣaghīr*, vol. II, p. 473.

68. al-Shawkānī, *Nayl al-Awṭār*, vol. VII, p. 12. See also Aḥmad Muṣṭafā al-Marāghī, *Tafsīr al-Marāghī*, 2nd edn., Cairo, Maṭba^cat Muṣṭafā al-Bābī al-Ḥalabī, 1953, p. 83.

69. al-Kāsānī, *Badā'i^c*, vol. VIII, p. 111; al-^cĪlī, *Ḥurriyyāt*, pp. 312-13.

70. al-Shawkānī, *Nayl al-Awṭār*, VII, 6.

71. al-^cĪlī, *Ḥurriyyāt*, p. 331.

72. al-Shawkānī, *Nayl al-Awṭār*, VII, 13.

73. Abū Dāwūd, *Sunan*, VI, 328.

74. Muḥammad ibn Aḥmad ibn Rushd al-Qurṭubī, *Bidayāt al-Mujtahid wa Nihāyat al-Muqtaṣid*, Cairo, Muṣṭafā al-Bābī al-Ḥalabī, 1401/1981, II, 334; al-^cĪlī, *Ḥurriyyāt*, p. 329.

75. al-Kāsānī, *Badā'i^c*, VII, 237; Ramadan, *Islamic Law*, p. 156.

76. Ibn Rushd, *Bidāya,* II, 310.

77. Ibid.

78. Shaltūt, *al-Islām*, p. 326.

79. ^cAwdah, *al-Tashrī^c al-Jinā'i*, II, 123.

80. Sayyid Abu'l-A^clā Mawdūdī, *Naẓariyyat al-Islām al-Siyāsiyyah*, translated from Urdu by Khalīl Ḥasan al-Iṣlāḥī, Beirut: Dār al-Fikr, n.d., p. 443.

81. Bayhaqī, *Sunan al-Kubrā*, X, 137; Zaydan, *Niẓām al-Qaḍā fi'l-Sharī^cah al-Islāmiyyah,* Baghdad, Maṭba^cat al-^cĀnī, 1404/1984, p. 136.

82. Wāfī, *Ḥuqūq al-Insān*, p. 109.
83. Ibn Qayyim al-Jawziyyah, *Iʿlām*, I, 72.
84. Muḥammad ʿAbduh, *Risālat al-Tawḥīd*, p. 188.
85. See for details al-ʿĪlī, *Ḥurriyyāt*, p. 324.
86. Cf. Maḥmūd Shaltūt, *Fiqh al-Qur'ān wa'l-Sunnah*, Kuwait, Maṭabiʿ Dār al-Qalam, n.d., p. 69; ʿUthmān, *al-Fikr al-Qānūnī al-Islāmī: Bayn Uṣūl al-Sharīʿah wa Turāth al-Fiqh,* Cairo: Maktabah Wahbah, n.d., p. 269; see also Zuḥaylī, *al-Fiqh al-Islāmī*, VII, 586.
87. Cf. Khallāf, *al-Siyāsah*, p. 94.
88. Ibid.
89. Cf. ʿAbduh, *al-Islām wa'l-Naṣrāniyyah*, p. 19; and *Risālah al-Tawḥīd* p. 185.
90. al-Mawardī, *Aḥkām*, p. 22.
91. al-ʿĪlī, *Ḥurriyyāt*, p. 319.
92. Cf. Mutawallī, *Mabādi'*, p. 397.
93. Qāḍ, *Naẓariyyat al-Dawlah*, p. 69.
94. Madkūr, *Maʿālim al-Dawlah*, p. 422.
95. See for details al-Māwardī, *Aḥkām*, p. 143; al-ʿĪlī, *Ḥurriyyāt*, p. 325.
96. Abū Yūsuf, *al-Kharāj*, p. 144.
97. Yūsuf al-Qaraḍawī, *Fiqh al-Zakāh*, 3rd edn., Beirut, Mu'assasat al-Risālah, 1397/1977, I, 98-99.
98. Abū Zahrah, *Tanẓīm al-Islām*, p. 31.
99. Shaltūt, *al-Islām*, p. 464.
100. More generally, there are over two hundred admonitions against injustice in the Qur'ān, and no less than almost a hundred expressions outlining the notion of justice, in either direct or indirect speech; cf. Majid Khadduri, *The Islamic Conception of Justice*, Baltimore, The John Hopkins University Press, 1984. pp. 9-10.
101. Rashīd al-Ghanoushī, *Ḥuqūq al-Muwāṭanah: Ḥuqūq Ghayr al-Muslim fi'l-Mujtamaʿ al-Islāmī*, 2nd edn., Herndon, VA: International Institute of Islamic Thought, 1413/1993, p. 48.
102. Maḥmaṣṣānī, *Arkān*, p. 260.
103. Rahman, 'The Status of the Individual in Islam', p. 323.
104. Maḥmaṣṣānī, *Arkān*, p. 261.
105. al-Suyūṭī, *al-Jāmiʿ al-Ṣaghīr*, vol. II, *ḥadīth* no. 7684; Maḥmaṣṣānī, *Arkān*, p. 267.
106. al-Qaraḍāwī, *al-Khaṣā'is*. p. 84.
107. ʿAwdah, *al-Tashrīʿ al-Jinā'i*, I, 35.
108. Abū Dāwūd, *Sunan*, *Kitāb al-Ādāb*, *ḥadīth* no. 5116.
109. Madkūr, *Maʿālim*, p. 104.
110. Al-Ghanoushī, *Ḥuqūq al-Muwāṭanah*, p. 72.

111. Mutahhari, *Fundamentals of Islamic Thought*, p. 95.

112. Ibid., pp.95-7.

113. See al-Shāwī's introduction to al-Ghanoushī's, *Ḥuqūq al-Muwāṭanah*, pp. 26-27.

CHAPTER THREE

Justice (ᶜ*Adl*)

I. Meaning and Definition

Literally ᶜ*adl* means placing something in its rightful place; it also means according equal treatment to others or reaching a state of equilibrium in transactions with them (*al-taswiyah fi'l-mu*ᶜ*āmalah*). ᶜ*Adl* (also ᶜ*adālah*) thus signifies moral rectitude and fairness since it means that things should be where they belong. Justice is closely related to equality in that it aims for a state of equilibrium in the distribution of rights and duties, and advantages and burdens in the community. Justice and equality are, however, not identical in the sense that, under certain circumstances, justice may only be achieved through inequality or an unequal distribution of wealth.[1] Justice is, in many ways, a universal concept in that its basic meaning does not seems to vary a great deal between the major legal traditions of the world.

Aristotle defined justice as avoiding too much or too little in the distribution of things, and readjusting and compensating where the balance has been disturbed. The two aspects of justice, namely corrective justice and distributive justice in this definition, both conceive of justice as a social concept as it subsumes social relations, and will have little meaning if it were applied to an individual in total isolation from society. Yet in both Islamic and Western thought, justice is also understood as a moral virtue and an attribute of personality within or outside the social context. Ancient Greek thought conceived of justice as an aspect of the character of the individual. Plato thus characterised justice as the right alignment of the individual soul, and Aristotle considered it one of the virtues needed to lead an excellent life.

In his *Republic*, Plato advanced the view that justice consists of harmonious relations between the various parts of a social organism. Every citizen must do his duty in his appointed place, and do that for which his nature is best adapted. Plato thus envisaged an ideal but class-oriented society in which people were naturally unequal, yet justice was a paramount virtue, administrated by the philosopher King. The state of the *Republic* was therefore an executive state, governed by the free intelligence of the best men rather than by the rule of law. Justice, too, was to be administrated under the rule of men rather than the rule of law. Aristotle's concept of justice was rooted in equality, moral virtue, and the just distribution of wealth. Yet he too regarded the individual as having a fixed role or status in a well-defined social structure. The concept of individual virtue was related to the fulfilment of the particular social role and duty that was incumbent upon a person. Virtue and justice were, thus, closely associated with the social structure. The individual self was no self at all, and evaluative questions were largely questions of social fact.[2]

Cicero's *De Officiis*, and natural law theory, also discuss justice as a virtue grounded in the inner character of men according to the 'law of nature', a quality on the basis of which men are called good men. Cicero spoke of natural law as 'right reason in agreement with nature from which there can be no dispensation either by the senate or the people'. To run counter to or try to restrict this natural law is immoral. Justice is thus closely linked with an assumed 'law of nature' that is grounded in the physical and psychic constitution of man. Nature demands of man a certain amount of food and sleep and has endowed him with reason, love, liberty and ownership, traits that no adequate theory of justice can overlook. The classical theory of natural law thus assumes that 'there are certain principles of human conduct, awaiting discovery by human reason, with which man-made law must conform if it is to be valid'.[3] Christian thinkers of the medieval period who initially found it difficult to embrace this theory were later persuaded to identify the law of nature with the law of God. The church thus became the exponent of natural law, and maintained that natural law was a product of the will of God and conformed to His prescriptions.[4]

Justice is not synonymous with equality, nor with 'just deserts', nor even with moral uprightness. It is rather a process, a complex and shifting balance between many factors, some of which are also relative and changeable. Equality has meant different things to different peoples and cultures. At a time when technology was not sufficiently developed to provide educational facilities for all, it was not necessarily a capricious decision to restrict all forms of higher education to men on the grounds that the women were needed at home. Similarly, there is no universal agreement on what does and does not constitute unreasonable discrimination.

John Rawls' influential work, *A Theory of Justice*, marked a return to the social contract tradition of the seventeenth and eighteenth century philosophers. What principles would a group of free and rational persons choose to govern their basic social and political institutions if they were brought together in an imaginary 'original position' of equity and fairness for this purpose? The main agenda is to agree on a set of principles to distribute fundamental rights and duties in a manner that can be described as just. A crucial feature of this original position is that its participants are ignorant of their personal characteristics, their social position and their historical period. This 'veil of ignorance' makes the decision impartial and unanimity on it possible. In these conditions, a person will choose the general principle that all social values, including liberty, opportunity and income, should be equally distributed unless an unequal distribution of these values is to everybody's advantage. Any social and economic inequality that is tolerated must benefit the least advantaged members of society. It is claimed that the social contract theory has the advantage of conveying the idea that the principles of justice are those that would be chosen by rational persons, and that the theory of justice is a part of the theory of rational choice.[5]

The classical connection between justice and individual virtue is very different from the contemporary concern with justice. Modern theorists conceptualise justice as an issue for the individual and the state to determine the principles for a relationship between the individual and political institutions, to determine rights among individuals; and also to determine the terms on which the products of social and economic cooperation will be distributed.

As a technical term, 'social justice' (*al-ʿadālah al-ijtimāʿiyyah*) is often equated, in both its English and Arabic usage, with economic justice. Social justice subsumes economic justice, but the two are not identical. Both are concerned with the equitable distribution of wealth in society which implies that economic justice is, however, an essential component of social justice. Economic justice is possible to achieve without social justice, but not vice versa. Social justice will not, for instance, accept a situation in which political powers and liberties are unjustly distributed, yet this would not be a problem for economic justice. Social justice is thus a broader concept as it refers to the structure and policies of a society, and to its political, legal, economic and social institutions.[6]

Let us now turn to the Muslim point of view. *Qaḍā'*, the Arabic word for adjudication, or judicial decision-making, literally means execution, that is, of the ruling, or *ḥukm,* of the *Sharīᶜah*. The literal meaning of *qaḍā'* is also reflected in its juridical application where *qaḍā'* is defined as declaring the *ḥukm* of the *Sharīᶜah* concerning a dispute in a manner that binds the disputing parties.[7] What this means is that a judge does not make the law; his duty is to declare and apply it to the dispute brought before him. It also means that a judicial decree does not render permissible what is forbidden or vice versa. Since the judge declares the ruling of the *Sharīᶜah*, and not his own opinion, for the purpose of implementation in a particular case, the ruling so arrived at is deemed to be enforceable and binding upon its declaration. The prompt enforcement of valid judicial decisions, which is a basic postulate of *qaḍā'* in Islam, is also founded on the analysis that judicial decisions are verified and pronounced by knowledgeable judges of upright character in order to resolve disputes among people. Judicial decisions should not therefore be delayed, as an unwarranted delay could be prejudicial, and may well undermine the substance of justice. Justice, in order to be effective, must, in other words, be swift, and justice delayed can often mean justice denied.

The majority (*jumhūr*) of the Muslim scholars maintain the view that judicial decisions are declaratory in character, and rely only on evidence that is presented in court rather than on any hidden truth not supported by evidence. Judicial decisions, according to this view, do not establish the truth; they merely seek to declare the truth as the evidence indicates. Imām Abū Ḥanīfah has held, on the other hand, that judicial decrees are necessarily concerned with the truth, and they affect not only the apparent (*ẓāhir*) but also the inner (*bāṭin*) state of things especially in the sphere of contracts and dissolutions (*al-ᶜuqūd wa'l-fusūkh*). Thus if a man claims that a certain woman was married to him but she denies it, and then the man manages to bring two false witnesses and proves his claim, and a judge consequently declares them a married couple, she becomes lawful to him. Similarly, if a judge orders separation or declares the same couple divorced, the decree is enforceable, even if the man denies the divorce, provided that the judge does not know that the witnesses were false and also that the matter fell within his proper jurisdiction.[8]

Justice is a collective obligation (*farḍ kifā'ī*) of the entire community, which must be maintained at all times and never abandoned, although in practice it may only be discharged by those who are best qualified to do so. The obligation is more specifically addressed to those who are of the highest integrity, knowledgeable about the *Sharīᶜah* and are capable of performing the task. The initial rulings of the leading *madhāhib* had it that a *qaḍī* (judge) must be a *mujtahid,* who was capable of interpreting the law and formulating independent judgements. Only in situations of necessity where a *mujtahid* is difficult to find was an imitator (*muqallid*) allowed to be appointed as judge. Whoever fulfils the necessary qualifications, whether a man or a woman, may be appointed to judicial office. This last point has, however, evoked differential responses from the *madhāhib.* The majority have held, as noted in the previous chapter, that women are not qualified to be judges, a ruling based on a rather vague analogy with the office of the Imām. Imām Abū Ḥanīfah has held that women are qualified to hold judicial office in all disputes except in the prescribed offences (*ḥudūd*), and in cases involving the implementation of just retaliation (*qiṣāṣ*). Ibn Jarīr al-Ṭabarī has held on the other hand, and rightly so, that women are qualified to be judges in all disputes. Al-Ṭabarī held that the most important qualification a person must possess to be a judge is erudition in the *Sharīᶜah*, and a difference of gender is not relevant to this.

Al-Ṭabarī considered the analogy between the judge and the Imām to be invalid as it was an analogy with a discrepancy (*qiyās maᶜ al-fāriq*). This is because the Imām is in theory the leader in *jihād,* which is why only a man is qualified to become Imām. But since the judge does not have to lead the army in war, a woman is equally qualified for appointment to judicial office.

II. The Qur'ānic Vision of Justice

Justice is a supreme virtue and it is, in all its various manifestations, one of the overriding objectives of Islam to the extent that it stands next in order of priority to belief in the Oneness of God (*tawḥīd*) and the truth of the Prophethood (*risālah*) of Muḥammad ﷺ. One of the leading Companions, ᶜAbd Allāh ibn Masᶜūd, is reported to have said: 'To sit as a judge [in a dispute] between two people is of greater merit to me than seventy years of worship.'[9] 'To render justice', al-Sarakhsī wrote, 'ranks as the most noble of acts of devotion next to belief in God; it is the greatest of all the duties entrusted to the prophets [...] and it is the strongest justification for the vicegerency of man [*khilāfah*] on the earth.'[10] The Prophet ﷺ declared in a *ḥadīth* that 'there are seven categories of people whom God will shelter under His shadows on the Day when there will be no shadow except His. [One is] the just leader [*imām ʿādil*].'[11]

سبعة يظلّهم اللّه في ظله يوم لا ظلّ إلا ظلّه ، ا لإمام العادل

God spoke through His Messenger in a *ḥadīth qudsī* in these terms: 'O my servants! I have forbidden injustice for Myself and forbade it also for you. So avoid being unjust to one another.'[12]

يا عبادي، إني حرّمت الظلم على نفسي وجعلته بينكم محرماً
فلاتظالموا

Elsewhere the Qur'ān declares that 'God Commands justice [*al-ʿadl*] and fair dealing [*al-iḥsān*]' (al-Naḥl, 16:90)

إن اللّه يأمر بالعدل والإحسان.

and 'O you who believe, be upright for God, [and] bearers of witness with justice' (al-Mā'idah, 5:8).

يا أيها الذين آمنوا كونوا قوامين للّه شهداء بالقسط.

It is thus concluded that justice is an obligation in Islam and indulgence in injustice is therefore *ḥarām*.[13]

The centrality of justice to the value structure of Islam is vividly portrayed in the following Qur'ānic *āyah*:

> We sent Our Messengers with clear signs and sent down with them the Book and the Measure in order to establish justice among the people. (al-Ḥadīd, 57:25)

لقد أرسلنا رسلنا بالبيّنات وأنزلنا معهم الكتاب والميزان ليقوم الناس بالقسط.

The phrase 'Our Messengers' confirms that justice has been the goal of all revealed the scriptures known to mankind. This text also indicates that justice must be administered in accordance with the revealed law and measured by its standards. Ibn Qayyim al-Jawziyyah grasped the essence of this Qur'ānic declaration when he observed that 'justice is the supreme goal and objective of Islam. God has sent scriptures and messengers in order to establish justice among people [...] Any path that leads to justice is an integral part of the religion and can never be against it'.[14] Ibn Qayyim has thus confirmed that even if nothing can be found in the *Sharīʿah* to indicate the direction of justice, it should still be attempted, and the results of such an effort will always be in harmony with Islam. The path to justice is for the most part shown and regulated by revealed law, but since justice is an overriding objective, the quest towards it is not just confined to justice under the rule of law, but should be pursued at all levels, within or outside existing law. To quote Ibn Qayyim again: 'The Lawgiver has not confined the ways and means of attaining justice, or any of its signs and indications, to the exclusion of other evidence [...] He declared justice as His overriding objective and also explained some of the means of attaining it, but then commanded that it should be the basis, generally, of all adjudication and government.'[15]

This also implies that no specific approaches in the realms of either philosophy, social policy or law, are recommend to the exclusion of others. Islam's approach to justice must remain therefore comprehensive and all-embracing, and any path that leads to justice is deemed to be in harmony with the *Sharīʿah*. The *āyah* under discussion is also explicit on the point that justice must be administered through correct guidelines and standards that are set by divine revelation. The Qur'ān clearly envisages justice being administered under the rule of law.

Al-Qaraḍāwī's understanding of the injunctions of the Qur'ān and the *Sunnah* on justice also lead him to the conclusion that they do not lay down any specific framework for how they should be implemented. The precise manner of enforcing the commands and prohibitions of the *Sharīʿah* on justice is therefore open to interpretation and *ijtihād*. From its simple origins during the times of the Prophet ﷺ and the Rightly-Guided Caliphs, the judicial branch of the Islamic state underwent development in subsequent periods, when new jurisdictions, such as that of the *maẓālim*, were added and refined over time. God Most High has demanded justice but has not specified the route that leads to it, or the means by which it can be obtained, nor has He declared invalid any particular means or methods that can lead to justice. All means, procedures and methods that facilitate, refine and advance the cause of justice, and do not violate the *Sharīᶜah* are therefore valid.[16]

This may also be said, al-Qaraḍāwī adds, of *ḥisbah*, that is, enjoining good and forbidding evil, which started in a simple form in the early days of Islam but acquired various features and ramifications over time. Some present-day government ministries and departments, such as those of health, social affairs, municipalities, transport and police, are now discharging duties that were at one time or another entrusted to the *muḥtasib.* These may all be said to be the proper manifestations of that principle.[17]

The Qur'ānic standards of justice transcend considerations of race, religion, colour and creed as Muslims are enjoined to do justice to their friends and foes alike, and to be just at all levels 'even if it is against yourselves, your parents and your relatives, or whether it is against the rich or the poor' (al-Nisā', 4:135).

كونوا قوّامين بالقسط شهداء للّه ولو على أنفسكم أو الوالدين
والأقربين، إن يكن غنيا أو فقيرا.

According to another Qur'ānic address, 'Let not the hatred of a people swerve you away from justice. Be just, for this is closest to righteousness.' (al-Mā'idah, 5:8)

ولا يجرمنّكم شنآن قوم على ألا تعدلوا، اعدلوا هو أقرب للتقوى.

With regard to relations with non-Muslims, the Qur'ān further provides: 'God forbids you not from doing good and being just to those who have neither fought you over your faith nor evicted you from your homes' (al-Mumtaḥinah, 60:8).

لا ينهاكم اللّه عن الذين لم يقاتلوكم في الدين و لم يخرجوكم
من دياركم أن تبروهم و تقسطوا إليهم.

Qur'ān commentators have concluded that these rulings apply to all nations and the followers of all faiths, indeed to the whole of mankind. Justice is a Qur'ānic obligation, which is why the Prophet ﷺ was told: 'If you judge, judge between them with justice' (al-Mā'idah, 5:42)

و إن حكمت فاحكم بينهم بالقسط.

and 'We have revealed to you the Book with the truth, that you may judge between people by what God has taught you' (al-Nisā', 4:105).

إنا أنزلنا إليك الكتاب بالحق لتحكم بين الناس بما أراك اللّه.

The Imām is required to appoint judges, as the Qur'ān enjoins: 'O you who believe, be maintainers of justice' (al-Nisā', 4:135).

يا أيها الذين أمنوا كونوا قوّامين بالقسط.

Furthermore, the Prophet ﷺ was asked to declare: 'Say: I believe in the Book which God has sent down, and I am commanded to judge justly between you' (al-Shūrā, 42: 15).

قل آمنت بما أنزل اللّه من كتاب وأمرت لأعدل بينكم.

This *āyah* also indicates the Qur'ān's image of itself: the Book that God sent down is devoted mainly to laying down the principles of the faith and justice. Sayyid Quṭb has drawn, from his reading of the Qur'ān, the conclusion that justice is an inherent right of all human beings under the *Sharīᶜāh*.[18] The same conclusion is drawn by Muḥammad Afzal Zullah, the Chief Justice of Pakistan as he then was, when he reflected on the value of justice in relation to the belief in the oneness of God (*tawḥīd*) and the prophethood (*risālah*) of Muḥammad ﷺ. In his view, given the high profile of ᶜ*adl* in the Qur'ān, it comes in order of priority next only to *tawḥīd*, and therefore 'justice is a fundamental right of everyone without any discrimination whatsoever'.[19]

The objectivity of Islamic justice is also affirmed by the fact that the basic blueprint and agenda for justice is enshrined in the divine text of the Qur'ān. Since no human agency has the authority to abrogate or change the Qur'ān, the basic standards of justice in Islam stand above the relativity of time and place.[20] This timeless commitment to justice is accentuated in a text when God Most High declares justice as the seal of His illustrious speech: 'The word of thy Lord finds fulfilment in truth and justice; none can change His words' (al-Anᶜām, 6:115).

و تمت كلمة ربك صدقا وعدلا، لامبدّل لكلماته.

The Qur'ānic conception of justice, according to Abū Zahrah, is that of absolute justice (*al-ᶜadālah al-muṭlaqah*), as it is all-embracing, non-partisan and universal. Abū Zahrah hastens to add, however, that the other legal systems of the world, all have their distinctive approaches to justice, but most of these are relative and bear the influence of such factors as the state of material progress, historical reality and philosophical outlook.[21] Abū Zahrah has in this connection recounted an incident in which someone asked the noble Prophet ﷺ if he could summarise Islam in a few words for him. The Prophet ﷺ, in response, recited this Qur'ānic passage: 'God commands justice, beneficence [*iḥsān*] and giving [of your wealth] to kith and kin, and He forbids indecency, evil and lawlessness' (al-Naḥl, 16:90).[22]

إن اللّه يأمربالعدل والإحسان وإيتاء ذيالقربى وينهى عن
الفحشاء والمنكر والبغى.

This passage refers to three virtues and three vices. The leading virtues noted here are all social since they encourage justice, beneficence and generosity to others.

The juxtaposition of *iḥsān* (being good to others) with *ᶜadl* tends to open up the scope of justice to considerations of equity and fairness. Whereas justice is primarily regulated by law, the scope of *iḥsān* is not restrained by conformity to formal rules.[23] *Iḥsān* can consist of forgiveness and returning good for evil, doing a good turn or being generous to those who may have neither claimed nor demanded justice. The reference to financial help in the text evidently accentuates the material dimensions of both

ʿ*adl* and *iḥsān*. To render justice is a trust (*amānah*) that God Almighty has conferred on man and, like all other trusts, its due fulfilment must be guided by a sense of responsibility beyond conformity to specific rules. The Qur'ān thus reads in an address to the believers, 'God commands you to render trusts to whom that they are due, and when you judge between people, judge with justice' (al-Nisā', 4: 58).

إن اللّه يأمركم أن تؤدّوا الأمانات إلى أهلها واذا حكمتم بين
الناس أن تحكموا بالعدل.

The fact that the reference to *amānāt* in this passage is immediately followed by a reference to justice implies that it is one of the most important of all *amānāt*.[24] The occurrence of *amānāt* in the plural also indicates that *amānāt* is a wider concept that includes among others government, giving testimony, taking care of orphans or of *waqf* property, and so on.[25] But, as indicated by the occasion of its revelation (*sha'n al-nuzūl*), the text under discussion was an address primarily to those in charge of the community affairs, the *ulū al-amr*, who are the main audience of Qur'ānic verses enjoining the *amānah* of establishing a just government.[26]

Justice in the Qur'ān is intertwined with the parallel concept of *khilāfah*, that is, the right to rule, or the vicegerency of man on earth. The relationship between these two is that justice is an essential component of *khilāfah* (Ṣād, 38:26). Since both justice and *khilāfah* partake of *amānah*, it follows that the Qur'ānic vision of justice extends to politics. This may be noted as a point of difference between Islamic and Western conceptions of justice. Western scholarship has seen justice as consisting of two main varieties: retributive and distributive justice. By contrast, Muslim jurists have related Qur'ānic justice to three major themes, which extend, in addition to the two familiar divisions, to selection and appointment of government officials. This must be in accordance with individual capabilities: the most qualified (*al-aṣlaḥ*) candidate among those available has to be selected.[27] This dimension of justice has been elaborated in a large number of *ḥadīth* and also in the precedent of the Rightly-Guided Caliphs.

The Qur'ānic conception of justice also extends to personal virtue and the standards of moral excellence that the believer is advised to attain as an integral part of God-consciousness and *taqwā*:

'Be just, for it is closest to *taqwā*' (al-Mā'idah, 5:8). The Prophet ﷺ himself instructed the believers to 'fear God and be just to your children'.[28] The Qur'ān also tells the believers that 'when you speak, speak with justice, even if it is against someone close to you'. (al-Anᶜām, 6:152)

واذا قلتم فاعدلوا ولو كان ذا قربى.

Having established the objectivity of its conception of justice, the Qur'ān also refers to its particular instances and contexts. One such instance is the requirement of justice in the treatment of orphans, which is the subject of several *āyāt* in the Qur'ān:

> And approach not the property of the orphan except in the fairest way until he attains the age of full strength, and give measurement and weight with justice. (al-Anᶜām, 6:152; see also al-Fajr, 89:17; al-Ḍuḥā, 93:9; al-Māᶜūn, 107:2)

ولا تقربوا مال اليتيم إلا بالتى هي أحسن حتى يبلغ أشده، وأوفوا الكيل والميزان بالقسط.

The reference to fair dealing in measurements and weights in the above text is also the subject of several other passages in the Qur'ān, where justice in market transactions is emphasised and it signifies the integrity of the person or persons involved in them. There is even a chapter in the Qur'ān (Sūra 83) bearing the title *al-Muṭaffifīn* (The Detractors in Giving Weights), where the text threatens with the wrath of God fraudulent dealers, 'those who demand full measure for themselves but give less than due measure when they give to others' (al-Muṭaffifīn, 81:2-3; see also al-Isrā', 17:35; al-Aᶜrāf, 7:85).

References to justice also occur in the context of polygamy, where the Qur'ān demands the equitable treatment of co-wives. The verse of polygamy actually begins with a reference to orphaned girls who, it is feared, could be exposed to depravation and injustice: when they reach marriageable age they may be taken in marriage, even polygamously (i.e. when there is an inequality in the numbers of men and women, as was the case after the battle of ᶜUḥud, when this *āyah* was revealed), but then the text instructs that 'if you fear that you cannot be just, then marry only one' (al-Nisā', 4:3).

وإن خفتم ألا تعدلوا فواحدة.

In the event where a conflict breaks out between the different sections of the Muslim community, the Qur'ān directs that efforts should be made towards reaching a just settlement:

> If two parties among the believers fall into conflict, try to make peace between them. But if one of them transgresses beyond bounds against the other, then fight the transgressing party until it complies with the commands of God. When it so complies, then make peace between them with justice. For God loves those who are just. (al-Ḥujurāt, 49:9)

وإن طائفتان من المؤمنين اقتتلوا فأصلحوا بينهما، فإن بغت إحداهماعلى الأخرى فقاتلوا التى تبغى حتى تفيء إلى أمر اللّه، فإن فاء ت فأصلحوا بينهما بالعدل وأقسطوا إن اللّه يحب المقسطين.

Military conquest is therefore not to be used as a means of crushing the vanquished party. All are entitled to justice, not just as a matter of conformity to rules, but also for the sake of gaining the pleasure of God. This also implies that devotion to a cause, country or people is not a valid ground for partisanship and compromise on justice. The nationalist sentiment that is sometimes used to justify loyalty at the expense of justice—such as when it is said 'my country, right or wrong'—will find little support in the Qur'ānic vision of justice. Loyalty to one's country and community is recommended, and so is self-exertion and sacrifice for a good cause, but not if these mean compromising on impartial justice.

III. The Islamic Judiciary

In Islamic legal theory the judge represents the authority of the Imām, and exercises power in the capacity of his *wakīl* (representative). The contract of *wakālah* (representation) is in principle open to the stipulation of the principal (*muwakkil*), that is the Imām, in such ways as he deems to be in the best interests of the community. But even when the Imām appoints a judge, he does not forfeit his right to act as a judge himself. For the administration of justice is one of the basic obligations of an Imām. When the Imām acts as a judge, however, he is in theory subject to precisely the same rules as are applicable to the *qāḍī* in regard to stating the grounds of his decision, and the admissibility of witnesses. The majority of jurists have held that in his capacity as *muwakkil*, the Imām has the right to remove the *qāḍī* from office. The Shāfiʿīs and some Ḥanbalīs have added that such a removal must be on grounds of public interest (*maṣlaḥah*). For the Imām has appointed the judge in pursuit of public interest, and so long as the judge discharges his duties with competence, the Imām is not entitled to remove him.[29]

Scholars are divided in their response to the question of whether Islamic law validates an independent status for the judiciary. The precedent of the second Caliph ʿUmar and other Rightly-Guided Caliphs indicates, as Maḥmaṣṣānī observed, that they upheld and respected the independence of judicial office.[30] There are reports, for example, that the Caliphs ʿUmar and ʿAlī had occasion to appear before the *qāḍī* as parties to litigation, and both exhibited sensitivity and concern about being given preferential treatment in court. This precedent sustains the conclusion, as one observer points out, that the judge can accept a suit against the head of state himself and try him in an open court; and 'this feature of the Islamic judiciary is an index of its independent status'.[31] There are also reports, as Ṭamawī has noted, that under the Umayyads (c. 661 AH/750 AD), judges enjoyed considerable freedom and were unhindered in the exercise of independent *ijtihād*.[32] Whereas the caliphal office had hitherto combined judicial functions, the founder of the Umayyad dynasty, Muʿāwiyah, was the first to relinquish all his judicial functions to appointed judges.[33] Another observer has qualified this conclusion by saying that during the era of Umayyads, 'the judiciary was fully independent from the executive [...] but this independence was confined to civil cases and private wrongs'.[34]

Muḥammad Salām Madkūr and ʿAbd al-Munʿim Aḥmad have both observed that there is no specific mandate in the *Sharīʿah* either for a separation of powers or for a concentration of powers. There was no pressing need for a mandate on this in earlier times, and the matter has consequently remained open. This explains the disagreement among modern jurists on whether or not Islam envisages a separation of powers and assigns an independent status for the judiciary.

Yet there is nothing in the *Sharīᶜah* against adopting a regime of the separation of powers if this is deemed to be more suitable for serving the ideals of justice under contemporary conditions.[35] ᶜAbd al-Munᶜim Aḥmad has added to this analysis that in practice, a line of separation between the judiciary, the legislative and executive departments of the Islamic state can be distinguished from the time of the Abbasids, but the early jurists did not articulate the form or substance of this separation. The judiciary remained under the executive, and the Caliph himself often exercised judicial powers. The second Caliph, ᶜUmar ibn al-Khaṭṭāb, was the first to delegate his judicial functions to the judges he appointed.[36]

The emergence and gradual crystallization of the four schools of law during the early Abbasid period, around the third century AH/tenth century AD, imposed new restrictions on the independence of judges. The establishment of these schools implied that the law had already been expounded and elaborated to an advanced level. And yet the plurality of legal schools and diversity of their doctrines had given rise to confusion and disparity in court decisions, which is why it became the policy of Islamic governments to adopt one or the other of these schools as their official *madhhab*. Thus the judges in Iraq were bound to follow the Ḥanafī school, whereas Egypt followed the Shāfiᶜī school, and the Mālikī school found followers in the Maghreb. Consequently, restrictions were brought to bear on the exercise of independent *ijtihād*. From then onward, judges were expected to follow the views of the established schools. There were also instances of executive interference in the judiciary, which were on the whole accountable for the fact that many a pious Imām like Abū Ḥanīfah, his disciple Ẓufār, and Aḥmad ibn Ḥanbal, all refused to serve as judges under the Abbasids.[37] The new restrictions that confined the scope of *ijtihād* to a particular school was clearly a departure from the precedent of the early Caliphs and an unwelcome imposition on the freedom of the judges. Al-Māwardī (d. 450 AH/c.1070 AD), himself a *qāḍī*, found this unacceptable when he expounded the doctrine, and wrote that the judge must exercise his own *ijtihād*, and in doing so he is not bound to adhere to the rulings of the school to which he subscribes: if he is a follower of the Shāfiᶜī school, he is not bound by the rulings of this school unless his own *ijtihād* leads him to it; should the *ijtihād* he arrives at favour the opinion of Abū Ḥanīfah, he should then act upon it accordingly.[38] This concern for the independence of *ijtihād* led the Ḥanbalī jurist, Ibn Qudāmah, to the following conclusion:

> It is not permissible [*lā yajūz*] to appoint a *qāḍī* on condition that he adjudicates according to a particular school. This is the ruling of the Shāfiʿī school and I know not of any disagreement on its validity. For God Most High has enacted righteousness as the criterion of justice, and righteousness cannot be confined to one particular school. Hence if the *qāḍī* is appointed with such a condition, the condition is null and void.[39]

The Abbasid Caliph Hārūn al-Rashīd was the first to establish a centralised judiciary and appoint the *mujtahid* Abū Yūsuf (d. 798 AD) as chief justice (*qāḍī al-quḍāt*). Hārūn al-Rashīd is also reported to have relinquished supervision of the judiciary to Abū Yūsuf, and made no judicial appointments without his recommendation.[40] The *qāḍī al-quḍāt* exercised judicial authority (*wilāyat al-qaḍā'*) in the capacity of a *ḥākim* (ruler), not a *mu'aẓẓaf* (task officer). The difference between the two is that the former is vested with general authority whereas the latter has no general powers. Furthermore, in his capacity as head of the judiciary, the *qāḍī al-quḍāt* was not a deputy (*muʿāwin*) to the Caliph in judicial affairs, but an officer of state who was in charge of its judicial branch and did not need to consult the Caliph in respect of his professional decisions.[41]

In theory, the chief justice and other judges acquire their authority from the head of state by way of delegation (*wilāyah* or *tawliyah*). *Wilāyah* implies that the person to whom authority is delegated acquires total responsibility and applies his own discretion in the exercise of that authority. This is partly why it is a condition of appointment to judicial office that candidates are learned in the law and capable of discharging their duties without asking the Imām for detailed instructions.[42] There are many reports of incidents that show latitude and independence of character on the part of prominent judges, who were obviously anxious for the independence of justice.[43] A growing tendency for judges to acquire general authority in criminal affairs, which were hitherto either entrusted to the police or exercised by local governors can also be discerned. One also notes, as Fatḥī ʿUthmān elaborates, a gradual separation of powers taking place between the judicial and other organs of state.[44]

Notwithstanding some of these positive developments, historical practice on the independence of the judiciary is on the whole inconsistent and uninspiring in that, for the most part, Abbasid rulers impinged on the freedom of the judges. The executive did not always enforce judicial decrees and often exercised their own discretionary powers.[45] In neither of the two early periods (Umayyad and Abbasid) were judges immune from the vagaries of politics and interference in their affairs.[46]

A judge who is anxious about the adverse repercussions of his decision can hardly be effective in translating the ideals of legal theory into his quotidian decisions. Similarly, an effective mechanism for judicial review cannot be expected to function in an environment where rulers and governors have powers not only in regard to the appointment and dismissal of judges but are at liberty also to exercise judicial powers themselves. Practical irregularity eventually tainted the vision of justice in society, and its leaders, with the result that the theory itself was affected by the exigencies of practice. Legal theory has consequently followed a course that falls short of giving full expression to the Qur'ānic ideals of impartial justice. It is not surprising therefore to find that modern constitutional law in those present-day Islamic countries that proclaim the judiciary to be an independent organ of the state is in substantial harmony with the Qur'ān.

A look at the Qur'ānic text that envisages the possibility of disputes arising between the ruler and ruled will confirm the necessity of an independent judiciary in an Islamic polity. The text in question enjoins the believers to 'obey God and obey the Messenger and those who are in charge of affairs among you. Should you dispute over a matter, then refer it to God and the Messenger (al-Nisā', 4:59)'.

أطيعوا اللّه و أطعيوا الرّسول وأولى الأمر منكم، فإن تنازعتم في
شيء فردّوه الى اللّه والرسول.

This text is clear on the point that both the ruler and ruled are subject to the ordinances of the *Sharīᶜah*. It is also implied in this text that people are entitled to disagree with their leaders. In the event of a disagreement, the final arbiter between them, as the text provides, is the law of God and the ruling of His Messenger. To facilitate proper implementation of this text there must be, as Asad and Khālidī have both observed, an independent judiciary with full powers to adjudicate between the citizen and state.[47] This may take, as Khālidī further observes, the form of the historical *maẓālim*, with powers to adjudicate cases involving state officials, or it may take a different form. In either case, 'it is essential that the head of state should have no powers to dismiss or replace the leading judges of the land'.[48]

Furthermore, Islamic constitutional theory is explicit that the community may depose the head of state in the event of manifest aberration or a loss of mental and physical capacity. The judiciary may thus be called upon to discharge the very sensitive task of impeaching the head of state and declaring him disqualified. This will be almost impossible unless the judiciary is fully independent and judges enjoy total security of office.

A court of general jurisdiction, known as *diwān al-maẓālim*, was established under the Abbasids and was vested with powers to receive and adjudicate complaints against government officials. It was also authorised to review the decisions of the *Sharīᶜah* courts upon appeal by aggrieved parties. It was a powerful tribunal that combined, in al-Māwardī's phrase, 'the justice of the *qāḍī* with the power of the sovereign'. As a general court of jurisdiction, its powers were not amenable to specialisation (*takhṣīṣ*). Since the *maẓālim* looked into complaints against all departments of government and adjudicated all disputes, its jurisdiction was not capable of dismemberment, except in one respect, that is, territorial. The basic purpose of the creation of this powerful tribunal was to ensure government under the rule of law, so that abuse of power by influential persons and state dignitaries did not take place and they could not escape the law merely due to their capacity for resisting it. The *maẓālim* had powers to adjudicate disputes between the citizen and state, and also acted as a high court of appeal. The very establishment of *maẓālim* was indicative of the need then felt that the judiciary must enjoy full powers and be able to act independently to ensure government under the rule of law.[49]

IV. Appellate Review: Its Validity and Scope

Contrary to the picture many commentators have drawn in which Islamic law does not recognise appellate review and jurisdiction, my own enquiry into this subject shows conclusively that it does. This is not a conclusion based merely on interpretational grounds but is supported by a consistent line of juristic doctrine among the *fuqahā'*. The scope of this study does not permit a detailed enquiry into the subject. However, I propose to give the gist of my research here and refer the reader for further detail to the article on this I presented to an international conference in London in 1991.[50]

The Qur'ān and the *Sunnah* admit, in principle, the possibility of errors in judicial decisions, even when they are made by the recipients of divine revelation. The Qur'ān, for example, refers to an incident in which the prophet David adjudicated a dispute that was brought to him regarding the ownership of a flock of sheep. The relevant Qur'ānic passage (Ṣād, 38: 20-26) indicates that David rushed to pass a judgement on the basis of a mere claim without giving the defendant an adequate opportunity to present his case. This manner of adjudication, as the text runs, was erroneous and therefore provoked God's admonition, which was communicated to David, as the Qur'ān declares, in the following terms: 'O David, We have made you a vicegerent on earth, so judge among people with truth and follow not the [vagaries] of desire' (Ṣād, 38: 26).

ياداوود إنا جعلناك خليفة في الأرض، فاحكم بين الناس بالحق
ولا تتبع الهوى.

The Qur'ān likewise speaks of the differing understanding and judgement of the same dispute by two prophets-cum-judges, namely David and Solomon. It is thus stated that each rendered a decision concerning a dispute about the destruction of agricultural crops belonging to one of the disputants by the straying sheep of the other. The Qur'ānic text (al-Anbiyā', 21:78-79) then continues to praise both for their wisdom and knowledge but adds the phrase that 'We, gave Solomon the right understanding of the issue.'

ففهمناها سليمان وكلا آتينا حكما وعلما.

The Prophet Muḥammad ﷺ is widely known to have made the following statement, in which he clearly admits the possibility of error occurring in his own adjudication:

> I am but a human being. When you bring a dispute to me, some of you may be more eloquent in stating their cases than others. I may consequently adjudicate on the basis of what I hear. If I adjudicate in favour of someone something that belongs to his brother, let him not take it, for this would be like taking a piece of fire.[51]

إنما أنا بشر، وأنكم تختصمون إليّ، فلعل بعضكم أن يكون ألحن بحجته من بعض فأقضي نحو ما أسمع، فمن قضيت له بحق أخيه شيئا فلا يأخذه فإنما أقطع له قطعة من النار.

No one is therefore immune from error, and error in judicial decisions is an ever-present possibility. A gross error of judgement that leads to a miscarriage of justice must therefore be rectified.

When a judge makes an erroneous decision despite his attempt to render a correct one through self-exertion and *ijtihād,* the decision so arrived at is deemed to be valid and enforceable. An error in *ijtihād* in other words affects neither the credibility of the judge nor his integrity; his good intention and effort are still commendable and worthy of reward, as in the following *ḥadīth*:

> When a judge exerts himself and gives a right decision, he will have a double reward, but if he errs in his judgement after exerting himself he will still merit one reward.[52]

الحاكم اذا اجتهد فأصاب فله أجران، و إن اجتهد فأخطأ فله اجر.

On the authority of this *ḥadīth* and other supportive evidence, the *ᶜulamā'* have reached the conclusion that judicial decisions that are based on sound *ijtihād* are not reviewable merely on grounds that another judge might take a different view of the same issue. The issuing judge himself is, however, at liberty to correct his own error and amend his initial *ijtihād*. In the event, though, where the error consists of a departure from the clear principles of the *Sharīᶜah*, the decision is open to review not just by the issuing judge, but also by the head of state and other judges who represent his authority.[53] But if the error that originates in the personal reasoning of the judge amounts to a gross error of judgment of a kind that could not be the result of sound *ijtihād* and leads to a manifest miscarriage of justice, then the decision is reviewable and may be reversed on the analysis that it represents a departure from the justice ordained by God and His *Sharīᶜah*. It is then necessary to declare the erroneous decision invalid through a review procedure, for it neither collapses nor becomes automatically invalid unless it is set aside by another judge.[54]

The right of appeal also emerges from the Qur'ānic text (al-Nisā', 4:59) in which it is laid down that when people dispute the decision of those who are in charge of affairs, the matter should be referred to God and to the Messenger ﷺ. Now if a party challenges the court decision and pleads that the law has not been properly applied, there ought to be a court of appeal to review the case and determine the validity of such an appeal.[55]

One of the most widely quoted authorities in support of judicial review in Islamic law is a letter that the second Caliph, ᶜUmar ibn al-Khaṭṭāb, wrote to his judge, Abū Mūsā al-Ashᶜarī. This letter, although open to interpretation in parts, is nevertheless clear on the necessity of correcting an erroneous decision, be it by the judge who is addressed himself or by other judges. In this letter, the Caliph refers to justice as a firm obligation (*farīḍa muḥkamah*) under the *Sharīᶜah*, and asks the judge, al-Ashᶜarī, to:

> Use your own understanding and judgement when disputes are placed before you [...] Let all men be equal in your sight, in your court and in your judgement, so that the strong may not hope to sway you into injustice, nor is the weak led to despair in your justice. The burden of proof lies on the shoulders of the plaintiff and the oath is upon the denying party. Compromise is permissible among litigants unless it renders into *ḥalāl* [lawful] what is forbidden [*ḥarām*] or forbids what is lawful. And let not a judgement that you rendered yesterday, and then upon reflection and reconsideration you find that it was incorrect, deter you from returning to the truth. For truth is timeless and returning to truth is better than continuing in falsehood. [56]

Several conclusions have been drawn from this letter and they are not always in agreement. Some of the obvious conclusions drawn are that the head of state is entitled to issue instruction to the judges; and that there needs to be no conflict between the independence of the judiciary and the right of the head of state (or those who represent him, such as a superior judge) to advise, consult and instruct judges as and when necessary. Indeed the Caliph is under a duty to supervise the affairs of the judiciary and take all measures that are conducive to the efficient administration of justice in the courts.[57]

This letter is self-evident on the point that the issuing judge may review his own decision and correct any error he may detect in it at any stage prior to enforcement. There is, however, disagreement on the issue of whether the contents of this letter also accommodate judicial review by another judge. The Ḥanafī jurist al-Sarakhsī has reached the conclusion that either the issuing judge or another judge may review the initial judgement. This letter, according to al-Sarakhsī, indicates that when an error becomes apparent to the *qāḍī*, it is for him to reverse his own decision, and he should not allow loss of face to deter him from doing so. Al-Sarakhsī continues:

> When the *qāḍī*'s decision is brought before another *qāḍī*, following the former's death or departure from office, and the latter disagrees with it, if it is a matter on which the jurists are in disagreement, then according to *ijmāᶜ*, the decision is not reviewable in matters that are open to *ijtihād*. If the second judge reverses the decision, he will have acted contrary to *ijmāᶜ*. But if the initial decision is in clear violation of the text and *ijmāᶜ*, then it is reversible.[58]

Al-Sarakhsī thus clearly visualises that a judicial decision may be reviewed by either the issuing judge himself or by another judge.

There is also a difference of opinion on whether the Caliph ᶜUmar's letter validates a review of the initial decision only in that case or in other similar cases also subsequently encountered. According to one interpretation the initial decision remains enforceable and may be neither reviewed nor reversed. The judge may, however, subsequently review his earlier *ijtihād* in a similar case. This is considered the preferable of the two views on the analysis that *ijtihād* can be erroneous, but the court decision that is based on it remains enforceable. This is the conclusion that Ibn Qayyim al-Jawziyyah has drawn, as he paraphrases the relevant part of the letter as follows:

> When you wish to carry out fresh *ijtihād* in a subsequent case, let not your initial *ijtihād* deter you from doing so. For *ijtihād* is liable to change and the first *ijtihād* is no impediment to a variant *ijtihād* in a similar case, if you are convinced of its validity and truth. For truth commands priority at all times.[59]

Notwithstanding such differences of interpretation, it should be clearly stated that judges have the authority under Islamic law to review their own decisions, whether such decisions are flawed by personal erroneous reasoning, or by a departure from the clear injunctions of the *Sharīʿah*. The jurists of the various schools have spoken at length on the grounds of judicial review and the principles that regulate this subject. These may be summarised as follows:

(a) When the court decision is based on a cause that is in reality non-existent; for example when a decision is based on perjury that has specified a ground, which is, however, not true.[60]

(b) When a serious fault comes to light in the evidential basis of the decision. It becomes known, for example, that the witnesses were unreliable and failed to fulfil the requirements of admissibility. The reason for this is that the *Sharīʿah* does not permit judicial decisions to be based on questionable grounds.[61]

(c) When the evidence on which the decision is based is contrary to obvious facts.[62]

(d) When new evidence comes to light after adjudication. Ibn Rushd al-Qurṭubī raises the question of whether it is permissible for a *qāḍī* to admit evidence after the issue of a judgement. Al-Qurṭubī adds that the *ʿulamā'* are in disagreement, but the best view of the Mālikī school is that such evidence is permissible in matters pertaining to the Rights of God, or public rights, such as crimes and penalties, but not admissible in regard to the Rights of Man, that is private litigation and civil claims.[63] It is one of the recognised grounds of appeal if the defendant proffers evidence that was unknown to him prior to adjudication.[64]

(e) When a decree adversely affects the right of someone who is not a party to the dispute.[65]

(f) When a decree is beyond the specified jurisdiction of the court.[66]

(g) When there is an irregularity in procedure, such as when a court decision is based on a mere claim, and is issued prior to granting the defendant an opportunity to state his case. If this is deliberate, the decision must be reversed, otherwise a review is granted so as to rectify the irregularity.[67]

The judge must specify the grounds of his decision and the authority on which it is founded. A judicial decision that fails to indicate these is reviewable according to the Ḥanafīs. The Shāfiʿīs are basically in agreement with the Ḥanafīs on this point.[68] The Shāfiʿī jurist Ibn Abī al-Dām al-Ḥamawī confirmed that the cause of the decision (*sabab al-ḥukm*) must be indicated, but if the decision is based on the confession of the defendant and the *qāḍī* merely states that the necessary proof has been supplied to his satisfaction, this is sufficient. If the evidence, in other words, is self-explanatory, then a specific statement by the *qāḍī* on the grounds of the decision is not required, but such a statement is required when this is not the case.[69]

The *ʿulamāʾ* are in disagreement about whether the *qāḍī* may adjudicate on the basis of his personal knowledge without any further evidence. Only the Ḥanafīs permit this, provided that such knowledge is founded on observed facts during the adjudication and trial itself, when, for example, the *qāḍī* incidentally hears a person speaking to another and confessing something. The Ḥanafīs permit adjudication on the basis of the personal knowledge of the *qāḍī* outside the prescribed offences, known as the *ḥudūd*. The Ḥanafīs have also held that in the event where the *qāḍī* issues a decision based on his personal knowledge, and it later transpires that he had confused the facts, then such a decision is liable to review and may be reversed.[70]

As stated earlier, a judicial decree must originate in the personal judgement and *ijtihād* of the *qāḍī* himself. When this is not the case and the *qāḍī* issues a decision that disagrees with his own judgement, his decision is reviewable. Examples of this are when the judge conforms to the wishes of another person of influence, or when he adopts the *ijtihād* of another person contrary to his own beliefs. The judge must always act upon his own conviction. This rule is, however, primarily addressed to the *qāḍī* who is also a *mujtahid*. But if the judge happens to be an imitator (*muqallid*) who follows the rulings of the school to which he belongs, then his decision is reviewable only if it disagrees with the dominant ruling of that particular *madhhab* (legal school).[71]

The jurists are in agreement that a judicial decision that is manifestly oppressive, whether deliberately or otherwise, is basically null and void, and therefore liable to reversal, initially by the issuing judge himself, who must instruct the parties to seek a review, or failing this, the Imām or his representatives are duty-bound to reverse it. In the event where an oppressive decision is implemented, if it is intentional, such as where bribery or personal prejudice are involved, the *qāḍī* must personally bear the consequences. If the decision has inflicted corporeal punishment, the *qāḍī* is liable, according to the majority of jurists, with the exception of the Ḥanafīs, to just retaliation, that is, in cases where retaliation is deemed to apply. Some jurists, including Imām al-Ḥaramayn al-Juwaynī, have upheld the same ruling in the event of a serious neglect of duty, such as the failure of the *qāḍī* to inquire into the admissibility of witnesses. This, in their view, is quasi-intentional (*shibh al-ʿamd*) and entails personal liability. If the decision inflicts a financial loss, in cases of both intentional and quasi-intentional miscarriages of justice, the *qāḍī* bears personal liability. If the *qāḍī* is unable to pay, the state must indemnify the injured party for the losses. The judge must be removed from office and punished for misconduct. He is also disqualified from holding judicial office in the future, and his testimony is inadmissible even after repentance.

In the event where a miscarriage of justice is attributable to someone other than the *qāḍī* himself, such as perjury that has survived after due enquiry and cross-examination, especially where the witnesses of probity (*tazkiyah*) have confirmed the upright character of the witnesses of proof, then in all such cases of perjury, the witnesses of proof in the first place, but also the witnesses of probity, are liable to retaliation or financial compensation as the case may be.[72]

V. Court Procedure

The procedural aspects of the administration of justice are regulated under the general heading of *ādāb al-qaḍā'* and *muḥākamāt*. The role and purpose of court procedure is to facilitate efficiency and ensure that adequate time and attention is given to the material aspects of disputes, and also to establish objectivity and coherence in trial proceedings. Court procedures are designed to ensure a calm and peaceful environment in the courtroom, which is conducive to scrutiny and impartial assessment. They safeguard the courtroom environment from unfair and haphazard practices that compromise the ideals of justice. Court procedures in every legal system reflect the standards of care and refinement in the system, and the necessary safeguards that are taken against distortion and abuse. The simple and direct trial procedures that were adequate for earlier communities are no longer sufficient for more complex societies, where progress in various fields has opened new avenues for more sophisticated levels of abuse. Hence the integrity of a procedural system is tested by its openness to development and growth. Since procedural matters in the Islamic judiciary are open to considerations of public policy (*siyāsah sharʿiyyah*), the process must always remain open to adjustment and reform. Procedural refinement is undoubtedly a cumulative process, yet the vital role of some of the basic rules of fair trial can hardly be overestimated at any given time. In this connection, attention will be drawn to some of the rules of fair trial that were laid down by the Prophet ﷺ and subsequently by his Companions. Note, for instance, the *ḥadīth* in which the Prophet ﷺ instructed ʿAlī ibn Abī Ṭālib, upon sending the latter as judge to the Yemen, as follows:

> When the litigants appear before you, do not decide for one until you hear the other. It is more likely that by doing so the reasons of a judgement will become clear to you.[73]

إذا جلس إليك الخصمان فلا تقض بينهما حتى تسمع من الآخر كما سمعت من الأول، فانك إذا فعلت ذلك تبين لك القضاء.

Although *ex parte* judgement or *qaḍā' ʿala al-ghā'ib* has been felt to be permissible in exceptional situations, many jurists have quoted the above *ḥadīth* as an authority to overrule the validity of *ex parte* judgement. This is definitely *ultra vires* in cases where the defendant is present in the locality or within reach. The Ḥanafīs have proscribed judgement *in absentia* except in situations of necessity, whereas the Mālikī, Shāfiʿī and Ḥanbalī schools permit it when the claimant has decisive evidence and long distance presents a problem for the other party. But this applies only to civil claims, and not to criminal disputes wherein *ex parte* judgement is generally not valid.[74]

Ibn Qudāmah has held that the scope of the above *ḥadīth* has been narrowed down, in so far as the rights of human beings (*ḥuqūq al-ādamiyyīn*) are concerned, by another *ḥadīth*, which seems to have validated adjudication *in absentia*.[75] According to this *ḥadīth*, when Hind, the wife of Abū Sufyān, complained to the Prophet ﷺ that Abu Sufyān was a niggardly man who did not give her enough maintenance for her and her child, the Prophet ﷺ instructed her as follows:

> Take what is sufficient for you and your child in a decent manner [or according to custom].[76]

خذي لك ولوالدك ما يكفيك بالمعروف.

This *ḥadīth* has provoked many comments from the jurists, some of whom have suggested that it applies to a particular situation, namely that of a married couple. Some commentators have, however, by analogy, extended the application of this *ḥadīth* to the case of a debtor who refuses to respond to a court summons. *The ḥadīth* is, in any case, held to be of particular import and does not validate *ex parte* judgement generally.

The requirement that the disputing parties, especially the defendant, must be given equal opportunity to present his or her evidence is also upheld by another *ḥadīth*, which provides that 'the Prophet, peace be on him, decreed that the litigating parties should sit in front of the judge'.[77] There is yet another *ḥadīth*, narrated by Ibn ᶜAbbās, in which the Prophet ﷺ said:

> If people were to be granted what they claim on the basis only of their claims, they would claim the blood and property of others; but the oath is on the shoulder of the defendant.[78]

لو يعطى الناس بدعواهم لادّعى ناس دماء رجال وأموالهم ولكن اليمين على المدعى عليه.

In addition to its basic meaning, this *ḥadīth* is expressive also of the apprehension that false and malicious claims might damage the reputation and good name of upright individuals, which is why the judge is authorised to reject a malicious claim and even punish a false accuser. In the absence of any other evidence to establish his claim, the last request that the claimant can make is to put the defendant on oath either to admit or reject the claim. This is also the subject of an equally important *ḥadīth*-cum-legal maxim, which simply declares that: 'The onus of proof is on the claimant but the defendant takes an oath.'[79]

Al-bayyinah in this *ḥadīth* is a derivative of *bayan*, which means to explain and clarify. Hence the claimant is expected to make his claim clear and specific, and support it by clear evidence. *Bayyinah* includes all forms of evidence, including witnesses, circumstantial evidence, expert opinion and documentation, and in some cases even the personal knowledge of the judge. The last two *ḥadīth* between them also provide basic authority for the principle of original non-liability (*al-barā'a al-aṣliyyah*), also referred to as the presumption of innocence. A mere claim that is not substantiated by clear evidence, in other words, is not enough to overrule the basic position of the *Sharīᶜah* that people are not liable to anything and are presumed innocent unless they are proven to be guilty. Court claims must be clear and specific, so as to be capable of being proven or rebutted by evidence. The subject-matter of a court claim must also be capable of constituting the substance of a valid demand that is put to the defendant. No one, for example, can sue another for failure to give in charity. The jurists have defined the claimant (*muddaʿī*) as one who cannot be compelled to pursue his claim if he wishes to abandon it. The defendant (*muddaʿā ʿalayhī*) is the person who does not have that choice, and may consequently be compelled to respond to a valid claim.[80] A claim (*daʿwā*) is considered basically weak, as it usually seeks to overrule the existing *status quo*, that is, the original non-liability of the defendant, and does not carry any weight unless it is supported by evidence. According to normal procedure, when a defendant denies the truth of the claim made by a plaintiff, the latter is called upon to provide evidence. The judge then ascertains the veracity of that evidence, which in the case of witnesses is through the procedure of *tazkiyah*, that consists of the verification of the character and reliability of the witnesses of proof.[81]

The Islamic judiciary is basically monolithic in that the courts of the *Sharīʿah* are courts of general jurisdiction for all types of disputes. Everyone must be treated equally, and there is in principle no recognition of specialised jurisdictions for members of different professions, such as civil servants, soldiers, industrialists and the like. Nor is there any recognition of special privileges for ministers, parliamentarians, or the head of state.

Historical precedent has favoured a single judge presiding over the court and representing the imām in a particular locality and court. But many Ḥanafī jurists and some jurists from the Ḥanbalī and Shāfiʿī schools have held that there is no objection to a plurality of judges determining cases in consultation with one another. For the judge represents the imām, and the latter may, in his capacity as the principal party, decide to appoint one or more judges, in which case they will sit on a panel and make consultative decisions.[82]

The Qur'ān also validates arbitration (*taḥkīm*) as a method of dispute settlement on the basis of an agreement between the parties (cf. al-Nisā', 4:35). Reconciliation and resolution, even of court cases, by mutual agreement of the disputing parties is generally recommended, so much so that all courts should encourage it prior to litigation.[83]

The administration of justice is a cardinal duty of the state. Thus it is administered free of charge and the state may not charge any fees for providing judicial services. The doors of the court must remain open to the public, and no secrecy is permitted in trial proceedings.

Nor is secrecy permitted in regard to the locality where a court holds its sessions unless this is for special and exceptional reasons. The judge may not, however, divulge what his judgement will be before the court hearing. The disputing parties must also be present at the time the court announces its judgement. Normal procedure also requires that the reasons and causes of court decisions are specified in writing, and that the court delivers a copy of its written judgement to each of the disputing parties.[84]

The court normally may not delay its judgement once the grounds and conditions of judgement have been duly identified and completed.[85] The disputing parties are entitled to represent themselves before the court, or to appoint representatives to act on their behalf. The attorney or counsel in this case acts in the capacity of a *wakīl* who is basically answerable to his or her principal. This right is equally available to the head of state, who may appoint a *wakīl*, usually the public prosecutor, to represent him in the court of justice. The Ḥanafī ʿ*ulamā'* have expressed some reservation about the validity of *wakālah* in *ḥudūd* and *qiṣāṣ* crimes on the analysis that the basic task of the court in such cases is to validate the evidence, and in this matter, there is little room for representation. The generally accepted position has it, however, that representation is valid in all disputes, including the *ḥudūd* and *qiṣāṣ*.[86]

Three types of procedural systems are known in the history of court proceedings relating to criminal trial: the accusatorial, the inquisitorial and a mixed system that combines elements of both. The accusatorial trial system has been in use for longer, and its view of criminal action is that it is a dispute shared between two parties of equal status. Within this system, the judge is precluded from engaging in pre-trial investigation, and mainly plays the role of balancing the evidence and the manner in which it is presented by the disputing parties without influencing the process of its discovery.

In the inquisitorial system, investigation and indictment are carried out by a judicial magistrate. The trial judge, too, plays a role in gathering evidence, and asks questions during the trial; his role is not merely confined to balancing and evaluating the relative weight of the evidence presented to him. The Islamic trial system is inclined towards the inquisitorial systems but also tends to combine elements of both. The judge has a role to play in the admission or rejection of evidence and claims that are presented to the court both before and during the trial. The judge thus questions the disputing parties and witnesses during the conduct of a trial, and generally controls courtroom proceedings. Yet the judge is normally not involved in pre-trial proceedings pertaining to the conduct of investigation and the collection of evidence. The *qāḍī* must also avoid addressing either of litigants in such a way as to support their claim or draw their attention to ideas about how to support it. The judge must also refrain from giving tendentious advice that might suggest things to the witness regarding the factual knowledge behind his or her testimony.[87]

As noted previously, court procedure pertaining to the conduct of investigation, prosecution and trial in the Islamic judiciary is determined by the political authority in accordance with the broad terms of a *Sharīᶜah*-oriented policy (*siyāsah sharᶜiyyah*). The ruler is accordingly authorised to determine rules and procedures that are deemed to be in the best interests of justice, and in harmony with the letter and spirit of the *Sharīᶜah*. These policies do not determine the *Sharīᶜah* itself, but the best ways and means by which it can be administered.[88] As a part of *siyāsah sharᶜiyyah,* the imām may impose jurisdictional limits on the powers of the court in accordance with the principle of *takhṣīṣ al-qaḍā'* (specification of court jurisdiction). These may be territorial, based on types of disputes such as criminal, civil and commercial, or may consist of quantitative limits such as imposing monetary or time limits on the length of custodial sentences that the court can impose, or imposing time limits on the hearing of claims. *Takhṣīṣ al-qaḍā'* authorises the imām to specify the jurisdiction of existing courts, or to create new ones as he deems necessary for the efficient administration of justice.[89] As already indicated, the setting up of appellate tribunals, whether general or specialised, and defining their jurisdictions, fall within the purview of a *Sharīᶜah*-oriented policy.

The doctrine of *siyāsah* equips the head of state with discretionary powers to take all the steps that are deemed necessary to secure benefit (*maṣlaḥah*) for the people, and establish good government.[90] 'There is nothing in Islam', Khallāf has observed, 'against establishing a judiciary consisting of specialised and well-defined spheres of jurisdiction, a judicial order in which the administration of justice is ensured by guarantees in respect of the enforcement of court decisions and the independence of the judiciary, as well as the nature of its relations with the other organs of state.'[91] Matters pertaining to court organisation, are, for the most part, procedural in character, and there is rarely, if ever, a definitive text in the *Sharīᶜah* to restrict the scope of *siyāsah sharᶜiyyah* on procedural matters. Hence, the discretionary powers of the head of state in this area remain, by and large, unrestricted.[92] Furthermore, it has been correctly observed that modern statutory legislation on court procedure and judicial review in present-day Muslim countries is generally in agreement with the *Sharīᶜah* and properly falls within the scope of *siyāsah sharᶜiyyah*.[93]

The judge exercises considerable discretion in the determination of the quantum of *taᶜzīr* punishments, but has no such powers in regard to the *ḥudūd* and *qiṣāṣ* offences. In regard to the latter, the judge exercises some discretionary power, which is usually in favour of the accused in respect mainly of determining the admissibility of evidence against him. Even in *taᶜzīr* punishments, the judge cannot create the offence, but only determines the punishment deemed most suitable under the circumstances.

Unlike the common law system, which subscribes to the doctrine of *stare decisis*, in the Islamic judiciary judges are not bound by the decision and precedent of the higher courts. This is partly a consequence of the independence of the jurist-*mujtahid* and judge, who must be at liberty to follow his own understanding of the *Sharīᶜah* and his convictions on how to administer justice. The legal maxim that '*ijtihād* is not overruled by its equivalent [*al-ijtihād lā yunqaḍ bi-mithlihi*]' means in this context that if two qualified judges who are capable of utilising the source evidence of *Sharīᶜah* in a dispute before them arrive at two different conclusions, provided that both comply with the basic requirements of valid legal reasoning and *ijtihād*, they are both equally valid, and one does not prevail over the other. A binding system of judicial precedent on the other hand requires the judge to follow the decision or precedent set by a superior judge. This is akin to judicial imitation (*taqlīd*) which is deemed to compromise the independence of the *mujtahid*.

VI. Distributive Justice

One of the principal themes that have become the focus of attention in the writings of Western commentators on distributive justice is the identification of the criteria on which distribution should be based. Equality is generally voiced as one of these criteria. Another is individual need, which many have held should be the basis of an individual's entitlement from the public purse. Still others have spoken of individual merit and contributions to the common wealth as better criteria for its valid distribution. There are still others who maintain that distribution should be by reference to the ethical norms of what might seem to be justified and right. The pro-liberty philosophers, including Bentham, Austin and Mill maintained, on the other hand, that granting maximum liberty to the individual, limited only by the liberty of others, and the operation of a free market, will guarantee social justice. Utilitarian philosophers of the nineteenth century, including Bentham and Mill, held that the maximisation of utility, the common good and the interests of people should be of primary concern to distributive justice. The course or policy that is adopted must, in other words, bring greatest benefit to the largest number. Modern commentators on the subject, including John Rawls, who emphasise rights, seek to displace utilitarian conceptions of justice as the appropriate paradigm. Utilitarianism has also suffered a decline partly because of its neglect of individual differences: the happiness of each person should not count equally in the total without regard for his or her past behaviour. An increase in total happiness might be unfairly purchased at the price of the pain of innocent individuals. The problem thus remains as to which of these approaches to distribution is the most convincing.[94]

Distribution on the basis of equality tends to ignore relevant differences, such as the case of those who might have dependents to feed or large medical bills to pay. It is therefore said that a satisfactory understanding of equality requires that individual circumstances and needs should be taken into account. Distribution on the basis of need alone also ignores the question of how much is deserved and who has contributed more. The fact that A has worked hard and B has not is surely an important factor in determining a just distribution. Furthermore, determining the needs of individuals is a difficult and changeable process. Legal philosophy has thus envisaged different approaches to distributive justice. The governing criterion could be one that looks to the past behaviour of individuals, their present situations, or their future happiness and the social good. The lack of consensus outlined previously has led some commentators to deny that any single principle of distribution will be adequate, and maintain that combining two or more into a single formula seems almost as arbitrary.

Islam's approach to distributive justice is embedded in the notion of human fraternity (*al-ikhā' al-insānī*) and cooperation (*taʿāwun*), principles that find explicit affirmation in the Qur'ān. In more than one place, the Qur'ān affirms the fraternity of mankind, their unity of origin, and equality in the eyes of the Creator. Thus according to a Qur'ānic address:

O mankind! Keep your duty to your Lord Who created you from a single soul and created its mate of the same [kind] and created from these many men and women. And keep your duty to God, by Whom you demand your rights from one another, and [observe] the ties of kinship. (al-Nisā' 4:1)

يا أيها الناس أتقوا ربّكم الذى خلقكم من نفس واحدة و خلق منها زوجها و بث منهما رجالا كثيرا و نساء، واتقوا اللّه الذى تساءلون به والأرحام.

The Qur'ān thus highlights the bond of unity among human beings in the expression *al-arḥām* (ties of kinship), a specific term that is usually employed in the Qur'ān in the context of inheritance and blood relations within the family (i.e. *dhawū al-arḥām*). The *āyah* thus began with describing the entire human race as being of the same ancestry, and then advised all people to be mindful of their ties of kinship with one another. The fraternity of man in the Qur'ān has been re-enforced, in the case of Muslims, by their fraternity with the hole of mankind, and there is no conflict between this and the Qur'ānic declaration that 'the believers are brethren' (al-Ḥujurāt, 49:10).[95]

إنما المؤمنون اخوة.

Fraternity among the believers has, in turn, a bearing on the faith of every Muslim, as expounded in this *ḥadīth*: 'None of you is a [true] believer unless you like for your brother that which you like for yourself.'[96] According to another *ḥadīth*, 'The faithful are to one another like [parts of] a building, each part strengthening the other.'[97] In yet another *ḥadīth*, it is stated that 'every Muslim is a brother to his fellow Muslim, neither wronging him nor allowing him to be wronged'.[98]

لايؤمن أحدكم حتى يحب لأخيه ما يحب لنفسه.
المؤمن للمؤمن كالبنيان يشد بعضه بعضا.
المسلم أخوالمسلم لا يظلمه ولا يسلمه.

The Qur'ān enjoins the believers to 'co-operate in good work and righteousness, and co-operate not in hostility and sin' (al-Mā'idah, 5:2).

تعاونوا على البرّ والتقوى ولا تعاونوا على الإثم والعدوان.

Co-operation in good work underscores the moral substance of fraternity. *Al-birr* refers mainly to the decent and fair treatment of others (*ḥusn al-muᶜāmalah*) by being pleasant and courteous to them, and being generous in helping those who are in need.[99] This is the purport of another Qur'ānic passage that reads: 'You shall not attain virtue [*al-birr*] unless you spend [on others] of what you like for yourselves' (Āl Imrān, 3: 92).

لن تنالو البرّ حتى تنفقوا مما تحبّون.

The Qur'ān also emphasises that *al-birr* requires a sense of sincerity in giving when it declares that 'it is not a virtue to turn your faces [in prayer] to the East and the West; but virtue is to have faith in God and the Last Day [...] and spend of your wealth out of love for Him on the near of kin and the orphans and the needy (al-Baqarah, 2:177)

ليس البرّ أن تولوا وجوهكم قبل المشرق و المغرب، ولكن البرّ من آمن بالله واليوم الآخر [...] وآتي المال على حبه ذوي القربىٰ و اليتامىٰ و المساكين.

The Caliph ᶜAlī's reading of these passages led him to the conclusion that 'God Most High has made it obligatory on the rich to provide for the poor with what is adequate for them' (cf. al-Dhāriyat, 51:19). Another prominent Companion, Abū Dharr al-Ghaffārī, went so far as to say that it was impermissible for a Muslim to accumulate wealth beyond his needs, and that surplus wealth in the hands of the rich should be expended on community welfare.[100] Be that as it may, Muslim jurists have held that acquisition of wealth through lawful means is not against the teachings of Islam. And lastly, it is a manifestation of fraternity and co-operation that the *Sharīᶜah* forbids usury (*ribā'*) and profiteering (*iḥtikār*) on the one hand, and encourages the giving of benevolent loans (*qarḍ ḥasan*) to those in need, even if they are not very poor, on the other.

The *Sharīᶜah* also seeks to bring about the equitable distribution of wealth through its social support system (*al-takāful al-ijtimāᶜī*), which can be seen in four areas of co-operation as follows:[101] (1) *takāful* within the family, which is manifested in a regime of maintenance (*al-nafaqāt*) for close relatives, and provisions relating to inheritance and bequest; (2) *takāful* within the community mainly through the distribution of revenues from *zakāh* (legal aims); (3) co-operation among smaller groups and associations, such as neighbours and local residents; and (4) voluntary charities and atonements (*al-ṣadaqāt wa'l-kaffārāt*) including charitable endowments (*al-awqāf*).[102]

Maintenance or *nafaqah* normally includes food, clothing, dwelling, education, marriage, and also services and medical treatment for the ill and the disabled.[103] Close relatives may be entitled to obligatory maintenance without consideration for individual need, such as in the case of one's wife; or it may be on the basis of need alone and provided even if the recipient is able to earn a living, such as in the case of one's parents; or it may be based on need but given only when the recipient is unable to earn a living, such as in the case of one's adult offspring, and with regard generally to other relatives.

This last condition, that the recipient must be unable to earn a living, is to encourage people to occupy themselves with productive work.[104] Parents are an exception to the rule of need because of the Qur'ānic call that they should in all cases be treated with *iḥsān* (al-Nisā', 4:36). Reasons for the inability to earn a living include being a minor, illness, chronic blindness, and being a student engaged in the pursuit of knowledge, on condition, however, that the student is successful at his/her studies. A student who is unsuccessful therefore loses his right to *nafaqah*.[105] There is some disagreement among the jurists on this, but the Ḥanafīs have held that the rules of *nafaqah* apply to Muslim and non-Muslim relatives alike, and that unity of religion is not a requirement.[106] And lastly, the duty of *nafaqah* falls on the state in respect of those poor and needy members of community who are unable to work and have no one to support them.

Bāqir al-Ṣadr's contribution to the debate on income and wealth distribution is not as concerned with the relative shares of income and wealth as it is with the provision of basic needs so that all men can live with dignity. He has distinguished three groups in society:

(1) those who can provide, through ability and talent, a high standard of living for themselves; (2) those who can satisfy their basic needs through their work; (3) the physically or mentally weak who cannot sustain themselves through their efforts.

Society has an obligation to help the latter, but not so as to penalise the first group. For penalising work is tantamount to dealing a heavy blow to the most important power that pushes the economic system ahead.[107] Both Umar Chapra and Nejatullah Siddiqi refer to al-Ṣadr in their own works. Chapra cites with approval al-Ṣadr's view that poverty and deprivation are caused by the absence of a morally defined framework of human relationships between the rich and the poor. Siddiqi supports al-Ṣadr's case for a minimum guaranteed standard of living for all in an Islamic state.[108]

Unlike Christianity and Judaism, which designated charity a moral duty of the rich, in Islam *zakāh* was elevated into a pillar of the faith and a legal obligation. *Zakāh* is a tangible manifestation of fraternity and co-operation in the Muslim community. It is payable at an annual rate of about two and a half per cent on surplus assets, but the precise amount varies with reference to the type of assets. Since *zakāh* is a pillar of the faith, it is levied only on Muslims; non-Muslim citizens pay a poll-tax (*jizyah*), which is at about the same rate as *zakāh*. The Qur'ān designates *zakāh* as a right of the poor in the wealth of the rich (al-Dhāriyāt, 51:19) which is paid in order to free and purify property from the claims of those entitled to a share in it (al-Tawbah, 9:103). Being a right, *zakāh* is recoverable by legal means, not just while a person is alive but also from his estate after his death. *Zakāh* is a special tax earmarked for distribution among specific target groups, namely the poor, the needy, the insolvent debtor and a number of other classes of people (eight classes are mentioned in the Qur'ān—al-Tawbah, 9:60). Entitlement to *zakāh* and other welfare assistance is generally determined on the basis of need but government authorities may exercise a certain amount of discretion in determining the manner and quantum of its distribution.[109] Reports indicate that the Prophet ﷺ used to give, when distributing state revenues to the public, two portions to a married person, and only one to a single person.[110] It is also reported that the Caliph ʿUmar ibn al-Khaṭṭāb entitled a married person who had a child to a larger portion of assistance from the state funds, and the amount gradually increased as the child grew older.[111] Without entering into details, the public treasury (*bayt al-māl*) has been divided into four sections, namely the land and poll tax division, which provides funds for general state expenditures and assistance to the poor among non-Muslims; the spoils of war division, which is to fund general state expenditures and the maintenance of poor Muslims to the extent of supporting them for one year; *zakāh* collections, which are to be expended as the Qur'ān has specified (al-Tawbah, 9:60); and unclaimed assets including escheat and unowned property, which are exclusively spent on the poor, including for their medical treatment, maintenance, funeral expenditures and so forth.[112] We may note here, in passing, the view commonly held by contemporary Islamic economic writers that *zakāh* and the Islamic inheritance system are insufficient in themselves to ensure a just distribution of resources in the community.[113]

It may further be added, on an historical note, that during the time of the first Caliph, Abū Bakr, the renowned Companion Khālid ibn al-Walīd signed a treaty with the Christians of Ḥīrah in Iraq in which he committed the public treasury to assist those of them who were unable to work because of old age, poverty and illness, and exempted them from the *jizyah* for as long as they resided in Muslim territories.[114] The Caliph ʿUmar assigned welfare allowance to those in need, both Muslims and non-Muslims. It is reported that on one occasion he exempted an elderly Jew, whom he met in the market-place, from the payment of poll-tax and assigned an allowance for him from the *bayt al-māl*. He told the keeper of the *bayt al-māl* that it was 'unfair that we ate from the fruit of his youth and then let him down in his old age'.[115] This is evidently a recognition of individual merit and contribution in the distribution of wealth. Reports also have it that in one of his night tours of Medina, the Caliph ʿUmar heard the cries of a child and alerted the mother to this, but a little later he noted that the infant was crying again and this time he rebuked the mother who said in response that she was weaning the child but this had not worked out very well. Upon further investigation, it turned out that the child was being weaned too early because the Caliph only entitled weaned children to welfare assistance. The Caliph then changed his policy and issued orders that entitled all children to welfare assistance. [116]

There is much emphasis in the Qur'ān and the *Sunnah* on co-operation between neighbours, on voluntary charity, hospitality for travellers, on expiations (*kaffārāt*) and charitable endowments (*awqāf*—usually for local welfare purposes) that the jurists have elaborated, and they all have the common objective of helping the poor and facilitating equitable distribution 'so that wealth does not circulate only among the rich' (al-Ḥashr, 59:7).

لكيلا يكون دولة بين الأغنياء.

Imam Mālik, Ibn Ḥazm and al-Qurṭubī have held that when the *zakāh* revenue is insufficient to support the poor in a neighbourhood, district or village, additional taxes may be levied on the rich to provide the poor with their necessities, and it becomes the duty of the rich to pay these.[117] Attention may also be drawn here to the pact of fraternity that the Prophet ﷺ endorsed between some individuals among the Immigrants and later among the Immigrants and Helpers, who consequently used to regard one another as real brothers and shared their food and shelter. Abū Zahrah has recounted this and suggested that this Prophetic *Sunnah* should be emulated and revived.[118] There are also provisions in the sources on atonements (*kaffārāt*) for deliberately breaking of the fast during Ramaḍān, for accidental homicide, for a certain type of divorce known as *al-ẓihār*, for futile oaths, and for certain omissions/irregularities in the Ḥajj ceremonies, all of which usually consist of providing food and clothing to the poor, and contribute to a fair distribution of wealth.[119] The Qur'ān also enjoins kindness (*iḥsān*) to three types of neighbours: the neighbour-cum-relative, the neighbour who is not a relative, and one's companions in a journey (al-Nisā', 4:36). Ibn Ḥazm's reading of the source evidence on hospitality for travellers persuaded him to say that serving them is obligatory for a day and a night. 'Acts of Kindness among Neighbours [*al-Māʿūn*]', is the title of a Qur'ānic sūra, where it is declared on a striking note:

> Woe to those who pray, but who do not think of what it means; those who do an act of goodness in order [merely] to be seen, and refrain from [a small] act of kindness. (al-Māʿūn, 107: 4-7)

فويل للمصلين الذين هم عن صلاتهم ساهون الذين هم يراء ون و يمنعون الماعون.

Commentators have understood *al-māʿūn* as meaning being helpful in small things, such as lending a utensil to a neighbour and small acts of generosity.

Islam has envisaged a diverse system of distribution, which aims to achieve a variety of goals. The purpose is not only to eradicate poverty and prevent the concentration of wealth in the hands of the rich alone, but also to alleviate other kinds of hardships, such as by extending help to travellers even if they are not poor, or to debtors even if they have some property, or to relatives who may not be in need, and so forth. Some distribution also occurs in the form of atonements and acts of piety and devotion. The system is committed not only to establish justice but also to promote mutual affection and kindness in the community. A variety of redistributive measures are employed, some of which are compulsory and others voluntary, just as there are measures that are permanent, such as those concerning *zakāh* and inheritance, and measures that can be brought in when needed (additional taxation, for example). The permanent measures aim to curb excessive deviation from the basic scheme, whereas temporary measures may be taken in response to exceptional circumstances. The emphasis is on equity but not on equality in personal income levels and wealth. There is recognition in the system that insisting on absolute equality in disregard of personal merit, need, and contribution can lead to injustices. Justice itself is the supreme objective of Islam, and the quest for it is not limited to a particular methodology or framework. Any approach or formula that leads to justice and is designed for the purpose of attaining a just distribution of wealth is therefore deemed to be acceptable.

From its essentially individualist conception in the nineteenth century, justice as translated into law in Western jurisdictions has, in the course of the twentieth century, assumed a predominantly social character. As a consequence of the acute awareness of the hazards facing individuals because of such catastrophic events as World War I, the economic depression of late 1920s and early 1930s, the rise of Fascism and Nazism, and World War II, idealistic aspirations to protect human beings have been manifested and reasserted worldwide, and formulated in such documents as the Universal Declaration of Human Rights of 1948. More pragmatically, Western states have shouldered much greater social responsibilities. Generally, since World War II, the rising rates of higher tax brackets, state or communal subvention of welfare programmes in education and health, and restrictive provisions limiting the autonomy of individual transactions, including unfair competition regulations, consumer protection and the like, have consistently created what the French term the economic and legal *dirigisme*, or state-directed activities. The general trend in Western Europe is still along the lines of welfare states and service states, of which the former stresses the recipient side and the latter the supplying side. The two sides have the idea of social justice in common.[120]

While Western discourse on social justice is predominantly philosophical, the Islamic approach is basically legal, which is determined, in its broad outline, by the directives of the Qur'ān and the *Sunnah*. Whereas Western philosophical discourse is preoccupied by considerations of rationality and theoretical paradigms, the juristic approach of the *Sharīʿah* is primarily concerned with laying down a set of principles and rules that are expressive of diversity in outlook and treating each case on its merit rather than by concern for adherence to a predetermined philosophy. The Islamic conception of social justice thus depicts a mixed picture that tends to combine a multiplicity of influences. This might prove difficult to achieve under the more heavily philosophical approaches that are part of Western discourses on justice. The relative absence of a parallel discourse among Muslim writers can be partially explained by the reluctance on the part of Muslim jurists to subject the normative guidelines of the Qur'ān and the *Sunnah* to philosophical argumentation. The juristic approach attempts to comprehend and interpret the Qur'ān and the *Sunnah*, whereas the philosophical approach is not bound by the concerns of adherence to an authoritative framework. Yet philosophers, too, have somehow felt the need to commit themselves to their own theoretical paradigms that are rooted, not in any commitment to the authority of divine revelation, but in the rationalist concerns of consistency and coherence. Having said this, the two approaches are not inherently opposed to one another since they subscribe to a set of values that are, in the final analysis, upheld by each.

VII. *Siyāsah Sharʿiyyah* (*Sharīʿah*-Oriented Policy)

This is a broad doctrine of Islamic public law that authorises rulers and judges, that is, the *ulū al-amr*, to determine the manner in which the *Sharīʿah* should be administered. A ruler may accordingly take discretionary measures, enact rules and initiate policies as he deems appropriate in the interests of good government, provided that no substantive principle of the *Sharīʿah* is thereby violated. The discretionary powers of the *ulū al-amr* under *siyāsah sharʿiyyah* are particularly extensive in the field of criminal law. The *ulū al-amr* may thus decide on rules and procedures to discover truth and determine guilt. With regard to the substantive law of crimes too, the *ulū al-amr* have powers to determine what behaviour constitutes an offence and what punishment is to be applied in each case.

Penalties that are imposed at the discretion of a judge are known as *ta*ᶜ*zīrāt*. As a branch of *siyāsah*, *ta*ᶜ*zīr* (lit. deterrence) takes into consideration the nature of the offence and the particular circumstances of the offender. The judge may thus determine the punishment of *ta*ᶜ*zīr* in each case according to his own observations and personal *ijtihād*.

The ᶜ*ulamā'* have used *siyāsah shar*ᶜ*iyyah* for different purposes. Literally, it means *Sharī*ᶜ*ah*-oriented policy, or government in accordance with the *Sharī*ᶜ*ah*. In this sense, *siyāsah shar*ᶜ*iyyah* applies to all government policies, whether in areas where the *Sharī*ᶜ*ah* provides explicit guidance or otherwise. In its juridical usage, however, *siyāsah shar*ᶜ*iyyah* implies decisions and policy measures taken by the imām and the *ulū al-amr* on matters for which no specific ruling can be found in the *Sharī*ᶜ*ah*. In this sense, *siyāsah shar*ᶜ*iyyah*, as Khallāf observed, is tantamount to acting on a *maṣlaḥah*, or public interest, that the Lawgiver has neither upheld nor overruled. '*Siyāsah shar*ᶜ*iyyah* denotes, in other words, the administration of public affairs in an Islamic polity with the aim of securing the interest of, and preventing harm to, the community, in harmony with the general principles of the *Sharī*ᶜ*ah*, even if this disagrees with the particular rulings of the *mujtahids*.'[121] *Siyāsah* may thus entail adopting policies and enacting laws in all spheres of government, in the areas of domestic or foreign relations, and constitutional, fiscal, administrative or judicial affairs. All measures taken to facilitate the efficient management of public affairs fall within the purview of *siyāsah* provided that they do not violate the clear injunctions of the *Sharī*ᶜ*ah*.

According to Ibn Qayyim, *siyāsah shar*ᶜ*iyyah* does not necessarily mean conforming to the explicit rules of the *Sharī*ᶜ*ah*: 'Any measure that actually brings people closer to beneficence [*ṣalāḥ*] and furthest away from corruption [*fasād*] partakes of just *siyāsah*, even if it has not been approved by the Prophet, or regulated by divine revelation. Anyone who says that there is no *siyāsah shar*ᶜ*iyyah* where the *Sharī*ᶜ*ah* itself is silent is wrong.'[122]

*Siyāsah shar*ᶜ*iyyah* is thus characterised by its essential harmony with the spirit and objectives of the *Sharī*ᶜ*ah*, sometimes even at the risk of abandoning the letter of the law. Commentators have illustrated this by reference to a decision of the Caliph ᶜUmar ibn al-Khaṭṭāb concerning the *muᶜallafāt al-qulūb*. These were persons of influence whose friendship and co-operation were regarded as beneficial for the victory of Islam. The Qur'ān (al-Tawbah, 9:60) had assigned a share for them in the *zakāh* revenues, which the Caliph discontinued saying that 'God has exalted Islam and it is no longer in need of their favour'. The Caliph thus departed from the letter of the Qur'ān in favour of its general purpose, and his ruling is considered to be in harmony with the spirit of the Qur'ān.[123]

The *fuqahā'* have also used *siyāsah sharᶜiyyah* in the sense of implying flexibility (*tawsiᶜah*) for rulers and judges in their decisions. In this way, *siyāsah* is used to denote discretionary powers: when a decision is said to have been taken as part of the *siyāsah* of a ruler or judge, this is tantamount to saying that it was a discretionary decision, provided of course that it did not contravene the *Sharīᶜah*. Al-Qarāfi has thus spoken of the need for *tawsiᶜah* in the rulings of the *Diwān al-Maẓālim* and in the actions of the police in their efforts to curb criminality and corruption. He has quoted in authority the *ḥadīth* that 'harm [*ḍarar*] may neither be inflicted nor reciprocated'. Al-Qarāfi has also referred to an incident where the Prophet ﷺ suspected a man, during the course of a military expedition, of being a spy, and punished the suspect until he made a confession.[124]

ᶜ*Adl* or justice in its juridical sense may sometimes conflict with the requirements of a judicious policy. This may be illustrated by an incident that took place during the time of the second Caliph, ᶜUmar ibn al-Khaṭṭāb. The Caliph used to receive complaints against his officials at public gatherings. On one such occasion, a member of the public complained against the governor of Egypt, ᶜAmr ibn al-ᶜĀṣ, that the governor had flogged him with one hundred lashes for no apparent cause. When the Caliph was convinced that the punishment was unwarranted, he asked the plaintiff to retaliate. ᶜAmr ibn al-ᶜĀṣ, who was present on the occasion, intervened, and said that retaliation in this case might be in harmony with the dictates of justice, yet it was unwise to flog a governor in a public gathering. The Caliph agreed and the matter was settled through financial compensation.[125]

The later-day jurists (*al-muta'akhkhirūn*) have, however, used the term *siyāsah sharᶜiyyah* in a more restricted sense, that is, to imply the administration of penalties meted out by rulers and judges in order to combat criminality and evil.[126] Ibn ᶜĀbidīn has thus described *siyāsah sharᶜiyyah* as an intensification of penalties for crimes concerning which the *Sharīᶜah* has a ruling, but where the penalty in question needs to be increased due to the hideous nature of the crime.[127] Al-Māwardī has spoken in similar terms, but has mentioned in this connection rulers and judges (*umarā' wa quḍāt*), adding that the former exercise *siyāsah* whereas the latter implement the rules (*aḥkām*) of the *Sharīᶜah*, and refers by way of illustrations to investigative detention by police as a manifestation of *siyāsah*.[128] This sort of distinction does not, however, feature prominently in other works on the subject. The extra-textual applications of *siyāsah* are illustrated by reference to the fact that rulers have sometimes ordered the killing of criminals who robbed houses at times when calamities such as fire, earthquake and war caused the occupants to flee, or when kidnappers terrorised people and inflicted suffering on the parents and relatives of victims. But to confine *siyāsah* to the administration of penalties is not totally justified, for *siyāsah* has much wider scope, and can equally apply in other areas of government.

The Qur'ānic authority for *siyāsah* can be found in a number of its injunctions, especially those that enjoin the promotion of good and the prevention of evil on the believers.[129] *Siyāsah sharᶜiyyah* is thus an instrument in the hands of the *ulū al-amr* by which they may discharge their duty. But more specifically, the Qur'ānic command ordering to the believers to 'obey God, obey the Messenger and those who are in authority among you' (al-Nisā', 4:59) provides the necessary authority for *siyāsah*. Obedience to the *ulū al-amr* is thus a Qur'ānic duty for Muslims provided that the *ulū al-amr* themselves comply with the dictates of the *Sharīᶜah*.[130] The preceeding Qur'ānic *āyah* in the same sūra (al-Nisā', 4:58) has also been quoted as the authority for *siyāsah* in regard to the selection and appointment of government officials. The text thus provides that 'God commands you to hand over the trusts [*al-amānāt*] to whom they belong, and when you judge between people, judge with justice'. Ibn Taymiyyah's renowned book, *al-Siyāsah al-Sharᶜiyyah fī Iṣlāḥ al-Rāᶜī wa'l-Raᶜiyyah* (On the Benefits of *Siyāsah* for both the Ruler and Ruled), as the author explains, is a commentary on this single *āyah* of the Qur'ān. Ibn Taymiyyah has stated that the Qur'ānic concept of trusts in this *āyah* has been interpreted by the following *ḥadīth*: 'When a person is entrusted with authority over the affairs of believers, and he in turn delegates this authority to another, while he could find a more competent person for the task, he has betrayed God and His Messenger.'[131] More generally, however, since the application of *siyāsah* is not confined to a particular area in the management of public affairs and applies generally to all subjects of concern to good government, all of the Qur'ānic *āyāt* that can be quoted for justice, benefit (*maṣlaḥah*), the removal of hardship (*rafᶜ al-ḥaraj*) and the elimination of corruption and oppression can be quoted in support of *siyāsah*. References have been made in particular to the two Qur'ānic *āyāt* proclaiming that 'God does not intend to put you in hardship' (al-Mā'idah, 5:6);

وما يريد الله ليجعل عليكم من حرج.

and that 'He has not made religion a means of imposing hardship upon you' (al-Ḥajj, 22:78).

ماجعل عليكم في الدين من حرج.

Then the Qur'ānic text proclaiming that 'God commands justice [*al-ᶜadl*] and benevolence [*al-iḥsān*]' (al-Nahl, 16:90)

إن الله يأمر بالعدل و الإحسان.

as well as the *ḥadīth* declaring that 'religion is good advice' (*al-dīnu al-naṣīḥatu*) all provide supportive evidence for *siyāsah*.[132]

Siyāsah in its widest sense has five purposes: the protection of faith, life, intellect, lineage, and property.[133] The *ᶜulamā'* are unanimous on the point that the protection of these values constitutes the ultimate objective of the *Sharīᶜah* itself, despite the fact that a specific reference to this group of values can be found neither in the Qur'ān nor the *Sunnah*. General consensus (*ijmāᶜ*) on the protection of these values is not based on any particular provision of the Qur'ān or the *Sunnah*, but on the overall contents of these source-texts and on the numerous commands and prohibitions that are designed to protect these values. The same can be said of the Qur'ānic verses that enjoin on the community the pursuit of good and prevention of evil. The good and evil are nowhere listed exhaustively in the Qur'ān or the *Sunnah*, but can be known through a general investigation of these sources. But even so, as al-Shāṭibī pointed out, right and wrong cannot be known in detail in advance without referring to particular acts and their surrounding circumstances.[134] Hence the *ulū al-amr* must have powers to uphold and protect the values and objectives of the

Sharīᶜah, and be able to order punishment for conduct that violates the sanctity of these values. It is on the strength of this argument that some jurists have added to these five values a sixth, namely the 'elimination of corruption', so as to enable the ruler to penalise conduct that amounts to corruption even if it does not violate any of the five values in question, and even if no specific ruling for it could be found in the *Sharīᶜah*.[135]

Ibn Qayyim has divided *siyāsah* into two types: unjust (*siyāsah ẓālimah*), which the *Sharīᶜah* forbids, and just (*siyāsah ᶜādilah*), which serves the cause of justice. Since justice is the overriding goal of *siyāsah ᶜādilah*, it is an integral part of the *Sharīᶜah* and is always in harmony with it. 'We merely call it *siyāsah* because of the linguistic usage, but it is nothing other than the justice ordained by God and His Messenger.' The Prophet ﷺ has occasionally ordered flogging or doubled the amount of compensation in mitigated cases of theft, and gave orders to smash the container in which wine was found. Ibn Qayyim continues: 'Whoever sets free the accused, after his taking an oath [as to his innocence], stating that there should be no punishment without the testimony of just witnesses, even though he has a reputation for corruption and robberies, verily acts contrary to *siyāsah sharᶜiyyah*'.[136]

It is not just *siyāsah* to persist in refusing to hear all claims which are not accompanied by upright witnesses. Indeed the judge is authorised to admit witnesses of lesser qualification (*ghayr ᶜudūl*) if this proves to be the only way of protecting the rights and properties of people.[137] In their efforts to protect people against aggression, the most capable of rulers have exercised intuitive judgement (*farāsah*) and taken decisions on the basis of circumstantial evidence (*amārāt*).[138] A just *siyāsah* requires that the judge does not set dangerous criminals free merely due to an insufficiency of evidence, but should detain them until the truth emerges. It would be patently tyrannical, on the other hand, to exercise the same degree of severity on every accused person, especially first-time offenders who have no criminal record.[139]

The ruler is advised to be gentle in implementing the *Sharīᶜah*, and to verge on the side of leniency where there is a choice between leniency and harshness. The removal of hardship from, and bringing ease to, the people is a general principle of the *Sharīᶜah* which is derived from the Qur'ān: 'God intends every facility for you and He does not intend to put you in difficulty' (al-Baqarah, 2:185; see also al-Ḥajj, 22:78).

يريد الله بكم اليسر ولا يريدبكم العسر.

In support of this, Ibn Taymiyyah quoted the *ḥadīth* that 'gentleness does not fail to create beauty whereas harshness is most likely to lead to ugliness'.

الرفق لايكون في شيء إلا زانه ولاينزع من شيء إلا شانه.

The Prophet ﷺ has also said: 'God loves gentleness [*al-rifq*] and gives what He gives through gentleness not through harshness [*ᶜunf*]'.[140]

إن الله يحبّ الرفق وهو يعطي في الرفق مالم يعط في العنف.

According to another *ḥadīth*, Abū Burdah reported that when the Messenger of God sent Muᶜādh ibn Jabal and Abū Mūsā al-Ashᶜarī to the Yemen, he told them: 'Be gentle to people and not harsh with them; bring them good tidings of mercy and do not scare them, and do not incite them to aversion'.[141]

يسرا ولا تعسرا و بشرا ولا تنفرا.

Commenting on this *ḥadīth*, Ibn Taymiyyah observed it is not benevolent (*iḥsān*) to citizens to leave them to do what they like, or avoid doing what they dislike. The essence of *iḥsān* is to ask them to do what is beneficial for them in this world and meritorious in the next, even if they happen to dislike this. However, when a ruler asks his subjects to do what they dislike, he must do so with gentleness, and avoid inciting people to aversion to the *Sharīᶜah*.[142]

To conclude, the availability of some discretionary power in the administration of justice is in principle accepted in all legal systems. It is the scope and dimension of such powers that are the main cause of concern, and the chief reason behind efforts to develop adequate controls on their exercise. The need to regulate the use of discretionary powers is particularly pressing in the field of criminal law, where citizen are exposed to the use of coercive power. It is in this area that the principle of the rule of law acquires especial significance.

Given the increasing complexity of government in modern times, it would seem good *siyāsah* to define and restrict discretionary powers, especially regarding *taʿzīr*, to reasonable limits. The bulk of civil and criminal law in present-day Muslim countries has, in any case, been either codified or extensively regulated by statutory legislation. Parallel to this development, a deliberate effort has also been made, almost everywhere, to regulate by means of legislation the exercise of *taʿzīr* on the part of the *Sharīʿah* courts. All this may be said to fall within the ambit of good *siyāsah*. The purpose is not, of course, to eliminate discretionary power or to overrule *taʿzīr* punishment altogether. It is rather to regulate the exercise of discretionary power and to provide appropriate guidelines for it.

NOTES

1. Diyā' al-Dīn al-Rīs, *al-Naẓariyyāt al-Siyāsiyyah al-Islāmiyyah*, 7th edn., Cairo, Dār al-Turāth, n.d., p. 328; ʿAmmāra, *al-Islām wa'l-Ḥuqūq al-Insān*, p. 65; Anwar Ahmad Qadri, *Islamic Jurisprudence in the Modern World*, 2nd edn., Lahore, Shah Muhammad Ashraf Press, 1987, p. 480.

2. Cf. Edgar Bodenheimer, *Jurisprudence, the Philosophy and Method of the Law*, 2nd edn., Englewood Cliffs (New Jersey), Prentice Hall, 1991, pp. 179-89; R.M.W. Dias, *Jurisprudence*, 5th edn., London, Butterworth, 1985; Stephen Mulhall and Adam Swift, *Liberals and Communitarians,* Oxford, Blackwell, 1992, p. 80.

3. H.L.A. Hart, *The Concept of Law*, Oxford, Clarendon Press, 1961, p. 186.

4. Bodenheimer, *Jurisprudence*, p. 212.

5. John Rawls, *A Theory of Justice*, Cambridge, Harvard University Press, 1971, pp. 11ff.

6. J. Arthur & N. Shaw, *Justice and Economic Distribution*, 2nd edn., Englewood Cliffs (New Jersey), Prentice Hall, 1991, p. 5; Nait-Belkacem, 'Social Justice', in Gauhar (ed.), *The Challenge of Islam*, London, The Islamic Council of Europe, 1978, p. 48.

7. Cf. Zaydān, *Niẓām al-Qaḍā'*, p. 12: '*al-qaḍā' huwa al-ikhbār ʿan ḥukn sharʿī ʿalā sabīl al-ilzām*'. See also al-Zuḥaylī, *al-Fiqh al-Islāmī*, VI, 785.

8. Al-Zuḥaylī, *al-Fiqh al-Islāmī*, VI, 756.

9. Ibid., VI, 740.

10. Shams al-Dīn al-Sarakhsī, *al-Mabsūṭ*, Beirut: Dār al-Maʿrifah, 1406/1986, XVI, 59-60.

11. Muslim, *Mukhtaṣar Ṣaḥīḥ Muslim*, p. 147, *ḥadīth* no. 537.
12. Al-Tabrīzī, *Mishkāt*, vol. II, *ḥadīth* no. 2325
13. Cf. al-Zuḥaylī, *al-Fiqh al-Islāmī*, VI, 718.
14. Ibn Qayyim al-Jawziyyah, *al-Ṭuruq al-Ḥukmiyyah*, p. 16.
15. Ibn Qayyim al-Jawziyyah, *Iʿlām*, IV, 373.
16. Yūsuf al-Qaraḍāwī, *Madkhal li-Darāsah al-Sharīʿah al-Islamiyyah*, Cairo, Maktabah Wahbah, 1411/1991, p. 177.
17. Ibid., p. 178.
18. Sayyd Quṭb, *Fī Ẓilāl al-Qur'ān*, Beirut: Dār al-Shuruq, 1397/1977, II, 689.
19. Muhammad Afzal Zullah, 'The Application of Islamic Law in Pakistan', presentation given at the International Islamic University Malaysia, 6 September 1991, where the present writer was a participant.
20. Muhammad Muslehuddin, *Philosophy of the Islamic Law and the Orientalists*, 2nd edn., Lahore, Islamic Publications Ltd., 1980, p. 106
21. Abū Zahrah, *Tanẓīm al-Islām*, p. 31.
22. Ibid.
23. See for a discussion of this *āyah* and some of its other juristic implications, Kamali, *Principles of Islamic Jurisprudence*, pp. 225ff.
24. Cf. al-Rāzī, Fakhr al-Dīn b. ʿUmar, *al-Tafsīr al-Kabīr* (also known as *Mafātīḥ al-Ghayb*). Beirut: Dār al-Fikr, 1398/1978, III, 353.
25. See for details, Kamali, 'The Limits of Power in an Islamic State', pp. 323-53.
26. Ibn Taymiyyah, *al-Siyāsah al-Sharʿiyyah fī Iṣlāḥ al-Rāʿī wa'l-Rāʿiyyah*, ed. Abd al-Raḥmān b. Qāsim, Beirut: Mu'assasat al-Risālah, 1398AH, p. 6.
27. Ibid., p. 5; Aḥmad, *Uṣūl al-Niẓām*, p. 229.
28. Al-Nawawī, *Riyāḍ al-Ṣāliḥīn*, *ḥadīth* no. 1872.
29. Al-Qurṭubī, *Bidāya*, II, 461; Ibn Ḥazm, *Muḥallā*, IX, 435; Zaydān, *Niẓām*, p. 51; Shaykh Taqī al-Dīn al-Nabhānī, *Muqaddimat al-Dustūr*, Kuwait, no publisher given, 1964, p. 216.
30. Maḥmaṣṣānī, *Arkān*, p. 98.
31. Farooq Hasan, *The Concept of State and Law in Islam*, New York, University Press of America, 1981, p. 43.
32. Sulaymān al-Ṭamāwī, *al-Sulṭāt al-Thalāth fi'l-Dasātir al-ʿArabiyyah wa'l-Fikr al-Siyāsī al-Islāmī*, 2nd edn., Cairo, Dār al-Fikr al-ʿArabī, 1973, p. 401; Muḥammad Fārūq al-Nabhān, *Niẓām al-Ḥukm fi'l-Islām*, Kuwait: Jāmiʿat al-Kuwait, 1974, p. 623.
33. ʿAjlānī, Muḥammad Munīr, *ʿAbqariyyāt al-Islām fī Uṣūl al-Ḥukm*, Beirut: Dār al-Nafā'is, 1405/1985, p. 342.
34. Ghulam Murtaza Azad, *Judicial System of Islam*, Islamabad: Islamic Research Institute, 1987, p. 50.

35. Madkūr, *Maᶜālim*, pp. 441-443.

36. Aḥmad, *Niẓām*, p. 192.

37. Al-Ṭamāwī, *al-Sulṭāt*, p. 401; Nabhān, *Niẓām*, p. 623; Muḥammad Salām Madkūr, *al-Qaḍā' fi'l-Islām,* Cairo: Dār al-Nahḍah al-ᶜArabiyyah, 1964, p. 30.

38. Al-Mawardī, *Aḥkām*, p. 64.

39. Ibn Qudāmah, *al-Mughnī*, II, 308.

40. ᶜAjlanī, ᶜ*Abqariyyah*, p. 343; Ṭamāwī, *al-Sulṭāt*, p. 402; Nabhān, *Niẓām*, p. 624.

41. Madkūr, *Qaḍā'*, p. 31.

42. Nabhān, *Niẓām*, p. 624; Nabhānī, *Muqaddimah*, p. 206.

43. ᶜUthmān, *Fikr*, p. 321.

44. Ibid., p. 304.

45. Mutawallī, *Mabādi'*, p. 230.

46. Al-Ṭamāwī, *al-Sulṭāt*, p. 403.

47. Muhammad Asad, *Principles of State and Government in Islam*, Berkeley (California), University of California Press, 1966, p. 66; Khālidī, *Qawāᶜid*, p. 211.

48. Ibid., p. 211.

49. Al-Ṭamāwī, *al-Sulṭāt*, p. 413; al-Nabhānī, *Muqaddimah*, p. 213.

50. Mohammad H. Kamali, 'Appellate Review and Juridical Independence in Islamic Law', in C. Mallat (ed.), *Islam and Public Law*, London, Graham & Trotman, 1993, pp. 49-85.

51. Abū Dāwūd, *Sunan*, vol. VIII, p. 1016, *ḥadīth* no. 3576.

52. Ibid., III, 1013, *ḥadīth* no. 3567.

53. Zaydān, *Niẓām*, p. 277.

54. Cf. Farīd Muḥammad Wāṣil, *al-Sulṭah al-Qaḍā'iyyah wa Niẓām al-Qaḍā' fi'l-Islām*, 2nd edn., Cairo, Maṭbaᶜat al-Amānah, 1983, p. 278;

55. Zaydān, *Niẓām*, p. 83. See for detail, Kamali, 'Appellate Review', pp. 49-85.

56. Cf. Azad, *Judicial System*, p. 104

57. Al-Māwardī, *Aḥkām*, pp. 59-60; Ibn Qayyim al-Jawziyyah, *Iᶜlām*, I, 85-6. An English translation of this letter appears in K. M. Ishaque, 'Al-Aḥkām al-Sulṭāniyyah', in *Islamic Studies* 4 (1965), pp. 289ff.

58. Burhān al-Dīn Ibn Farḥūn, *Tabṣirat al-Ḥukkām fi Uṣūl al-Aqḍiyah wa Manāhij al-Aḥkām*, ed. Ṭāhā ᶜAbd al-Raūf Saᶜd, Cairo, Maktabat al-Kulliyyāt al-Azhariyyah, 1406/1986, I, 77; Ẓāfir al-Qāsimī, *Niẓām al-Ḥukm fi'l-Sharīᶜah wa'l-Ta'rīkh,* 2nd edn., Beirut: Dār al-Nafā'is, 1977, p. 185; Zaydān, *Niẓām*, p. 75.

59. Al-Sarakhsī, *al-Mabsūṭ*, XVI, 62.

60. Ibn Qayyim al-Jawziyyah, *Iᶜlām,* I, 94-5.

61. Wāṣil, *al-Ṣulṭah*, p. 267
62. Ibid., p. 268.
63. ʿUthmān, *al-Fikr al-Qānūnī*, p. 314.
64. Al-Qurṭubī, *Bidāyat*, II, 475.
65. ʿUthmān, *al-Fikr al-Qānūnī*, pp. 314-15
66. Ibid.
67. Ibid.
68. Ibid.
69. Madkūr, *Qaḍā'*, p. 67.
70. Shihāb al-Dīn al-Ḥamawī, *Kitāb Ādāb al-Qaḍā'*, ed. Muṣṭafā al-Zuḥaylī, Damascus, Dār al-Fikr, 1402/1982, p. 488.
71. Madkūr, *Qaḍā'*, p. 69; Nabhānī, *Niẓām*, p. 84.
72. Ibid., p. 64.
73. Al-Sharbīnī, *al-Mughnī*, IV; Wāṣil, *al-Sulṭah*, p. 280.
74. Al-Bayhaqī, *al-Sunan al-Kubrā*, X, 137.
75. Cf. al-Zuḥaylī, *al-Fiqh al-Islāmī*, VI, 498.
76. Ibn Qudāmah, *al-Mughnī*, IX, 109.
77. Al-Tabrīzī, *Mishkāt*, II, 1000, *ḥadīth* no. 3342.
78. Al-Shawkānī, *Nayl al-Awṭār*, VIII, 274; al-Zuḥaylī, *al-Fiqh al-Islāmī*, VI, 500.
79. Muslim, *Mukhtaṣar Ṣaḥīḥ Muslim*, p. 280, *ḥadīth* no. 1053; Ibn Qayyim al-Jawziyyah, *Ṭuruq*, p. 94.
80. Ibn Qayyim al-Jawziyyah, *Ṭuruq*, p. 94; also the *Mejelle* (art. 76).
81. Cf. al-Zuḥaylī, *al-Fiqh al-Islāmī*, VI, 775.
82. Ibn Qayyim al-Jawziyyah, *Ṭuruq*, pp. 96-98; Zarqā, *Sharḥ al-Qawāʿid*, pp. 369ff.
83. Cf. al-Zuḥaylī, *al-Fiqh al-Islāmī*, VI, 754.
84. Ibid., p. 756.
85. Cf. Zuḥaylī, *al-Fiqh al-Islāmī*, VI, 503; Qadri, *Islamic Jurisprudence*, pp. 492-496.
86. Ibid., p. 496.
87. See for details, Bandar ibn Fahd Suwaylim, *al-Muhtam: Muʿāmalatuh wa Ḥuqūquh fi'l-Fiqh al-Islāmī*, Riyad, al-Markaz al-ʿArabiyyah li'l-Dirāsāt al-Amniyyah, 1408/1978, pp. 291ff.
88. Cf. al-Zuḥaylī, *al-Fiqh al-Islāmī*, VI, 501.
89. Cf. Awad, 'The Right of the Accused under Islamic Criminal Procedure', in M. Cherif Bassiouni (ed.), *Islamic Criminal Justice System*, London and New York: Oceana Publications, 1982, pp. 93-4.
90. Al-Māwardī, *Aḥkām*, pp. 60-61.
91. For details on *siysāsah sharʿiyyah*, see Kamali, '*Siyāsah Sharʿiyyah* or the Policies of Islamic Government', *The American Journal of Islamic Social Sciences* 6

(1989), pp. 59 - 81.

92. Khallāf, *Siyāsah*, p. 50.

93. Wāṣil, *al-Sulṭah*, p. 260.

94. Ibid.

95. Cf. Bodenheimer, *Jurisprudence*, p. 20; John Arthur and William Shaw, *Justice and Economic Distribution*, 2nd edn., Englewood Cliffs (New Jersey), Prentice Hall, 1991, p. 7.

96. Al-Qaraḍāwī, *al-Khaṣā'iṣ*, p. 84.

97. Al-Nawawī, *Riyāḍ al-Ṣāliḥīn*, p. 113, *ḥadīth* no. 188.

98. Tabrīzī, *Mishkāt*, *ḥadīth* no. 4955.

99. Ibid., *ḥadīth* no. 4958.

100. Cf. al-Sibāʿī, *Ishtirākiyyāt*, p. 112.

101. Ibn Ḥazm, *al-Muḥallā*, VI, 158.

102. See for details al-Sibāʿī, *Ishtirākiyyāt*, pp. 133ff.

103. Cf. Abū Zahrah, *Tanẓīm*, 146ff.

104. Cf. Muḥyi al-Dīn al-Nawawī, *Minhāj et Talibin,* Eng. trans. E.C. Howard, Lahore: Law Publishing Co., n.d. pp. 390ff; al-Sibāʿī, *Ishtirākiyyāt*, p. 130.

105. al-Sibāʿī, *Ishtirākiyyāt*, p. 148.

106. al-Nawawī, *Minhāj*, p. 389; Abū Zahrah, *Tanẓīm*, p. 149.

107. Abū Zahrah, *Tanẓīm*, p. 147.

108. Muḥammad Bāaqiīr al-Ṣadr, *Iqtiṣādunā* (Our Economics), 13th edn., Beirut, Dār al-Taʿarruf li'l-Maṭbūʿātn.d., n.d, vol. 1, part 2, p. 120.

109. Cf. Rodney Wilson, 'The Contribution of Muhammad Baqir al-Sadr to Contemporary Islamic Economic Thought', *Journal of Islamic Studies* 9.1 (January 1998), p. 56.

110. This is partly due to the fact that two of the eight groups of people that the Qur'ān has specified are no longer in existence: these are the slaves and *mu'allafath al-qulūb* (people whose support was important for the success of Islam). Cf. Abū Zahrah, *Tanẓīm*, note 30, p. 187.

111. Cf. Thomas Hughes, *Dictionary of Islam*, Lahore, The Book House, n.d., p. 114 (under *fā'*).

112. Al-Ṭamāwī, ʿ*Umar ibn al-Khaṭṭāb*, p. 96.

113. Abū Zahrah, *Tanẓīm*, p. 152.

114. Cf. Wilson, 'The Contribution of Mauhammad Baqir al-Sadr', p. 53.

115. Abū Yūsuf, *Kitāb al-Kharāj*, p. 144.

116. Ibid., p. 126.

117. Al-Shawkānī, *Nayl al-Awṭār*, VII, 70; al-ʿĪlī, *Ḥurriyyāt*, p. 498.

118. Qurṭubī, *al-Jāmi*ʿ, II, 223; Ibn Ḥazm, *al-Muḥallā*, III, 560.

119. Abū Zahrah, *Tanẓīm*, p. 168; al-ʿĪlī, *Ḥurriyyāt*, p. 496.

120. See for details, al-Sibāʿī, *Ishtirākiyyāt*, p. 130ff.

121. Cf. Parviz Owsia, *Formation of Contracts: A Comparative Study under English, French, Islamic and Iranian Law*, London, Graham & Trotman, 1994, p. 50.

122. ʿAbd al-Raḥmān Tāj, *al-Siyāsah al-Sharʿiyyah wa'l-Fiqh al-Islāmī*, Cairo, Maṭbaʿah Dār al-Ta'līf, 1393/1953, p. 28; Khallāf, *al-Siyāsah*, p. 3.

123. Ibn Qayyim Ibn Qayyim al-Jawziyyah, *al-Ṭuruq*, p. 16.

124. Tāj, *al-Siyāsah*, p. 28.

125. Tūghān al-Ashrafī, *al-Muqaddimah al-Sulṭāniyyah fi'l-Siyāsah al-Sharʿiyyah*, ed. Muḥammad ʿAbd Allāh, Cairo: Maktabah al-Zahrā, 1418/1997 *al-Muqaddima*, p. 13; Tāj, *al-Siyāsah*, p. 28; Khallāf, *Siyāsahā*, p. 3.

126. Mutawallī, *Mabādi'*, p. 272.

127. Khallāf, *Siyāsah*, p.3.

128. Ibn ʿĀbidīn, *Ḥāshiyah*, IV, 15.

129. Aal-Māawardī, *Aḥkām*, p. 219.

130. Note e.g. the Qur'ān (Āl-ʿImrān, 3:104 and 110; al-Tawbah, 9:71 and 124).

131. Mohamed Selim el-Awa, *Punishment in Islamic Law*, Indianapolis, American Trust Publications, 1982, p. 116.

132. Ibn Taymiyyah, *al-Siyāsah*, p. 6.

133. Al-Ashrafī, *Muqaddimah*, p. 21.

134. Tāj, *Siyāsah*, p. 10.

135. Al-Shāṭibī, *Muwāfaqāt*, II, 7.

136. Ibn Farḥūn, *Tabṣirat al-Ḥukkām*, II, 106.

137. Ibn Qayyim al-Jawziyyah, *al-Ṭuruq*, p. 5.

138. Tāj, *Siyāsah*, p. 43.

139. Ibn Qayyim al-Jawziyyah, *al-Ṭuruq*, p. 28.

140. Tāj, *Siyāsah*, p. 42.

141. Both of these *ḥadīth* appear in Ibn Taymiyyah, *Siyāsah*, p. 145. See also Muslim, *Mukhtaṣar Ṣaḥīḥ Muslim*, p. 474, *ḥadīth* nos. 1784 and 1783.

142. Ibn Taymiyyah, *Siyāsah* p. 145. See also Muslim, *Mukhtaṣar Ṣaḥīḥ Muslim*, p. 294, *ḥadīth* no. 1112.

143. Ibn Taymiyyah, *Siyāsah*, pp. 144-5.

Conclusion

The three topics addressed in this volume all represent major civilisational themes and have been the focus of incessant deliberation, renewal and reform in the legal traditions of the world. They also represent ideals and values that partake of a continuous process rather than concrete and specifically defined projects. As such, they are the concern as much of law and legal reform now as they might have been in the formative stages of Islamic law. Every era, age and generation have posed issues of their own, and raised challenging questions in each of the three areas under review. No legal system has yet claimed to have delivered definitive solutions to all the issues of concern to freedom, equality and justice. The quest for more refined solutions and alternatives that can elevate the standards of attainment in all these areas needs, therefore, to be dynamic and resourceful. How vigorous, moderate or *laissez faire* one should be in approaching issues of concern to freedom, under a given set of circumstances, is a question that is not amenable to predetermined answers. The answers to this and other similar questions must remain changeable so as to suit the temper, philosophical outlook and immediate concern of every question, and take cognisance of the particularities of history and culture.

To develop a balanced attitude to and outlook on the ideals of liberty and justice, one must remain open to considerations of both continuity and change, of stability and dynamism. The pace of change in the present phase of history is probably more rapid than the history of civilisation has ever seen.

In the midst of a maelstrom of change in almost every sphere of contemporary society, globalisation is a latecomer, a phenomenon that has only just caught the attention of the leading thinkers of the present generation. The globalisation of information technology and finance has also meant the globalisation of civilisation and culture. The effect of globalisation on the issues of concern here has yet to be explored by means of fresh research. Yet one can hardly escape the general impression that globalisation tends to inflict hardship in unwanted places and among the weaker strata of humanity much faster that it can enable them to share good fortunes. The difficulties that are being experienced by the economics of the developing nations of Asia and Africa as a result of the financial crisis of the late 1990s, are associated with globalisation. The problems of the world, especially of the weaker nations, are shared problems, and geographical boundaries are of little use in averting them. This is not the place to expound further upon the issues of globalisation. But in the midst of all this, one is reminded of the benefits of moderation and restraint, and that the influences that lend support to a continuity of values are rooted in equality and justice.

World religious traditions have witnessed an upward trend of interest in the 1990s almost everywhere, partly due to the generally felt need for a balanced combination of influences, both in the national and international spheres of human relations. The rapid pace of life, in the midst of an overall emphasis on material gain as the overt manifestations of success, has clearly proved somewhat overwhelming, and the need is therefore felt for moderation and balance. Liberty and self-interest need to be tempered by responsibility and obligation towards others.

All religious traditions have taken a close interest in the basic humanitarian values that have been the subject of this presentation. Islam has often been characterised as a social uprising against injustice, a fact borne out by the degree of attention justice has received in the Qur'ān. This is also the case with regard to equality, which can easily be singled out as one of the outstanding contributions of Islam to global civilisation.

Notwithstanding the differences of language and style by means of which the Qur'ān and the *Sunnah* have addressed the subject of freedom, the basic characterisation of Islam as a natural religion (*dīn al-fiṭrah*), which takes the freedom and moral autonomy of the individual as one of the aims of a great deal of its teaching, has been elaborated in the relevant parts of this work. Freedom often constitutes the basic postulate of a great many of the Qur'ānic directives on such subjects as *tawḥīd*, *ḥisbah*, *nasīḥah* and *shūrā*.

Tawḥīd, the belief in one Almighty God who alone has control over the destiny of the believer, has a liberating effect on the personality and outlook of the individual. Similarly, the Qur'ānic principle of *ḥisbah,* which entitles the individual to promote a good cause and be an active participant therein, and gives him the right to prevent evil in situations where he is able to do so, takes for granted his basic liberty of action. This must originate in personal conviction, and any affirmative action that is taken in support of *ḥisbah* must also be purposeful and lead to positive results. *Ḥisbah* is a broad Qur'ānic principle, broad enough to encompass the government as a whole; and so is the effort, however slight, of an individual to remove a conflict or misunderstanding between two individuals, groups, friends, families or strangers; all of these partake of *ḥisbah. Ḥisbah* thus encourages the participation and involvement of the individual in society and sees him as a morally autonomous agent who is alert to the problems and concerns of the community in which he lives.

Naṣīḥah, or sincere advice, and *shūrā* (consultation), too, are Qur'ānic principles, which take for granted an individual's freedom to offer advice to another, whether a government leader, a friend or a fellow citizen, on a matter on which he can provide constructive and sincere advice. Similarly, the participant in *shūrā* must enjoy the freedom to deliberate on issues, and be able to formulate an opinion on them. *Shūrā* would be meaningless without granting its participants freedom of opinion and speech. As a principle, *shūrā* can equally relate to the political and economic affairs of the community, just as it can be used in the family affairs and business concerns of individuals. It is an inherently participatory process, and utilises individual liberty and initiative in the pursuit of socially constructive goals.

In the literary and legal spheres, the history of Islamic thought still bears vestiges of the early division between the rationalists (*ahl al-ra'y*) and traditionalists (*ahl al-ḥadīth*), of whom the former relied more on considered judgment and opinion, and the latter on textual guidelines, in the development of the *Sharīʿah.* The general climate of opinion eventually changed this course, and the bipartite model of earlier times gave way to the emergence of four leading schools of jurisprudence. During the course of the transition from one to the other, literally hundreds of sects, schools and movements emerged in all corners of the Islamic domain. The liberty of opinion and thought marked the history of the *ʿulamā'.* The main concern at this time, that is, during the fourth and fifth centuries Hijrah, was to impose restrictions on the freedom of *ijtihād* and encourage unanimity and consensus. This led to the so-called closure of the door of *ijtihād* (*insidād bāb al-ijtihād*), a self-imposed closure designed mainly to curtail the free exercise of opinion and reason in the development of Islamic legal thought. This is not the place to debate over the basic validity, or factual accuracy, of the so-called closure of the door of *ijtihād* and the ensuing prevalence of imitation (*taqlīd*) that dominated Islamic scholarship over the course of the following centuries. The general contours of this picture clearly confirm, however, that freedom, an outlook and philosophy that is *sui generis*, is incapable of regulating itself. What is more, however, there is a danger that the attempt to restrain or regulate the exercise of freedom can itself become unbalanced, even misguided. It is not certain to this day, for instance, whether or not the effort on the part of the *ᶜulamā'* of the Abbasid era to restrict the freedom of *ijtihād* and advocate imitation (*taqlīd*) inflicted a greater harm than the one it tried to contain.

The era of constitutionalism of the nineteenth and twentieth centuries was a response that subsequent generations of thinkers provided to the basic civilisational question of how to provide an authoritative blueprint for the valid exercise of freedom. Yet the era of constitutionalism has also shown that one can have a constitution, but there is no guarantee that the constitution itself will not be misinterpreted and abused. The issue here is also not just confined to the legal and political contexts. Thus the quest to find a balanced mix of guidance on liberty has been a challenging issue that has engaged thinkers throughout the history of ideas. Islamic responses to issues of concern to the present enquiry are formulated through the reading, in the first place, of the source-texts of the Qur'ān and the *Sunnah* on freedom, equality and justice. Observing these guidelines goes a long way towards moderating one's approach to the question of the exercise of freedom. But that is not enough. Every community and generation of Muslims will need to continue its quest to find the best methods by which to relate its reality and experience to the normative guidelines of the Qur'ān and *Sunnah*.

At the institutional level of applied jurisprudence, general consensus (*ijmāᶜ*) played an important role in ascertaining the acceptability or otherwise of new developments and *ijtihād* on issues of concern to liberty, equality and justice. *Ijmāᶜ* puts society's seal of approval on scholarly responses to new and unprecedented issues. This brings into focus the somewhat similar role played by judicial precedent in Western jurisprudence. Islamic jurisprudence has not validated binding judicial precedent in the same way as Western legal thought. The

Western legal doctrine of *stare decisis* makes judicial precedent a wholly binding legal source. The leading decisions of the higher courts in Common Law jurisdictions thus bind the lower courts to their application by analogy to similar cases. Judicial precedent provides a framework and process that ensures that the law moves apace with social reality and experience. It has the benefit of engaging courts of justice in legal construction and reform, while keeping in focus, in the meantime, practical legal issues that touch the lives of ordinary people. This process necessarily involves addressing the issues of justice, equality and freedom, and the manner in which they are translated into practical guidelines. Islamic jurisprudence has not embraced the idea of *stare decisis* partly because of the fact that Islamic law is governed by the given terms of the sacred text, and partly due to its concern for protecting the integrity *of ijtihād:* the judge and *mujtahid* must have the liberty to interpret the law themselves rather than be bound by the decision of another judge. Valid and sound as it may seem, the reality is somewhat less palatable for the Muslim observer, who sees that *ijtihād* has declined, but *stare decisis* has not, and that the latter has even found support in Muslim jurisdictions, such as Egypt, Malaysia and Pakistan. The latter two countries have retained binding judicial precedent and a common law-based judiciary as parts of their colonial legacy, parts that they obviously found worth preserving.

Eminent scholars and capable *mujtahids* do exist among the Muslims at large, but since the machinery of the nation-state and its (usually) Western-inspired constitution do not have a process for the *mujtahid* or of *ijtihād*, the creative thought and energies of these individuals are not being utilised. Some may well be making valuable contributions in their writings and publications, but their works nevertheless remain outside the decision-making processes of government. It would therefore be of benefit to society, and to the *ummah* at large, to take a positive view of *stare decisis* and see binding judicial precedent as a stimulus to legal reconstruction and *ijtihād*, rather than as a disincentive or unwarranted restriction on them. This can be the subject of a new constitutional formula, or of an amendment to the relevant provisions of the constitution in force. Every Muslim country could take into consideration its institutional framework, and the realities within and outside its judiciary, and determine its own approach to a binding system of judicial precedent. But to introduce reform measures along these lines, and take an affirmative stance on it at the earliest opportunity is advisable. I reach this conclusion partly because of the wide gap between the theory and practice of law in many Muslim jurisdictions. There is a need for a concerted effort not only at making the law more pragmatic but also at making it a tangible reality and a convincing apparatus.

Broadly speaking, Muslim countries are not particularly short of theoretical guidelines and constitutional formulae. What is really needed is to make them work and to make government under the rule of law a convincing prospect for citizens. Issues of freedom, equality and justice need not only theoretical deliberation and refinement, but a strong sense of commitment and purpose on the part of all concerned. Government leaders and law enforcement agencies have a special role to play in making government under the rule of law a process that will eventually inspire the citizen's loyalty and conviction. This can become a reality when citizens can expect that the law applies equally to all, and does-not make convenient exceptions for the powerful and the privileged. To achieve this is probably the greater part of the challenge facing contemporary Muslim societies at present, rather than engaging in theoretical deliberations alone, although in reality theory and practice are the two faces of the same coin and can hardly be divorced from one another.

Glossary

ʿ*abd*: slave.
adab al-qaḍā': juristic procedure.
ʿ*adālah*: justice.
*al-*ʿ*adālah al-ijtimā*ʿ*iyyah*: social justice.
*al-*ʿ*adālah al-muṭlaqah*: absolute justice.
ʿ*adl*: justice.
aḥkām: rules.
ahl al-dhimmah: people of the covenant.
*ahl al-ḥall wa'l-*ʿ*aqd*: those who loosen and bind, that is, the electoral college of elders who nominate the prospective Imām.
amān: safe conduct.
amānah: trust, which signifies a fiduciary concept, institution or relationship.
amārāt: circumstantial evidence.
ʿ*āmm*: general as opposed to specific.
arḥām: ties of kinship.
arjaḥ: most preferred.
ʿ*asabiyyah*: tribal kinship.
aṣlah: most qualified.
ʿ*ataqa*: to free.
ʿ*awfa*: exemption; pardoning.
āyah (pl. *āyāt*): a verse of the Qur'ān.
al-barā'ah al-aṣliyyah: original non-liability.
barā'at al-dhimmah: presumption of innocence.
bāṭin: inner.
*bay*ʿ*ah*: pledge of allegiance.
bayān: clarification, explanation.

bayt al-māl: public treasury.
bayyinah: evidence.
birr: virtue, good.
dār al-ḥarb: abode of war.
dār al-Islām: abode of Islam.
ḍarār: harm, injury, damage, prejudice.
daʿwā: claim (in a court).
daʿwah: call to religion or invitation to embrace Islam.
dhawū al-aḥrām: family relations and inheritance.
dhimmah: legal capacity of the individual.
dhimmī: free non-Muslim subjects living in Muslim lands, who, in return for capital tax payment, enjoy protection and safety.
diwān al-maẓālim: court of general jurisdiction vested with powers to receive and adjudicate complaints against government officials, established under the Abbasids Caliphate.
diyyah: blood money paid to the family of the victim of homicide or to the victim of injuries by the perpetrator.
faqīh: jurist.
farḍ ʿayn: emphatic personal obligation, often referring to religious duties, which are established by the decisive injunctions of the Qur'ān and the *Sunnah*.
farḍ kifā'ī: collective obligation of the community as a whole, which is discharged even if some, and not all, members of the community perform it.
farāsah: intuitive judgment.
farīḍah muḥkamah: firm obligation
fasād: corruption.
fatwā: considered opinion given by a qualified scholar, a *mufti* (jureconsult) or a *mujtahid*, concerning a legal religious issue; a religious edict.
fiqh: Islamic law as developed by Muslim jurists.
fuqahā: see *faqīh*.
ghayr ʿudūl: witnesses of lesser qualification.
ḥadīth: lit. speech; the reported sayings and teachings of the Prophet Muḥammad ﷺ. It is used interchangeably with the *Sunnah*.
ḥākim: ruler, governor.
ḥakam: arbitrator.
ḥalāl; legitimate; allowed by the *Sharīʿah*.
ḥanth: liability.
ḥaraj: harm.
ḥarām: totally forbidden.

ḥarbī: belligerent non-Muslim.
ḥaẓar: prohibition.
ḥiṣbah: promotion of good and prevention of evil. It is a collective obligation of the Muslim community to take an affirmative stand towards *ḥisbah* and put it into effect whenever the occasion arises.
ḥudūd: prescribed punishments which the Qur'ān or the *Sunnah* have determined for a handful of offences, including adultery and indefensible theft.
ḥukm: law, injunction or value of the *Sharīʿah* which seeks to regulate the conduct of competent individuals who are capable of bearing legal obligations.
ḥuqūq al-ādamiyyīn: right of human beings.
al-ḥuqūq wa'l-ḥurriyyāt al-iqtiṣādiyyah wa'l-ijtimāʿiyyah: socio-economic rights and liberties.
al-ḥuqūq wa'l-ḥurriyyāt al-maʿnawiyyah: intellectual rights and liberties.
al-ḥuqūq wa'l-ḥurriyyāt al-shakṣiyyah: personal rights and liberties.
ḥurr al-kalām: speech of high literary quality.
ḥurr al-karīm: person of integrity.
ḥurr: free.
ḥurriyyah: freedom.
ḥurriyyat al-ʿamal: freedom of work.
al-ḥurriyyah al-madaniyyah: civic liberty.
al-ḥurriyyah al-milkiyyah: freedom to own property.
al-ḥurriyyah al-shakhṣiyyah: personal freedom.
ḥurriyyat al-taʿallum wa'l-taʿlīm: freedom of education and dissemination of knowledge.
ḥurriyyat al-ʿaqīdah: freedom of faith.
ḥurriyyat al-tamalluk: freedom of ownership.
ḥusn al-muʿāmalah: good and fair treatment.
ʿibāḥah: permissibility (as opposed to prohibition).
ʿibādāt (pl. of *ʿibādah*): devotional matters and rituals of worship; often referring to obligatory duties such as the daily prayers, giving charity and fasting.
idhn: permission.
ijmāʿ: consensus of opinion, especially of the learned scholars of the *Sharīʿah*, over a legal or religious ruling.
ijtihād: lit, self-exertion; independent reasoning usually by a qualified person (i.e. *mujtahid*) in order to deduce the juridical ruling of an issue from the source materials of the *Sharīʿah*.
ijtihād ẓarfī: circumstantial *ijtihād*.
al-ikhā' al-dīnī: religious fraternity.

al-ikhāʾ al-insānī: fraternity of man.
ikhtiyār: choice; free will.
iḥsān: goodness; excellence; benevolence; fair-dealing.
iḥtikār: profiteering.
ᶜilm: knowledge, science.
imām ᶜādil: just leader.
istiṣḥāb: presumption of continuity.
jabbār: tyrant.
al-jabr wa'l-ikhtiyār: predestination and free will.
jihād: lit. striving; personal effort in the advancement of a sacred cause, struggle against the forces of evil; military campaign.
jizyah: the Islamic poll-tax levied on non-Muslims.
jumhūr: majority.
kaffārah (*pl. kaffārāt*): expiation.
kalām: lit. speech; the scholastic theology of Islam developed by such schools as the Ashᶜarites and Muᶜtazilites.
karīm: noble.
khalaṣa: to release, to free.
khalīfah: Caliph; vicegerent, successor.
kharāj: land tax.
khilāfah: the Qur'ānic doctrine of the vicegerency of man on earth; also refers to the historical caliphate.
khulᶜ: divorce initiated by the wife.
al-laqīṭ: foundling, abandoned child.
liᶜān: lit. cursing; imprecation which commonly refers to a form of divorce in Islamic law.
madhhab (pl. *madhāhib*): theological or legal school.
martabat al-ᶜawfa: state of forgiveness.
maṣlaḥah: public good, benefit or interest; often used in contradistinction to *mafsadah*, mischief, evil. The rules of the *Sharīᶜah* are all deemed to be for the realisation of the general benefit of the people.
māᶜun: acts of kindness among neighbours.
maẓālim (pl. of *maẓlimah*): complaint against government officials.
muᶜāhid: covenanted person.
muᶜallafāt al-qulūb: persons of influence whose co-operation and friendship was regarded as beneficial for the victory of Islam.
al-muᶜāmalah bi'l-mithl: reciprocal treatment.
muᶜāmalāt (sing. *muᶜāmalah*): civil or commercial transactions, often used in contradistinction to *ᶜibādāt*.
muḥākamāt (*muḥākamah*): judicial proceedings; hearing (in court).

mu^cāwin: deputy.
mu'azzaf: task officer.
mubārāt: divorce by mutual consent of husband and wife.
mudda^cā ^calayhi: defendant (in a court claim).
mudda^cī: plaintiff, one who institutes a court claim.
mudda^cī: claimant (in a court claim).
muḥtasib: regulator.
mujtahid: a competent scholar who is capable of conducting independent legal reasoning, or *ijtihād*.
muqallid: imitator, often used in contradistinction to *mujtahid*.
musayṭir: controller.
musta'mūn: non-Muslims temporarily resident in Muslim territory for a particular purpose.
muta'akhkhirūn: later-day jurists.
muwakkil : the principal party in a contract of agency.
muwāṭinūn: non-Muslim citizens of a Muslim state.
nafaqah: maintenance for close relatives.
naṣīḥah: sincere advice.
naṣṣ qaṭ^cī: clean text.
naẓar: observation.
qaḍā': the Divine decree.
qaḍā' ^calā al-ghā'ib: ex-parte judgement; ruling, judgment in absentia.
qāḍī: judge.
qā^cidah kulliyyah: legal maxim.
qarḍ ḥasan: benevolent loan given to those in need.
qawamah: maintenance; subsistence.
qawwām: provider.
qiṣāṣ: retaliation.
qiṣt: justice, fairness; just, fair.
qiwām: maintenance.
qiyās ma^c al-farīq: analogy with a discrepancy.
raf^c al-ḥaraj: removal of hardship.
ribā': usury.
rifq: gentleness.
risālah: the prophethood of Muḥammad ﷺ; message.
sabab al-ḥukm: cause of decision, ruling, judgement.
ṣabr: patience.
safīh: idiot.
ṣalāḥ: beneficence.
salam: forward sale, in which the price is paid at the time of the contract, but delivery is postponed to a future date.

sha'n al-nuzūl: the historical context for the revelation of a verse/verses of the Qur'ān

shibh al-ᶜamd: quasi-intentional.

shūrā: consultation.

siyāsah ᶜādilah: just policy.

siyāsah sharᶜiyyah: *Sharīᶜah*-oriented policy; often refers to discretionary decisions taken by the head of state or *qāḍī* in pursuit of public good, in response to emergency situations, or in cases where strict application of the established law would lead to undesirable results.

siyāsah ẓālimah: unjust policy.

sukhriyyah: mutual benefit.

ṣulḥ: settlement, compromise.

taᶜaqqul: rational judgment.

taᶜāwun: co-operation.

tābiᶜūn: follower, adherent, partisan.

tafakkur: thinking.

tafaqquh: understanding.

tahrīr: releasing, manumitting a slave.

al-takāful al-ijtimāᶜī: social support.

takhṣīṣ al-qaḍā': specification of court jurisdiction.

takhṣiṣ: specification.

taklīf: responsibility, accountability.

ṭalāq: divorce.

ṭalāq al-tafwīḍ: delegated divorce in which the husband delegates his power of unilateral *ṭalāq* to the wife.

taqlīd: lit. imitation; often implying an indiscriminate following of the *ᶜulamā'* of the past. It is often used in contradistinction to *ijtihād*.

taqwā: God-consciousness, piety.

al-taswiyah fi'l-muᶜāmalah: equality in treatment.

tawḥīd: belief in the Oneness of God.

tawsiᶜah: flexibility.

taysīr: bringing ease and facilitating difficult situations.

taᶜzīr: lit. deterrence or deterrent punishment which a *qāḍī* may impose at his discretion by reference to attending circumstances.

tazkiyah: probity, attestation of (a witness') honourable record, integrity.

ulū al-amr: lit. those with authority; government and community leaders, as well as *ᶜulamā'*, who exercise authority and influence in community affairs. The Qur'ān requires that they must be respected and obeyed.

ᶜulamā': religious scholars; theologians.
ummah: the Muslim community at large.
ᶜunf: harshness; violence.
al-ᶜuqūd wa'l-fusūkh: contracts and dissolutions.
wālī al-maẓālim: public grievances tribunal.
wakālah: the contract of agency, representation.
wakīl: legal representative, agent, attorney.
walāyah (also *wilāyah* - pl. *wilāyāt*): legal authority such as in the case of guardianship (*walī*) who exercises authority over his ward. *Walāyah* also means guardianship.
waqf (pl. *awqāf*): charitable endowment; a charitable trust instituted for the advancement of a good cause.
wazīr al-tafwīḍ: prime minister.
wazīr al-tanfīdh: ministerial portfolio.
wilāyah ᶜāmmah: public authority.
wilāyah khāṣṣah: private authority.
wilāyat al-qaḍā': judicial authority.
zakāh: lit. purity; legal alms incumbent upon a Muslim, to help the poor and the needy, at the rate of approximately two and a half per cent, payable annually on certain types of assets held for over a year.
ẓāhir: apparent.
ẓann: conjecture, supposition.
ẓihār: a type of divorce.

Bibliography

ʿAbd al-Bāqī, Fu'ād, *al-Muʿjam al-Mufahras li-Alfaẓ al-Qur'ān al-Karīm*, 2nd edn., Cairo: Dār al-Fikr, 1402/1981.

ʿAbduh, Muḥammad, *al-Islām wa'l-Naṣrāniyyah maʿ al-ʿIlm wa'l-Madaniyyah*, 6th edn., Cairo: Maṭbaʿat Nahḍah, 1375/1956.

—*Risālat al-Tawḥīd*, 6th edn., Cairo: Dār al-Manār, 1973.

Abū Dāwūd, *Sunan Abū Dāwūd*, Eng. trans. Aḥmad Ḥasan, 3 vols., Lahore: Ashraf Press, 1984.

Abū Ḥabīb, Saʿdī, *Dirāsah fī Minhāj al-Islām al-Siyāsī*, Beirut: Mu'assasat al-Risālah, 1406/1985.

Abū Yūsuf, Yaʿqūb b. Ibrāhīm, *Kitāb al-Kharāj*, 5th edn., Cairo: al-Maṭbaʿah al-Salafiyyah, 1396AH.

Abū Zahrah, Muḥammad, *Tanẓīm al-Islām li'l-Mujtamaʿ*, Cairo: Dār al-Fikr al-ʿArabī, 1385/1965

—*al-Jarīmah wa'l-ʿUqūbah fi'l-Fiqh al-Islāmī,* Cairo: Dār al-Fikr al-ʿArabī, n.d.

—*Uṣūl al-Fiqh*, Cairo: Dar al-Fikr al-ʿArabī, 1377/1958.

al-ʿAbūdī, Muḥsin, *al-Ḥurriyyāt al-Ijtimāʿiyyah Bayn al-Nuẓūm al-Muʿāṣirah wa'l-Fiqh al-Siyāsī al-Islāmī*, Cairo: Dār al-Nahḍah al-ʿArabiyyah, 1410/1990.

ʿAfīfī, Muḥammad al-Ṣādiq, *al-Mujtamaʿ al-Islāmī wa-Uṣūl al-Ḥukm*, Cairo: Dār al-Iʿtiṣām, 1400/1980.

Aḥmad, Fu'ād ʿAbd al-Munʿim, *Uṣūl Niẓām al-Ḥukm fi'l-Islām*, Alexandria: Mu'assasat Shabāb al-Jāmiʿah, 1411/ 1991.

ʿAjlānī, Muḥammad Munīr, *ʿAbqariyyāt al-Islām fī Uṣūl al-Ḥukm*, Beirut: Dār al-Nafā'is, 1405/1985.

Al-Āmidī, Sayf al-Dīn, *al-Iḥkām fī Uṣūl al-Aḥkām*, 4 vols., ed. ʿAbd al-Razzāq ʿAfīfī, 2nd edn., Beirut: al-Maktab al-Islāmī,

1402/1982.

ᶜAmmārah, Muḥammad, *al-Islām wa Ḥuqūq al-Insān: Ḍarūrāt la Ḥuqūq*, Cairo: Dār al-Shurūq, 1409/1982.

Anderson, J.N.D., 'The Syrian Law of Personal Status', BSOAS XVII (1955), pp. 34-49.

Al-Anṣārī, ᶜAbd al-Ḥamīd, *al-Shūrā wa Āthāruhū fi'l-Dimuqrāṭiyyah al-Ḥadīthah*, 2nd edn., Cairo: al-Maktabah al-ᶜAṣriyyah, 1400/1980.

Arthur, John and Shaw, William, *Justice and Economic Distribution*, 2nd edn., Englewood Cliffs, New Jersey: Prentice Hall, 1991.

Asad, Muhammad, *Principles of State and Government in Islam*, Berkeley: University of California Press, 1966.

al-Ashrafī, Tūghān Shaykh al-Muḥammadī, *al-Muqaddimah al-Sulṭāniyyah fi'l-Siyāsah al-Sharᶜiyyah*, ed. Muḥammad ᶜAbd Allāh, Cairo: Maktabat al-Zahrā', 1418/1997.

Awad, M. Awad, 'The Rights of the Accused under Islamic Criminal Procedure', in M. Cherif Bassiouni (ed.), *Islamic Criminal Justice System*, London and New York: Oceana Publications, 1982.

ᶜAwdah, ᶜAbd al-Qādir, *al-Tashrīᶜ al-Jinā'ī al-Islāmī*. Beirut: Mu'assasat al-Risālah, 1403/1983.

Azad, Ghulam Murtaza, *Judicial System of Islam*, Islamabad: Islamic Research Institute, 1987.

Al-Badawī, Ismāᶜīl, *Daᶜā'im al-Ḥukm fi'l-Sharīᶜah al-Islāmiyyah wa'l-Nuẓūm al-Dustūriyyah al-Muᶜāṣirah*, Cairo: Dār al-Fikr al-Islāmī and Alexandria (Egypt): Mu'assasat Shabāb al-Jāmiᶜah, 1404/1984.

Badrān, Abu'l-ᶜAynayn Badrān, *Uṣūl al-Fiqh al-Islāmī*, Alexandria (Egypt): Mu'assasat Shabāb al-Jāmiᶜah, 1404/1984.

Al-Bahī, Muḥammad, *al-Dīn wa'l-Dawlah min Tawjīhāt al-Qur'ān al-Karīm*, Beirut: Dār al-Fikr 1391/1971.

Bassiouni, Cherif M. (ed.), *The Islamic Criminal Justice System*, London and New York: Oceana Publications, 1982.

Al-Basyūnī, ᶜAbd Allāh ᶜAbd al-Ghanī, *Naṣariyyat al-Dawlah fi'l-Islām*, Beirut: Dār al-Jāmiᶜiyyah, 1986.

Al-Bayhaqī, Aḥmad b. Husayn b. ᶜAlī, *al-Sunan al-Kubrā*, Beirut: Dār al-Fikr, n.d.

Bodenheimer, Edgar, *Jurisprudence, the Philosophy and Method of the Law*, 2nd edn., Englewood Cliffs, New Jersey: Prentice Hall, 1991.

Dias, R.M.W., *Jurisprudence*, 5th edn., London: Butterworth, 1985.

El-Awa, Mohamed Selim, *On the Political System of the Islamic State*,

Indianapolis (Indiana): American Trust Publication, 1980.
El-ᶜAwah, *Fi'l-Niẓām al-Siyāsī li'l-Dawlah al-Islāmiyyah*, Cairo: al-Maktab al-Miṣrī al-Ḥadīth, reprint, 1983.
—*Punishment in Islamic Law*, Indianapolis: American Trust Publications, 1982.
The Encyclopedia of Islam, new edn., Leiden: E.J. Brill, 1965.
Al-Farrā', Abū Yaᶜlā Muḥammad ibn al-Ḥusayn, *al-Aḥkām al-Sulṭāniyyah*, Cairo: Muṣṭafā al-Bābī al-Ḥalabī, 1357AH.
Al-Faruqi, Ismail R., 'Islam and Other Faiths', in Altaf Gauhar (ed.), *The Challenge of Islam*, London: The Islamic Council of Europe, 1978.
Gauhar, Altaf (ed.), *The Challenge of Islam*, London, The Islamic Council of Europe, 1978.
Al-Ghannushī, Rāshid, *Ḥuqūq al-Muwāṭanah: Ḥuqūq Ghayr al-Muslim fi'l-Mujtamaᶜ al-Islāmī*, 2nd edn., Herndon, VA: International Institute of Islamic Thought, 1413/1993.
Al-Ghazālī, Muḥammad, *Ḥuqūq al-Insān Bayn Taᶜālim al-Islām wa Iᶜlān al-Umam al-Muttaḥidah.* Alexandria (Egypt): Dār al-Daᶜwah li'l-Nashr wa'l-Tawzīᶜ, 1413/1993.
al-Ḥamawī, Shihāb al-Dīn b. Abū Isḥāq Ibrāhīm, *Kitāb Ādāb al-Qaḍā'*, ed. Muṣṭafā al-Zuḥaylī, 2nd edn., Damascus: Dār al-Fikr, 1402/1982.
Hart, H.L.A., *The Concept of Law,* Oxford: Clarendon Press, 1961.
Hasan, Farooq, *The Concept of State and Law in Islam*, New York: University Press of America, 1981.
Hughes, Thomas P., *Dictionary of Islam*, Reprint. Lahore: The Book House, n.d.
Ibn ᶜAbd Rabbih, Aḥmad al-Andalusī, *al-ᶜIqd al-Farīd li'l-Malik al-Saᶜīd*, 3rd edn., Cairo: Maṭbaᶜat Lajnat al-Ta'līf, 1384/1965.
Ibn ᶜĀbidīn, Muḥammad Amīn, *Ḥāshiyah Radd al-Mukhtār ᶜalā Durr al-Mukhtār*, 2nd edn., Cairo: Muṣṭafā al-Bābī al-Ḥalabī, 1386/1966.
Ibn ᶜĀshūr, Muḥammad al-Ṭāhir, *Maqāṣid al-Sharīᶜah al-Islāmiyyah*, Tunis: Maṭbaᶜat al-Istiqāmah, 1966.
Ibn al-Athīr, ᶜAlī ibn Aḥmad ibn Abī al-Karam, *al-Kamil fi'l-Ta'rīkh*, Cairo: Maṭbaᶜat al-Shaykh Aḥmad al-Bābī al-Ḥalabī, 1303AH.
Ibn Farḥūn, Burhān al-Dīn Ibrāhīm b. ᶜAlī, *Tabṣirat al-Ḥukkām fī Uṣūl al-Aqḍiyah wa Manāhij al-Aḥkām*, ed. Ṭāhā ᶜAbd al-Ra'ūf Saᶜd. Cairo: Maktabat al-Kulliyyāt al-Aẓhariyyah, 1406/1986.
Ibn Ḥanbal, Aḥmad, *Musnad al-Imām Aḥmad Ibn Ḥanbal*, 6 vols., Beirut: Dār al-Fikr, n.d.

Ibn Ḥazm, Abū Muḥammad ʿAlī b. Aḥmad b. Saʿīd, *al-Fiṣal fi'l-Milal wa'l-Ahwā' wa'l-Nihal*, Cairo: Maktabat al-Salām al-ʿĀlamiyyah, n.d.

—*al-Iḥkām fī Uṣūl al-Aḥkām*, ed. Aḥmad M. Shākir, 4 vols., Beirut: Dār al-Āfāq al-Jadīdah. 1400/1980.

—*al-Muḥallā*, ed. Aḥmad M. Shākir, Cairo: Dār al-Fikr, n.d.

Ibn Hishām, ʿAbd al-Mālik, *al-Sīrah al-Nabawiyyah*, Cairo: Muṣṭafā al-Bābī al-Ḥalabī, 1936.

Ibn Kathīr, Ḥāfiẓ Abu'l-Fidā Ismāʿīl, *Tafsīr al-Qur'ān al-ʿAẓīm* (also known as *Tafsīr Ibn Kathīr)*, Cairo: Dār al-Shaʿb, 1393/1973.

Ibn Mājah, Muḥammad b. Yazīd al-Qazwīnī, *Sunan Ibn Mājah*, Istanbul: Cagli Yayinlari, 1401/1981.

Ibn Qudāmah, Muwaffaq al-Dīn Abū Muḥammad ʿAbd Allāh, *al-Mughnī*, Cairo: Maṭbaʿat al-Manār, 1367 AH.

Ibn Taymiyyah, Taqī al-Dīn Aḥmad, *Naẓariyyāt al-ʿAqd*, Beirut: Dār al-Maʿrifah, 1317 AH.

—*Majmūʿ Fatāwā Shaykh al-Islām Aḥmad Ibn Taymiyyah*, ed. ʿAbd al-Raḥmān b. Qāsim, Beirut: Mu'assasat al-Risālah, 1398 AH.

—*al-Siyāsah al-Sharʿiyyah fī Iṣlāḥ al-Rāʿī wa'l-Rāʿiyyah*, ed. Abd al-Raḥmān b. Qāsim, Beirut: Mu'assasat al-Risālah, 1398 AH.

Al-ʿĪlī, ʿAbd al-Ḥakīm Ḥasan, *al-Ḥurriyyāt al-ʿĀmmah*. Cairo: Dār al-Fikr, 1403/1983.

Iqbal, Muhammad, *The Reconstruction of Religious Thought in Islam*, Lahore: Shah Muhammad Ashraf Press, reprint, 1982.

Ishaque, K. M., 'Al-Aḥkām al-Sulṭāniyyah', *Islamic Studies* 4 (1965), pp. 275-314.

Al-Jaṣṣās, Abū Bakr Aḥmad ibn ʿAlī al-Rāzī, *Aḥkām al-Qur'ān*, Cairo: al-Maṭbaʿah al-Bahiyyah, 1347/1928.

Al-Jawziyya, Ibn Qayyim, *al-Ṭuruq al-Ḥukmiyyah fi'l-Siyāsah al-Sharʿiyyah*, ed. Muḥammad Jamīl Ghāzī, Jeddah: Maṭbaʿat al-Madanī, n.d. See also the Cairo edn. by al-Mu'assasat al-ʿArabiyyah, 1380/1961.

—*Iʿlām al-Muwaqqiʿīn ʿan Rabb al-ʿĀlamīn*, ed. Muḥammad Munīr al-Dimashqī, Cairo: Idārat al-Ṭibāʿah al-Munīriyyah, n.d.

Kamali, Mohammad Hashim, *Principles of Islamic Jurisprudence*, revised edition, Cambridge: The Islamic Texts Society, 1991.

—'Divorce and Women's Rights: Some Muslim Interpretations of S1:228', *The Muslim World* 74 (1984), 85-100.

—*Siyāsah Sharʿiyyah* or the Policies of Islamic Government', *The American Journal of Islamic Social Sciences* 6 (1989), 59-81.

—'The Limits of Power in an Islamic State', *Islamic Studies* 28 (1989), 323-353.
—'Appellate Review and Judicial Independence in Islamic Law', in Chibli Mallat (ed.), *Islam and Public Law*, London: Graham & Trotman 1993, pp. 49-85.
—*Freedom of Expression in Islam*, Cambridge: The Islamic Texts Society, 1997 and Kuala Lumpur: Ilmiah Publishers, 1998
—'Islamic Law in Malaysia: Issues and Developments', *Yearbook of Islamic and Middle Eastern Law,* vol. IV (1997-1998). London: Kluwer Law International, 1998, pp. 153-180.
—*Law in Afghanistan: A Study of the Constitutions, Matrimonial Law and the Judiciary*, Leiden: E. J. Brill, 1985.
Khadduri, Majid. *The Islamic Conception of Justice*, Baltimore: The John Hopkins University Press, 1984.
al-Khālidī, Maḥmūd ᶜAbd al-Majīd, *Qawāᶜid Niẓām al-Ḥukm fi'l-Islām*, Kuwait: Dār al-Buḥūth al-ᶜIlmiyyah, 1980.
Khallāf, ᶜAbd al-Wahhāb, *ᶜIlm Uṣūl al-Fiqh,* 12th edn., Kuwait: Dār al-Qalam, 1398/1978.
—*al-Siyāsah al-Sharᶜiyyah*, Cairo: al-Maṭbaᶜah al-Salafiyyah, 1350 AH.
Al-Kāsānī, *Badā'iᶜ al-Ṣanā'iᶜ*, Cairo: Maṭbaᶜat al-Istiqāmah, 1956.
al-Kurdi, Abdulrahman Abdulkadir, *The Islamic State: A Study Based on the Islamic Holy Constitution*, London and New York: Mansell Publishing Ltd., 1984.
Laylah, Muḥammad Kāmil, *al-Nuẓūm al-Siyāsiyyah,* Cairo: Dār al-Fikr al-ᶜArabī, 1963.
Lewis, Bernard, *The Middle East and the West*, London: Weidenfeld & Nicholson, 1967.
Luca, Costa, 'Discrimination in the Arab Middle East', in Willem A. Veenhoven ed., *Case Studies on Human Rights and Fundamental Freedoms*, vol. 1, The Hague, 1975, pp. 211-40.
Madkūr, Muḥammad Salām, *al-Fiqh al-Islāmī*, 2nd edn., Cairo: Maṭbaᶜat al-Fajālah, 1955.
—*Maᶜalim al-Dawlah al-Islāmiyyah:* Maktabat al-Falāḥ, 1403/1983.
—*al-Qaḍā' fi'l-Islām*, Cairo: Dār al-Nahḍah al-ᶜArabiyyah, 1964.
Maḥmaṣṣānī, Subḥī Rajab, *Arkān Ḥuqūq al-Insān fi'l-Islām*, Beirut: Dār al-ᶜIlm li'l-Malāyīn, 1979.
Mallat, Chibli (ed.), *Islam and Public Law*, London: Graham and Trotman, 1993.
Marāghī, Aḥmad Musṭafā, *Tafsīr al-Marāghī*, 2nd edn., Cairo: Maṭbaᶜat Muṣṭafā al-Bābī al-Ḥalabī, 1953.

al-Māwardī, Abu'l-Ḥasan, *Kitāb al-Ahkām al-Sulṭāniyyah*, 2nd edn., Cairo: Muṣṭafā al-Bābī al-Ḥalabī, 1386 AH.

Mawdūdī, Sayyid Abu'l-Aᶜla, *Naẓariyyah al-Islām al-Siyāsiyyah*, translated from Urdu by Khalīl Ḥasan al-Islāḥī, Beirut: Dār al-Fikr, n.d.

The Mejelle: Being an English Translation of Majallah el-Akkam el-Adliya, trans. C.R. Tyser, reprint, Lahore: Law Publishing Co., 1967.

Montgomery-Watt, W., *Islamic Political Thought: the Basic Concepts,* Edinburgh: Edinburgh University Press, 1968.

Mulhall, Stephen and Swift, Adam, *Liberals and Communitarians,* Oxford, Blackwell, 1992.

Al-Mundhirī, Zakī al-Dīn ᶜAbd al-ᶜAẓīm, *al-Targhīb wa'l-Tarhīb*, 3 vols., Cairo: Muṣṭafā al-Bābī al-Ḥalabī, 1373/1954.

Muslehuddin, Muhammad, *Philosophy of Islamic Law and the Orientalists*, 2nd edn., Lahore: Islamic Publications Ltd., 1980.

Mutahhari, Ayatollah Murtaza, *Spritual Discourses*, Eng. trans. Alauddin Pazargadi, Albany (California): Muslim Students' Association in the U.S. A. and Canada (PSG), 1986.

—*Fundamentals of Islamic Thought: God, Man and Universe*, Eng. trans. R. Campbell, Berkeley, CA: Mizan Press, 1985.

Mutawallī, ᶜAbd al-Ḥamīd, *Mabādī' Niẓām al-Ḥukm fi'l-Islām*, Alexandria (Egypt): Mansha'āt al-Maᶜārif, 1974.

al-Nabhān, Muḥammad Fārūq, *Niẓām al-Ḥukm fi'l-Islām*, Kuwait: Jāmiᶜat al-Kuwait, 1974.

al-Nabhānī, Shaykh Taqī al-Dīn, *Muqaddimat al-Dustūr,* Kuwait, no publisher given, 1964.

Nait-Belkacem, Mouloud Kassim, 'The Concept of Social Justice in Islam', in Altaf Gauhar (ed.), *The Challenge of Islam*, London: Islamic Council of Europe, 1978.

al-Nawawī, Muḥyi al-Dīn Abī Zakariyā Yaḥyā, *Riyāḍ al-Ṣāliḥīn*, 2nd edn, by Muḥammad Nāsir al-Dīn al-Albānī, Beirut: Dār al-Maktab al-Islāmī, 1404/1984.

—*Minhāj al-Ṭālibīn*, Eng. trans. E.C. Howard, Lahore: Law Publishing Co., n.d.

al-Nishāpūrī, Muslim b. Hajjāj, *Mukhtaṣar Ṣaḥīḥ Muslim*, ed. Muḥammad Nāṣir al-Dīn al-Albānī, 2nd edn., Beirut: Dār al-Maktab al-Islāmī, 1404/1984.

Owsia, Parviz, *Formation of Contract: A Comparative Study under English, French, Islamic and Iranian Law*, London: Graham & Trotman, 1994.

Qāḍ, Samīr ʿĀliyah, *Naẓariyyat al-Dawla fi'l-Islām*, Beirut: al-Mu'assasah al-Jāmiʿiyyah, 1408/1980.
Qadri, Anwar Ahmad, *Islamic Jurisprudence in the Modern World*, 2nd edn., Lahore: Shaikh Muhammad Ashraf, 1981.
Al-Qaraḍāwī, Yūsuf, *al-Khaṣā'is al-ʿĀmmah li'l-Islām*, Cairo: Maktabat Wahbah, 1409/1989.
—*Fī Fiqh al-Awlawiyyāt: Dirāsah Jadīdah fī Ḍaw' al-Qur'ān wa'l-Sunnah*, Cairo: Maktabat Wahbah, 1416/1996.
—*Fiqh al-Zakāh*, 3rd edn., Beirut: Mu'assasat al-Risālah, 1397/1977.
—*Madkhal li-Dirāsah al-Sharīʿah al-Islamiyyah*, Cairo, Maktabat Wahbah, 1411/1991.
—*Bayʿ al-Murābaḥah li'l-ʿĀmir bi'l-Shirā'*, 2nd edn., Cairo: Maktabat Wahbah, 1409/1982.
al-Qāsimī, Ẓāfir, *Niẓām al-Ḥukm fi'l-Sharīʿah wa'l-Ta'rīkh*, 2nd edn., Beirut: Dār al-Nafā'is, 1977.
al-Qurṭubī, Muḥammad b. Aḥmad b. Rushd, *Bidāyat al-Mujtahid wa Nihāyat al-Muqtaṣid,* Cairo: Muṣṭafā al-Bābī al-Ḥalabī, 1401/1981.
al-Qurṭubī, Abū ʿAbd Allāh Muḥammad, *al-Jāmiʿ li-Aḥkām al-Qur'ān*, Cairo: Maṭbaʿat Dār al-Qur'ān, 1387/1954.
Quṭb, Sayyd, *al-ʿAdālah al-Ijtimāʿiyyah fi'l-Islām*, 4th edn., Cairo: ʿĪsā al-Bābī al-Ḥalabī, 1373/1954.
—*Fī Ẓilāl al-Qur'ān*, Beirut: Dār al-Shuruq, 1397/1977.
Rahman, Fazlur, 'The Status of the Individual in Islam', *Islamic Studies* 5 (1966), 319 - 33.
Ramadan, Said, *Islamic Law, Its Scope and Equity*, 2nd edn., Kuala Lumpur: Muslim Youth Movement of Malaysia, 1992.
Rawls, John, *A Theory of Justice*, Cambridge: Harvard University Press, 1971.
al-Rāzī, Fakhr al-Dīn b. ʿUmar, *al-Tafsīr al-Kabīr* (also known as *Mafātīḥ al-Ghayb*), Beirut: Dār al-Fikr, 1398/1978.
Riḍā, Muḥammad Rashīd, *Tafsīr al-Qur'ān al-Ḥakīm* (also known as *Tafsīr al-Manār*), Beirut: Dār al-Maʿrifah, 1328AH.
Al-Rīs, Ḍiyā' al-Dīn, *al-Naẓariyyāt al-Siyāsiyyah al-Islamiyyah*, 7th edn., Cairo: Dār al-Turāth, n.d.
Rosenthal, Franz, *The Muslim Concept of Freedom*, Leiden: E.J. Brill, 1960.
Russell, Bertrand. 'Freedom and Government', in Anshen, R.N. (ed.), *Freedom, Its Meaning*, New York: Macmillan, 1941.
Ṣaʿb, Ḥasan, 'al-Ḥurriyyah al-Falsafiyyah', in Jamīl Munayminah, (ed.), *Mushkilat al-Ḥurriyyah fi'l-Islām*, Beirut: Dār al-Kitāb al-Lubnānī, 1974.

al-Sadr, Muhammad Baqir, *Contemporary Man and the Social Problem*, Eng. trans. Yasin T. A. al-Jibouri, Tehran: World Organisation of Islamic Services, 1980.

—*Iqtiṣādunā*, 13th edn., Beirut: Dār al-Taᶜarruf li'l-Maṭbūᶜāt, n.d.

Al-Sanhūrī, ᶜAbd al-Razzāq, *Fiqh al-Khilāfah wa Taṭawwuruhā*, ed. Nādia al-Sanhūrī and Tawfīq Muḥammad al-Shāwī, Cairo: al-Hay'ah al-Miṣriyyah al-ᶜĀmmah li'l-Kitāb, 1989.

Said, Abdul Aziz, 'Precept and Practice of Human Rights in Islam', *Universal Human Rights*, Vol. 1 (Jan. 1979), pp. 63ff.

al-Sarakhsī, Shams al-Dīn, *al-Mabsūṭ*, 32 vols., Beirut: Dār al-Maᶜrifah, 1406/1986.

Al-Shāfiᶜī, Muḥammad ibn Idrīs, *Kitāb al-Umm*, ed. Muḥammad Sayyd Kaylānī, 2nd edn., Cairo: Muṣṭafā al-Bābī al-Ḥalabī, 1403/1983.

Shaltūt, Maḥmūd, *al-Islām, ᶜAqidah wa Sharīᶜah*, Kuwait: Maṭābiᶜ Dār al-Qalam, n.d.

—*Fiqh al-Qur'ān wa'l-Sunnah*, Kuwait: Maṭābiᶜ Dār al-Qalam, n.d.

al-Sharbīnī, Muḥammad al-Khaṭīb, *Mughnī al-Muḥtāj ilā Maᶜrifat Alfāẓ al-Minhāj*, Beirut: Dār al-Fikr, n.d.

al-Shāṭibī, Abū Isḥāq Ibrāhīm, *al-Muwāfaqāt fī Uṣūl al-Sharīᶜah*, ed. Shaykh ᶜAbd Allāh Dirāz, Cairo: al-Maktabah al-Tijāriyyah al-Kubrā. n.d.

al-Shawkānī, Yaḥyā b. ᶜAlī, *Irshād al-Fuhūl min Taḥqīq al-Ḥaq ilā ᶜIlm al-Uṣūl*, Cairo: Dār al-Fikr, n.d.

—*Nayl al-Awṭār: Sharḥ Muntaqā al-Akhbār*, Cairo: Muṣṭafā al-Bābī al-Ḥalabī, n.d.

al-Sibāᶜī, Muṣṭafā, *Ishtirākiyyāt al-Islām*, 2nd edn., Damascus: al-Dār al-Qawmiyyah li'l-Ṭibāᶜah wa'l-Nashr, 1379/1960.

Suwaylim, Bandar ibn Fahd, *al-Mutham: Muᶜāmalatuh wa Ḥuqūquh fi'l-Fiqh al-Islāmī*, Riyad: al-Markaz al-ᶜArabiyyah li'l-Dirāsāt al-Amniyyah, 1408/1978.

al-Suyūṭī, Jalāl al-Dīn, *al-Jāmiᶜ al-Ṣaghīr*, 4th edn., Cairo: Muṣṭafā al-Bābī al-Ḥalabī, 1954.

Al-Ṭabarī, Abū Jaᶜfar Muḥammad ibn Jarīr, *Ta'rīkh al-Rusul wa'l-Muluk*, Cairo: al-Maṭbaᶜah al-Tijariyyah, 1358/1939.

al-Tabrīzī, ᶜAbd Allāh al-Khaṭīb, *Mishkāt al-Maṣābīḥ*, ed. Muḥammad Nāṣir al-Dīn al-Albānī, 2nd edn., Beirut: al-Maktab al-Islāmī, 1399/1979.

Tāj, Abd al-Raḥmān, *al-Siyāsah al-Sharᶜiyyah wa'l-Fiqh al-Islāmī*, Cairo: Maṭbāᶜah Dār al-Ta'līf, 1393/1953.

Al-Ṭamāwī, Sulaymān, *al-Sulṭāt al-Thalāth fi'l-Dasātir al-ᶜArabiyyah wa'l-*

Fikr al-Siyāsī al-Islāmī, 2nd edn., Cairo: Dār al-Fikr al-ᶜArabī, 1973.
—*ᶜUmar ibn al-Khaṭṭāb wa Uṣūl al-Siyāsah wa'l-Idārah al-Ḥadīthah*, Cairo: Dār al-Fikr al-ᶜArabī, 1403/1983.
Al-Tirmidhī, Abū ᶜĪsā Muḥammad, *Sunan al-Tirmidhī*, Beirut: Dār al-Fikr, 1400/1980.
Ṭubliyah, Muḥammad al-Quṭb, *al-Islām wa Ḥuqūq al-Insān. Dirāsah Muqārinah*, 2nd edn, Cairo: Dār al-Fikr al-ᶜArabī, 1404/1984.
ᶜUthmān, Fatḥī, *al-Fard fi'l-Mujtamaᶜ al-Islāmī: Bayn al-Ḥuqūq wa'l-Wājibāt*, Cairo: al-Majlis al-Aᶜlā li'l-Shu'ūn al-Islāmiyyah, 1382/1962.
—*al-Fikr al-Qanūnī al-Islāmī: Bayn Uṣūl al-Sharīᶜah wa Turāth al-Fiqh*, Cairo: Maktabah Wahbah, n.d.
Al-Wāfī, ᶜAbd al-Wāḥid, *Ḥuqūq al-Insān fi'l-Islām*, Cairo: Maṭbāᶜat al-Risālah, n.d.
Wāṣil, Farīd Muḥammad, *al-Sulṭah al-Qaḍā'iyyah wa Niẓām al-Qaḍā' fi'l-Islām*, 2nd edn., Cairo: Maṭbaᶜat al-Amānah, 1983.
Weeramantry, J., *Islamic Jurisprudence: An Islamic Perspective*, Basingstoke(UK), Macmillan, 1988.
Wilson, Rodney, 'The Contribution of Muhammad Baqir al-Sadr to Contemporary Islamic Economic Thought', *Journal of Islamic Studies* 9.1 (1998), 46-60.
Yusrī, Aḥmad, *Ḥuqūq al-Insān wa Asbāb al-ᶜUnf fi'l-Mujtamaᶜ al-Islāmī fī Ḍaw Aḥkām al-Sharīᶜah*, Alexandria (Egypt): Mansha'at al-Maᶜārif, 1993.
al-Zarqā, Shaykh Aḥmad b. Muḥammad, *Sharḥ al-Qawāᶜid al-Fiqhiyyah*, ed. Muṣṭafā al-Zarqā, 3rd edn., Damascus: Dār al-Qalam, 1414/1993.
al-Zarqā, Muṣṭafā, *al-Madkhal al-Fiqhī al-ᶜĀm*, 3 vols., Damascus: Dār al-Fikr, 1967.
Zaydān, ᶜAbd al-Karīm, *al-Fard wa'l-Dawlah fi'l-Sharīᶜah al-Islāmiyyah*, Gary (Indiana): al-Ittihād al-ᶜĀlamī li'l-Munaẓẓamāt al-Ṭullābiyyah, 1390/1970.
—*Niẓām al-Qaḍā' fi'l-Sharīᶜah al-Islāmiyyah*, Baghdad: Maṭbaᶜat al-ᶜĀnī, 1404/1984.
al-Zuḥaylī, Wahbah, *al-Fiqh al-Islāmī wa Adillatuh*, 3rd edn., Damascus: Dār al-Fikr, 1409/1989.
Zuhayr, Muḥammad Abū al-Nūr, *Uṣūl al-Fiqh*, 4 vols., Cairo: Dār al-Ṭibāᶜah al-Muḥammadiyyah, c. 1372/1952.
Zullah, Muhammad Afzal, 'The Application of Islamic Law in Pakistan', presentation given at the International Islamic University Malaysia, 6 September 1991

Index

Abbasid, 90, 117, 118, 119, 120
ʿabd, 3, 8
ʿAbd Allāh ibn Masʿūd, 107
ʿAbduh, Muḥammad, 72, 78
Abū Bakr, 24, 56, 59, 60, 139
Abū Burdah, 148
Abū Ḥanīfah, 85, 86, 106, 107, 117
Abū Mūsā al-Ashʿarī, 123, 148
Abū Zahrah, Muḥammad, 5, 80, 92, 112, 140
adab al-qaḍā', 127
ʿadālah, 103
al-ʿadālah al-ijtimāʿiyyah, 105
al-ʿadālah al-muṭlaqah, 112
ʿadl, 93, 103, 112, 113, 146
ʿAlī ibn Abī Ṭālib, 72, 83, 84, 88, 116, 127-8, 136
aḥkām, 145
ahl al-dhimmah, 1
ahl al-ḥall wa'l-ʿaqd,
amān, 78
amānah, 20, 21, 59, 113, 145
amārāt, 147
ʿāmm, 84
ʿAmr ibn al-ʿĀṣ, 144
ʿAmr ibn Shuʿayb, 86
apostasy, 89
ʿAqabah, 72
Arberry, 65
arḥām, 51, 135
arjaḥ, 84
Aristotle, 103
ʿasabiyyah, 53
Asad, Muhammad, 119
aṣlah, 113
ʿataqa, 3
Austin, 134
ʿAwdah, ʿAbd al-Qādir, 7, 87, 94
ʿawfah, 3
ʿawqāf see *waqt*,
āyah, 10, 15, 16, 20, 25, 30, 31, 32, 47, 50, 51, 53, 58, 59, 60, 62, 64, 65, 66, 68, 74, 80, 81, 82, 84, 85, 91, 92, 93, 108, 109, 111, 114, 135, 145

al-barā'ah al-aṣliyyah, 3, 28, 129
barā'at al-dhimmah, 36, 39
Bassiouni, Cherif, 37
bāṭin, 106
bayʿah, 13, 24